D1606405

FASCISM

FASCISM

WHY NOT HERE?

BRIAN E. FOGARTY

Potomac Books, Inc.
Washington, D.C.

Library of Congress Cataloging-in-Publication Data
Fogarty, Brian E.
  Fascism : why not here? / Brian E. Fogarty. — 1st ed.
    p. cm.
  Includes bibliographical references and index.
  ISBN 978-1-59797-223-9 (alk. paper)
  1. Political culture—United States. 2. Fascism—United States. 3. National characteristics, American. 4. United States—Civilization. 5. United States—Politics and government—1989– 6. Political culture—Germany—History—20th century. 7. Fascism—Germany—History—20th century. 8. Germany—Politics and government—1918–1933. 9. Germany—Politics and government—1933–1945. 10. National characteristics, German. I. Title.
  E183.F64 2009
  306.20973–dc22

                                        2009015028

Printed in the United States of America on acid-free paper that meets the American National Standards Institute Z39-48 Standard.

The author's photo on the dust jacket is by Tony Nelson. Used with permission.

Potomac Books, Inc.
22841 Quicksilver Drive
Dulles, Virginia 20166

First Edition

10 9 8 7 6 5 4 3 2 1

In Memoriam

Edward T. Fogarty
September 30, 1922–June 6, 1944

CONTENTS

PREFACE

THIS BOOK BEGAN, as I suspect many do, with memorable teaching experiences. My most memorable have involved traveling with students and my former colleague Dale McGowan to Germany and Austria to study the relationship of German culture to the rise of National Socialism. In these trips, we focused on German music, and particularly the operas of Richard Wagner, as our entry point into German history, philosophy, and social thought.

Trying to get students, from their American point of view, to understand the Germans' descent into National Socialism was a great challenge for me as an educator. As I sought ways to help them grasp what it might have felt like to be an ordinary German citizen in the 1920s and 1930s, I drew parallels to the sorts of political and ideological struggles they could see in contemporary American politics in the wake of the 9/11 terrorist attacks: calls for bold and decisive leadership and for military vengeance, appeals to an arrogant sort of nationalism, a notable lack of dissent, acquiescence in greater government surveillance and arrest powers, a wartime mentality, and an almost pathological veneration of the common man against elites of all sorts. The whole thing ultimately rekindled in me the question that nags many of those who have studied the Third Reich: could it happen here? I'm grateful to both McGowan and our intrepid students for helping me find ways to address that question.

By lucky circumstance, I was up for sabbatical leave at about the time I began this project, and by even luckier circumstance, I was granted the Carol Easley Denny Award to help fund the research for this book. I am very grateful to St. Catherine University and to Charles Denny and the Denny family for their great assistance.

As writing progressed, I was helped by several cherished colleagues. Jeanne Emmons, professor of English at Briar Cliff University, read and critiqued the chapter on Romanticism. Jane Lamm Carroll, associate professor of history at St. Catherine, helped with Populism and Nationalism. Paul Schons, professor of German at the University of St. Thomas, helped with interpretations of German culture on several chapters. I am grateful to them and to many other supportive and helpful colleagues.

My wife, Cheryl, provided much critique and support and was helpful in innumerable other ways. My marriage to her is one more lucky circumstance.

—1—

INTRODUCTION

THE GEORGE W. BUSH ERA IS OVER. The 2008 elections confirmed a growing public disillusionment with the "bold leadership" and ideological fervor of the Bush administration, which was the last hurrah, for now, of the neoconservative movement. Postmortem analyses of the election results were stunning: the Republican ticket lost ground in virtually every state compared with the 2004 election, and it lost ground with most income groups, with Hispanics, with women, with young voters, and, of course, with African Americans. This latter finding was only the least obvious manifestation of the most stunning fact of all: the Bush legacy had become so discredited that the American people had elected a black president, something most people thought simply could not happen.

It seemed an overwhelming refutation of the many dire warnings—dozens of books, scores of magazine articles, and thousands of blogs—that had shouted of a coming era of totalitarianism, of one-party rule, of an end to the Bill of Rights, and even of fascism. Some explicitly claimed that America had already passed the point of no return and would follow Germany's earlier path into the dark night of a fascist state.

The warnings were not entirely implausible. It was true that a turgid sort of militarist nationalism had come to dominate the political discourse since the attacks of September 11, 2001, and American foreign relations had adopted an imperial arrogance that worried many at home and abroad. It was true that Congress had acquiesced in the rush to war in Iraq, as many likely opponents feared being stigmatized as soft on terrorism. Congress had also gone along with the Uniting and Strengthening America by

Providing Appropriate Tools Required to Intercept and Obstruct Terrorism (USA PATRIOT) Act, thereby legalizing a variety of intrusions into citizens' private lives as well as exceptions to their most fundamental legal rights. And in the climate of fear and anger that had been encouraged, the cooperation of Congress was not always even necessary. It was true that the administration on its own invented a new category of detainees who had neither the protections of prisoner of war status nor the rights of civilian criminal suspects. It was true that the president had adopted a policy of employing signing statements to selectively enforce laws passed by Congress according to his own agenda and ideology. It was true that in attempting to achieve a total partisan domination of the institutions of government, the administration had fired federal prosecutors who had not zealously enough pursued cases damaging to Democratic interests or had too zealously prosecuted the administration's friends. The administration similarly had interfered in various other components of the executive branch, including the regulatory powers of the Food and Drug Administration and the Federal Communications Commission, even going so far as to impose a litmus test on abortion attitudes when hiring staff workers for the Green Zone in Baghdad.[1]

But these issues did not sway voters in their choice at the polls. Polls showed that for the great majority of voters the most important issue in the election was the economy, followed by the failing and expensive Iraq War and by the fear of terrorism. Looking down the list, there were the usual concerns over taxation, moral issues, health care, education, and so on but not domestic surveillance, the rendition and torture of supposed enemy combatants, or the imprisonment of citizens without charge. These last three issues weren't even included among the questions the pollsters asked.[2]

One might also wonder whether the outcome would have been the same if the Iraq and Afghanistan wars had reached a successful conclusion, if John McCain had run a better-focused campaign aimed at centrist voters, if he had chosen a more competent running mate than Sarah Palin, or if he had been twenty years younger. Most of all, what if there had not been such a stunning financial and economic crisis, blossoming with such perfect timing to reinforce the Democratic message? What if there had been a significant terror attack during the fall of 2008? It's easy to forget that the two candidates were virtually tied in the polls just a few months prior to the election. It's also easy to forget that even with so many cards stacked against McCain's candidacy, 46 percent of the voters cast their ballots for the McCain-Palin ticket.

The Democrats did win the election but not because the nation heeded the warnings about the possibility of increased government intrusion and control. In fact, within days of the election, the conservative pundits and radio voices resumed their drumbeat of abuse on the president-elect. They claimed that he was a friend of terrorists, that he was vaguely foreign or un-American, that he was a dangerous radical or a Socialist or Communist. Rush Limbaugh gleefully sang a ditty titled "Barack the Magic Negro" on his broadcast. These critics' ratings had not suffered much: Limbaugh, Sean Hannity, Bill O'Reilly, William Bennett, and G. Gordon Liddy were still doing fine. In the end, the Democrats won the election because the neoconservative agenda had hit a couple of snags—that is, stagnation in Iraq and an economic crash. The elements of the McCain-Palin ticket that appealed to their voters were the same ones that had worked for George Bush and Richard Cheney: bold leadership; unilateral militarism; spread-eagle patriotism; an antiurban, anti-intellectual populism; a focus on national security fears; and maybe just a bit of racist jingoism. As it happens, these same cultural and ideological themes roused the Germans of the 1920s to support an upstart party called the National Socialist German Workers' Party—the Nazi Party.

This book is not about the excesses of the Bush administration, about conspiracies in high places, or about the evils of conservative politics. Rather, it is about the reasons Americans seem drawn from time to time toward a certain form of extremist politics called fascism. Concern about fascist tendencies in American life is not new; indeed, it has troubled Americans of various political and philosophical leanings since the coming of the Third Reich. As early as 1935, Sinclair Lewis's bestselling novel *It Can't Happen Here* struck a nerve in the American consciousness by postulating a takeover of the White House by a Nazi-like regime. Lewis had reason to worry; a wave of sympathy for National Socialist Germany was gaining popularity at the time, and for many of the same reasons the Nazis had been granted power in Germany. In the 1950s the witch hunts and Red-baiting of the Cold War era led many to decry the return of fascist leanings in American politics. As Americans entered the post-9/11 era—this age of continuous fear of terrorists and a growing government security apparatus—they were treated to a host of new comparisons. Most notable were Philip Roth's novel *The Plot Against America* and Joe Conason's

It Can Happen Here: Authoritarian Peril in the Age of Bush, both of which alluded strongly to Sinclair Lewis's nightmare scenario. Conason's book had the additional virtue of being nonfiction. But these warnings were not confined to the professional thinkers and writers. Worries about American totalitarianism are as old as the founding of the republic itself, and worries about the specter of fascism have been expressed many times—not always appropriately—by ordinary people whose frustrations with government have so often been summed up in the handy phrase "Isn't this how Hitler started?"

As a matter of fact, the events of the past several years did resemble the step-by-step dismantling of democratic institutions that occurred in Germany of the 1930s, if at a slower pace. There, as here, a democratically installed government with a weak mandate capitalized on fears of foreign and domestic conspiracy to centralize power in the executive. Key elements of the rule of law were suspended in the name of security, surveillance of foreign and domestic communication was undertaken, and the onset of war rendered dissent unpatriotic. Citizens were encouraged to report suspicious activity at airports and other public places. While the Bush administration could not criminalize its political opponents as the Nazis did, its proponents did not hesitate to denounce them as enemy sympathizers and defeatists. Explicit criminalization of its opposition was unnecessary, as the American Congress, media, and public had effectively silenced themselves. Few had the political strength to object.

It was this general acceptance of, and even demand for, restrictions of freedoms and aggrandizement of the executive that most resembled the German experience. If the excesses of the Bush era were a far cry from those of a fascist state, the Americans' underlying political feelings in the post-9/11 era were not so different from those felt by Germans in the 1920s. The events of 2001 through 2008 ought to raise deep questions about how Americans respond to a crisis: by compromising constitutional rights, by increasing surveillance of citizens, by demonizing legitimate opposition, by placing national unity above reasoned discourse, and most of all, by clamoring for bold and even reckless executive leadership in hopes of saving the day. In short, Americans have reacted to crisis in much the same way the Germans did in their hour of need after World War I. The difference is that Americans have not yet faced crises as deep and as threatening as those faced by the Germans, and thus we have been able to right ourselves before it was too late.

Still, the experience of the Bush era should raise questions in the minds of thoughtful Americans: how did we allow these excesses to happen? Why did the public acquiesce in the abridgement of the Bill of Rights, in reckless military adventure, and in government by executive fiat? What made it so difficult to oppose the administration's policies? Why couldn't the American people even muster a clear voting majority in the 2004 election, after most of these excesses were already known?

The simplistic answer is that the Bush administration seized excessive power through false claims, fear mongering, and divisive politics. But the sobering truth is that many Americans were well aware of these maneuverings and denied that they could be happening, rationalized them away, or simply went along with them anyway. And though many other Americans—maybe a majority—were horrified by these policies and by the whole tenor of the administration's philosophy of government, somehow they were unable to mount an effective opposition. Too often, what they had to say was the sort of thing that could not be said—that Americans do not have a monopoly on righteousness, that Iraq was not the enemy, that Islamic fundamentalism arose for a reason, that the world is not divided simply into the Good and the Evil, and riskiest of all, that the 9/11 attacks did not really "change everything"—and consequently, such truth tellers always seemed vaguely seditious.

This book rejects simplistic answers to our recent flirtation with fascism. Instead of asking what the Bush administration did to "seize" excessive power, it asks why Americans seem so ready to grant excessive power in times of crisis, as the Germans did in theirs. The answer lies in American values: the Bush administration was better attuned to a number of deeply held American ideals, yearnings, and assumptions than its opponents were, and it was thus generally able to marginalize those opponents. As it happens, these deeply held values also ran deep in German culture.

WHAT IS FASCISM?

There are two great difficulties in making an argument regarding fascist elements in American culture. The first is that the word "fascist" is so inflammatory that its very use immediately engages the wrong kind of response: that the speaker is simply against America and its ideals and seeks only to slander the country and its people. The second problem derives from the first: the word's only utility is as a slur and it has no real meaning, in the way curse words lose their literal meanings. Hence, we have seen in recent years rampant misuse of the term, almost always to defame or dismiss some group or opposing point of view. Calling people fascists even became something of a Washington fad for a while. Donald Rumsfeld did so by implication when he compared those against the Iraq War to Neville Chamberlain, who appeased Hitler in 1938. There followed a proliferation of supposed fascists, all sorts of them. In addition to anti–Iraq War fascists, there were Islamo-fascists, so dubbed by the Bush administration, who want to kill us and take over the world. Then there were the liberal fascists, described by Jonah Goldberg in his *Liberal Fascism: The Secret History of the American Left, from Mussolini to the Politics of Meaning.* In it, according to the publisher's press release, Goldberg argued that political correctness on campus and calls for campaign finance reform parallel the practices of the Third Reich. There had been for some time the branding of feminists as "Feminazis" by right-wing talk radio personalities. Finally, there were the usual cries of fascism applied to the right wing whenever they took up the issues of illegal immigrants, gun rights, or crime.

It has become common to equate any authoritarian sentiment or, for that matter, any restriction on individual license with fascism, especially when it's a restriction that one doesn't like. To apply the term to an organized proto-government like the Taliban's is at least appropriate in scale and intensity; it does fit most definitions of a brutally authoritarian regime. But that doesn't make its adherents fascists. The czars were authoritarian, too, and so were the Soviets, but they weren't fascists. The regimes of Idi Amin, François "Papa Doc" Duvalier, and the Bourbon kings of France were not fascist either. Not every case of a government pushing its citizens around qualifies as fascism.

Rather, fascism is a particular form of totalitarianism, one that enlists the citizens themselves to cooperate in their own oppression. A fascist regime—the National Socialists are the model here—is a genuine populist movement that derives its power from the people's yearning for national greatness, cultural purity, intense solidarity, and bold, authoritarian leadership to make it all happen. The National Socialists worked hard to make the German people believe that the regime was doing the people's work in crushing communism, in going to war to gain *lebensraum* (living space) in the east, and in ridding the country of Jews and other "non-German" elements. It exalted German culture—the "true" German culture—above all others and elevated the German people as well. Most of all, the National Socialists consistently promoted the idea of the unity and equality of all Germans through an end to political partisanship, to labor-management strife, and to political dispute. In short, they promised an end to the ills of democratic dithering and interest politics—an end to democracy itself. This message was the magic appeal of the Nazis—the final unification of the Germans into one people. If the leadership was harsh, it had to be so to achieve these goals, and citizens felt obliged to help accomplish them.

The Nazis came to power by campaigning for more than a decade on these themes, refining their approach, focusing their appeals, and reading the public mood until January 1933, when Hitler was handed the chancellorship in a brokered deal. They were not especially good administrators and their party was splintered into factions for most of its life, but they did possess one invaluable asset—their leader's ability to articulate the above themes in a way that resonated with the average German citizen. And even if a majority of the citizens weren't swayed, they were at least silenced by fear of being labeled defeatists by their fellow citizens.

The same themes that carried the Nazis to power can be found deep in the American political psyche as well. Under the fear of terrorism and the stress of war, the populist and nationalist elements of American political values came increasingly to the surface. The public and its representatives called for greater scrutiny of foreigners as well as for greater restrictions on immigration. The military was sanctified in every mention, whether in the media, at the ballpark, or in the schools. The country was divided into a "real" America, comprising small-town families whose kids played ball on a dirt field, and another one centered in large cities, where people read lots of books, questioned American policies, drove foreign hybrid cars, and sipped cappuccino. Voters rejected the presidential candidacies of Al Gore in 2000 and John Kerry in 2004 partly because both men were simply too erudite, too cautious, and too verbal. Instead, voters responded to the candidate who seemed more certain, more instinctive, more angry, more bold. And through it all, the voters' opinion of Congress was dismal.

The election of Barack Obama ran counter to most of these cultural themes, and that is what makes it remarkable. If the Obama presidency is effective at solving the current financial crisis, these themes will subside into the woodwork for a while, and we will undo the political damage of the Bush era. But America has buried political excesses before, only to see them return when times changed. Warren Harding's election, after the "Red Scare" of Woodrow Wilson's administration, brought a "return to normalcy," which lasted for a few decades. John F. Kennedy's election in 1960 effectively buried the remnants of McCarthyism. Lyndon Johnson's landslide in 1964 brought an end to Jim Crow racism and the beginning of the end of de facto discrimination. Jimmy Carter's win was a reaction to the era of Richard Nixon's enemies lists and secret investigations. Barack Obama's election will stand among these other turning points in the American political discourse.

But it is also true that none of these elections brought a permanent end to an ongoing agitation in American politics for greater government control over morals, over aliens and other marginal people, and over thought and at the same time expansion of American influence and control over the circumstances of other nations. There has always been a strong voice for increased executive power, for a bigger military, for restrictions on immigrants, for promotion of Americanism, for Christian dominance, for "common sense" in the face of Eastern intellectuals, for the rancher against the city folk. During the Bush years, these themes waxed in prominence and moved America toward fascism in a number of ways, but in the end, the country was saved from a dire outcome. But if the American voters were so smart in rejecting the Bush Doctrine in 2008, why didn't they do it in 2004?

The political winds change direction when crises strike. In 2008 the threat of economic collapse turned voters away from the arrogance of exceptionalism, from the sort of populism that rejects intellect and polish, from the taint of racism, and from a romantic desire for bold and reckless action. But the Obama era will not last forever, any more than Harding's return to normalcy or Kennedy's Camelot or Johnson's Great Society did. For that matter, it is not at all clear that the Obama administration will be able to save the country from ruin. What then? When we are visited by new crises in the right combination, we will be open to new fears, new suspicions, new enemies, new calls for obedience, new surveillance, and new compromises to the Constitution. We will move again in the direction of the self-oppression of fascist politics.

This book does not predict when this will happen or even whether it will. Rather, its purpose is to caution readers that it could happen, given the right circumstances. In the 1920s Germany was beset with a crushing military defeat, a failed economy, and the contempt of much of the community of nations. Without these conditions, it is almost certain Hitler's Nazis would have been just another fringe party consigned to history. Instead, these crises were fuel for a firestorm of frustration and then of hysteria for revolutionary and reckless change. It does not seem so impossible to imagine such crises befalling the United States. The following pages argue that should such dire events beset Americans, we could very likely respond in the same way.

—2—

CAUSE AND CULTURE

NINETEEN THIRTY-SIX WAS A GOOD YEAR to be a German. The economy had improved; at least what money the Germans had was worth something. The Treaty of Versailles had become an irrelevance as Germany chipped away at its restrictions. The 1936 Nazi Party rally was the best ever, even grander than the one immortalized in Leni Riefenstahl's *Triumph of the Will*, which had been released to international acclaim the previous year. Germany was regaining its standing among nations, symbolized by its hosting of both the Winter and Summer Olympic Games.

A German sitting in the Olympic Stadium that summer would have had reason to feel relief and pride. Still, there were worries. Progress had been made, but at what cost? Political and social discord had been quelled, but that had largely been accomplished by harassing or jailing opponents of the government, which now was synonymous with the party. The world was again paying attention to Germany, but it was not always the best sort of attention. The moral license and decadent entertainments of the past were rolled back, but it all seemed to put Germany out of step with the rest of the world.

More thoughtful Germans were concerned. The betterment of Germany had come with an increasingly overbearing political regime. The rule of law had been largely suspended, and people were looking over their shoulders and casting a wary eye on their neighbors. And the constant propaganda made it seem as if Germany was in an unending, shrill election campaign but with only one party contending. Still, if harsh measures had been taken, most seemed to agree that it was a fair price to pay for a better society. The world had again begun to make sense, and the Germans were enormously relieved. Even those who did not admire the führer had to give him credit as the architect of Germany's rebirth. If nothing else, he was a bold, audacious leader who inspired confidence, and that was worth a great deal.

Did those Germans seated in the Olympic Stadium know they were about to become part of the greatest evil of the twentieth century? Were they aware of the threat that Hitler and his party posed to their families, their neighbors, their country, their world? Could the Berliners, Nurembergers, Leipzigers, and the citizens of the other German cities and villages have foreseen their social, political, and moral destruction at the hands of the Nazis?

Of course not. Had they been able to see the future, even the most fanatical among them would have sent Hitler packing. But if the future that came to pass was unimaginable at the time, many in the crowd foresaw the possibility of increased political repression, expanded racist policies, war, and widespread suffering. Still, what could they do about it? How could they stop the political juggernaut they saw before them, powered by the upraised voices and raised right arms of so many of their fellow citizens? Better to bide their time, wait for the political winds to change, and hope for the best meanwhile. Maybe it wouldn't be so bad.

None of us can see the future, especially the unimaginable sort. Yet Americans have now and then had cause to worry just as those Germans did in the 1930s. Consider the U.S. anti-immigration laws of the early twentieth century, fueled by a vigorous eugenics movement; the militarist hysteria of the Spanish-American War, reprised by Woodrow Wilson during World War I; the Prohibition movement, which was at least partly aimed at controlling foreign elements like the Irish and the Germans; populist heroes like Father Charles Coughlin, Joseph McCarthy, and countless smaller fry who mixed jingoism and racism with their assaults on one "elite" or another; the fundamentalist fervor of the Scopes trial and a hundred prayer-in-the-schools battles; and the internment of American citizens of Japanese descent during World War II. And these examples are but momentary excesses compared to the destruction of native cultures and peoples and the long-lived institution of slavery. At times we Americans have been capable of the most egregious departures from our own ideals.

Nor can we ignore the recent outrages of the post-9/11 era, only now starting to be undone: imprisonment without charge of enemy combatants caged at Guantánamo and elsewhere with neither the protections of POW status nor access to the courts, domestic spying on Americans in direct defiance of the Constitution, Pat Robertson's prayer for vacancies on the Supreme Court (answered, it would seem, with Chief Justice William Rehnquist's death), and a sustained anti-knowledge movement led by the push for creationism and its "lite" version, intelligent design, in the public schools. We Americans have endured our share of demagogues and cranks over the years, but we have managed to shrug them off before it was too late. Yet McCarthy, Coughlin, and all the forgotten others gained notoriety precisely because their views struck a chord in the American consciousness. They had their time in the spotlight because Americans have always been too receptive to the simple answer, the jingoistic accusation, or the radical solution.

What we haven't had is a series of crises as deep and as threatening as those the Germans faced after 1918. Here was a people whose vaunted military had lost a ghastly total war, who became saddled with punitive economic and political penalties as a result of it, who had endured a revolution that created a leftist government in which they had little faith, who had suffered frightful economic instability, and who had witnessed unprecedented change in moral, social, and aesthetic values. These calamities were unlike any seen in the United States since the Civil War and maybe not even then. Would Americans still resist the appeals of the "next Hitler" if our current troubles were compounded—if, for example, our overextension in Iraq and Afghanistan were to become a genuine military debacle while energy shortages, deflation and recession, and more terrorist attacks at home rubbed raw the nerves of average Americans? Is it possible, given the right series of genuinely grave misfortunes, that Americans might embrace the sort of enthusiastic revolution that the National Socialists offered the Germans?

If in such times a charismatic orator and ardent nationalist were to hold a mass rally at Washington's Lincoln Memorial or Chicago's Grant Park or New York City's Ground Zero, would he or she draw a crowd? If such an orator were to bemoan the current state of affairs—global terrorism, military failure, moral decline, godlessness—and blame it all on the elites, the international capitalists, the Muslims, Hollywood, the banks, the press, the professors, and, most of all, the entrenched Washington bureaucrats, would the message be taken seriously? If he or she were to call for sweeping reforms of the schools, the sacking of subversive elements from government positions, redoubled surveillance and control of citizens, arrests without due process for suspicious foreigners, expulsion of Muslim immigrants, and wholesale impeachment of activist judges, would a majority of us object? Could we, in short, become collaborators in our own repression, as the Germans did? Could the United States become a fascist society?

THE "CAUSE" OF NAZISM

We can approach these questions by asking how fascism arose in Germany. The actual sequence of events is clear enough. After four years of blood-letting in World War I—a static, miserable idiocy that was supposed to have been over in a few months—Germany was defeated. The subsequent Treaty of Versailles included punitive reparations and loss of territory for Germany, humiliations that many Germans could not bear. The imperial government was discredited, and the general political and social chaos gave birth in 1918 to Germany's first republican government, born of revolution and the kaiser's abdication. The Weimar Republic, as it was called, was unprecedentedly liberal, democratic, and egalitarian. It accorded full civil rights to Jews, for example, and even included them in the government.

But the Weimar government struggled for legitimacy. Many Germans lamented the loss of the kaiser, the aristocracy, and, most of all, the old values. Many despised the Weimar government's endorsement of modern-ism in the arts and in political and social thought. Many more hated its willingness to pay war reparations and blamed its founders for signing the Treaty of Versailles in the first place. It wasn't helped by the currency crisis of 1923, during which the mark fell in value from four to the dollar to a breathtaking four billion to the dollar. It's no wonder that Germany was beset with coup attempts, assassinations, and general unrest.

The National Socialist Party capitalized on the Germans' anger and alienation and began to make gains in the parliament. Its popularity grew in fits and starts until, at the beginning of 1933, the Nazis had won enough seats to impose a deadlock on the selection of a new chancellor. Hitler pressured the aging President Paul von Hindenburg to allow him to form a government with himself as chancellor, after which the Nazis immediately began consolidating power by various legal and extralegal measures: staged riots, assassination of opponents, and new heights in political propaganda. As each new law was railroaded though the parliament, as each new fear was agitated, as each new spectacle was staged, Germany moved toward the passage of the Enabling Act of 1933, by which Adolf Hitler himself was declared the only law in Germany. It was ratified by 90 percent of the voters in a later plebiscite. The light of democracy had gone out.

Everybody has a theory about how and why the Nazis were able to take hold of German society. For many, it was the worldwide depression and the lingering effects of the currency crisis. Hitler's promise to repair the economy was a powerful vote getter, just as it is today in American politics. For others, the crisis was political, amounting to a loss of faith in the Weimar government's ability to maintain control. Still others point to the loss of the war as the source of bitterness and wounded national pride, which the Nazis promised to restore. A Marxian line of theory suggests that the whole thing was the product of the economic interests of the capitalist class, which helped install the Nazis to ward off the Bolsheviks. For many Germans, even today, the cause was the unfair and ruinous Versailles Treaty, with which the victorious allies of World War I humiliated and punished Germany beyond the breaking point. Then there is the popular and simplistic favorite: that a madman named Hitler took over Germany and turned it to his evil obsession with world domination.

So which of the theories is true? Which one fits the historical narrative? The answer, of course, is that they all do. Hitler really was a madman, given to dreams of greatness as the savior of the German people, to an abiding hatred of Jews, and to a predisposition toward violent headaches and fits of rage. The problem is there are plenty of such madmen in a country of any size. Surely the United States harbors thousands of potential Hitlers, but they don't usually rise to power, or if they do, the voters and the Constitution keep them more or less in check. So while we acknowledge Hitler's madness as a contributing cause of Nazism (a saner man wouldn't have created the regime he did), our question about the cause of Nazism has to focus upstream from Hitler's personality: what caused the Germans to put Hitler in power?

Certainly the ongoing sense of economic chaos in the 1920s helped make the Germans susceptible to the Nazis' appeals. And we also know that such chaos breeds social and moral disarray, as expressed by one contemporary observer of the Weimar era:

It was a time of intense revaluation—in the economy and culture, in material as well as psychological things. Rich people who could have afforded all the pleasures in the world were suddenly glad to have someone hand them a bowl of warm soup. Overnight little apprentices became powerful bank directors and possessed seemingly inexhaustible funds. Foreigners, some of the most impoverished of pensioners at home, could suddenly step out in Germany like princes. Everything seemed reversed.[1]

Long-standing social conventions seemed to lose their effect; after all, if the future looks bleak, one should live for today. All sorts of social, artistic, and sexual license threatened the traditions that Germans had revered for generations. Policies that accommodated such change and welcomed its instigators were themselves thought morally corrupt. As for political crisis, there is nothing like defeat in war to drive rifts into the social fabric. When the war is lost, it's hard to admit the valiant have died in vain.

Given recent events, one might imagine American society in such a circumstance someday: defeated in war, economically ruined, surrounded by enemies, friendless in the community of nations, beset by violence and terrorism, and subject to a deep sense of moral and spiritual malaise. How might Americans respond then? Would we fall back on the lofty principles of the Constitution, petitioning our representatives to make judicious and wise policy to facilitate our national recovery? Given our recent history in responding to threats, the answer would seem to be no.

The Germans, for their part, looked to a strong leader with ready explanations for their troubles and simple, moralistic solutions to them. Hitler and the Nazis offered them all. They called their program National Socialism, and it combined the nationalist anger of the political Right with the socialist impulse for equality and unity of the Left. To these appeals it added something that Benito Mussolini had brought to Italy—a strong central government that was not master of the people but the servant of their unitary and revolutionary will (which, of course, had to be shaped and united by the government itself). It disdained democracy as obsolete, or at least unfit for Germans, who shared a deep common bond of culture, place, and blood. This sort of political regime—uniting the Far Left and the Far Right under a radically activist government dedicated to the elevation of a tyrannical majority—falls under the generic name of fascism.

The Role of Culture
All of the theories of the Nazis' rise are true enough, but they fail to really explain events except by recourse to earlier events, which depend in turn

on even earlier ones, and so on in an infinite regress of previous causes. But there is a solution to this problem: the effect one historical event has on another is always influenced—moderated, exaggerated, or otherwise affected—by the more stable forces of culture. Would the loss of World War I, the subsequent treaty, the ensuing economic strain, and the other historical events have had the same effect on a people who were not as xenophobic, or authoritarian, or antidemocratic, or conformist as the Germans? Would the moral and artistic innovations of the Weimar era have seemed so threatening to a less aesthetically focused people? Would Jews have been so handy a scapegoat where anti-Semitism was less deeply rooted? Ultimately, the social, political, and economic events that we take to be the substance of history can best be understood by understanding the collective values, beliefs, aspirations, and fears of the people involved.

So we look to culture for the answers to the questions of why and how the Nazis rose to power in the first place. We recognize that the simplistic answer—that they (or Hitler personally) somehow seized power and bent the nation to their wishes—is inadequate. The Nazis worked hard for more than a decade to build their political base and throughout the twenties rode a wave of anger—anger over the unfairness of the Versailles Treaty, over foreign influence in German affairs, over the shaky economy, over the loss of the kaiser and the empire, over the democracy and modernism of the Weimar Republic, and over the defeat not only of German arms but of Germanness itself. Some of these sources of wrath were historical opportunities that had simply appeared at a lucky time for the Nazis. But many were deeply rooted in German culture, and the Nazis were just more skilled than others were at tapping into them. Their greatest strength was in translating economic and historical events into affronts to deeply held German values: Germany had lost World War I *because* of the treachery of the Versailles Treaty's signers, who had "stabbed Germany in the back." The economy was ruined *because* of the Jews. Modern art was unfathomable and decadent *because* of the influence of foreigners.

Thus the Nazis took power not by raw seizure but by appealing to values and beliefs close to the hearts of the German people. We know, for example, that anti-Semitism ran deep in Germany, and its target provided a handy enemy against which Germans could unite. The Germans were also fiercely nationalistic, having only just achieved unity as a nation in 1871 after centuries of division as a bagful of kingdoms, principalities, and duchies. The Germans seemed to have a deep yearning for community and order, which must have contributed to the Nazis' rise.

In fact, one can identify five central characteristics of German culture as essential in bringing about the rise of the Nazis:

Romanticism: Manifested in the romantic movement in art, music, literature, and political philosophy, this mode of thought valued feeling over reason, daring over prudence, and heroics over caution. It's what made it possible for the Germans to abandon reason in their political thought and to put their faith in a charismatic leader.

Nationalism: The Germans struggled for centuries for nationhood, and much of their social and philosophical thought concerned itself with the idea of Germanness. This emphasis led many Germans to reject the internationalist Weimar Republic and to endorse Nazi appeals to xenophobia and war.

Populism: This attitude was expressed as the elevation of the *volk*, the simple people of traditional German character and values. Populism was a central theme of National Socialist thought, and it helped weld the Left and the Right of the working class in a powerful movement against real and imagined elites.

Racism: The despised and oppressed "race" was the Jews, regarded clearly as a racial and not just a religious or ethnic group. Anti-Semitism's deep roots in Germany could be manipulated as a strong vote getter when used as an explanation for German suffering.

Authoritarianism: The Germans placed a good deal of faith in the authority not only of leaders but also of the community as a whole. This conviction made it possible for ordinary Germans to report their neighbors to the authorities for various transgressions and ultimately to acquiesce in their ghettoization, imprisonment, and destruction.

Without these elements of German culture, there could not have been a National Socialist state, at least not in the form it ultimately took. Without the strong nationalism, losing the war would not have been such a crushing blow, and perhaps the nation would not have endured the war for as long as it had in the first place. Without the anti-Semitism, the mountain of blame heaped on the Jews would not have scored points with voters. Without a strong current of authoritarianism, more Germans might have resisted the rise of the party or, at least, resisted the passage of such laws as the Enabling Act. Without the populism, Hitler and his henchmen would have been dismissed as uninformed rabble. Without the German penchant for romanticism, the Nazis would have seemed like a bunch of kooks.

But they didn't seem like that at all, at least not to enough Germans of the 1920s and 1930s. The Nazis harnessed the Germans' most cherished cultural traits by casting themselves as their truest champions. They extolled the romantic ideal of a singular leader who could lead the German people to greatness. They scorned all elites as useless parasites. They decried the influence of Jews in German life because they threatened the fundamental ideal of Germanness. Finally, they offered a hero who ignored petty legalisms and demanded total commitment to his pursuit of a greater German world. These ideals had been staples of Nazi philosophy since Hitler had written *Mein Kampf* and were refined into a coherent political platform throughout the 1920s as the party rose in popularity and support.

Ever Again?

All the theories pertaining to the Nazis' rise to power are true because historical events are always embedded in an entire world of other events, political movements, economic forces, cultural beliefs, strong personalities, and dumb luck. It took all of these things—the currency crisis, the loss of World War I, the Versailles Treaty, the authoritarianism, the anti-Semitism, the libertine culture of the Weimar era, and Hitler's own megalomania—to produce the calamity of the Nazi regime. In this sense, the rise of fascism in Germany, as well as the genocide it organized, was a singular historical event. All of those factors, in just that combination, will never be seen again.

But this conclusion doesn't mean fascism will never return or that there can never be another Hitler. On the contrary, the world has since seen many of the characteristics of fascism—authoritarian government, extreme militarism, officially sanctioned racism and genocide, total control of culture and media—in many political regimes since the end of the Nazi era. And we already recognize that there is no shortage of Hitlers in every country. For that matter, popular myth has it that the "next Hitler" has actually assumed power here and there already: Idi Amin, the Duvaliers, Pol Pot, Ayatollah Khomeini, Mu'ammar al-Gadhafi, Saddam Hussein, Kim Jong Il.

So while events can't ever play out exactly as they did in Germany in the 1920s and 1930s, certainly another fascist regime could arise, and there is little reason to believe that it can't happen in a nation as thoroughly modern and stable as the United States. As early as 1935, Sinclair Lewis thought it possible when he wrote *It Can't Happen Here*, and many other more or less articulate political and social theorists have harbored the same worry.

One of the most penetrating theorists on the history and rise of Nazism in Germany is George Mosse, who wrote in 1966:

> In the end, it is not likely that Europe will repeat the fascist or the National Socialist experience. However, the fragments of our Western cultural and ideological past which fascism used for its own purposes still lie ready to be formed into a new synthesis, even if in a different way. . . . Those ideals of mass politics upon which fascism built its political style are very much alive, for ours is still a visual age to which the "new politics" of fascism were so well attuned. . . . The danger of successful appeals to authoritarianism is always present, however changed from earlier forms or from its present worldwide manifestations.[2]

Novelist and essayist Umberto Eco believes the spirit of fascism is already pervasive. This generic fascist ideology, which he calls Ur-Fascism, "is still around us, sometimes in plainclothes. It would be so much easier, for us, if there appeared on the world scene somebody saying 'I want to reopen Auschwitz, I want the Black Shirts to parade again in the Italian squares.' Life is not that simple. Ur-Fascism can come back in the most innocent of disguises."[3]

THE RISE OF AMERICAN FASCISM

How might fascism arise in contemporary America? If we examine only the immediate historical events that tend to lead to such extremism, it's not so hard to imagine them occurring in the United States in the twenty-first century. The rise of a fascist regime could follow this scenario.

Though the Democrats took control of the White House in 2008, the government is unable to find an acceptable solution to the war on terrorism. Meanwhile, the worldwide recession deepens, and in its attempts to stimulate the economy, the Obama administration runs up massive deficits. Before long foreign investors lose their appetite for American bonds, and the United States no longer has the borrowing power even to incur the deficits. The treasury is forced to simply print more money, devaluing the currency and beginning a spiral of hyperinflation.

Because the war on terrorism can no longer be funded, troops are pulled out of Iraq and Afghanistan. The administration is branded as a dithering gang of defeatists, even traitors. While it tries to roll back some of the elements of the Patriot Act as well as other executive excesses, this effort only adds to the chorus of blame. In Iraq, dominant Shiites form a close alliance with Iran, effectively turning much of Iraq into an Iranian province. President Asif Ali Zardari's government in Pakistan falls, as does that of Hamid Karzai in Afghanistan, increasing instability in the region. Several major terrorist attacks strike the United States, but rather than discrediting the government, they serve to increase the public's demands for it to exert more control in the name of safety.

Muslim Americans and Arab Americans fall under increasing suspicion and sporadic attack. The government conducts occasional sweeps of mosques and Muslim community centers. Civilian crimes of vandalism and assault against Muslims and Arabs are prosecuted vigorously at first, but as prosecutors are punished at the polls for being soft on terror, they learn to focus their energies elsewhere. Thus such attacks gradually become normal and routine.

The public is restless and blames both parties for the government's ineffectiveness—the Republicans for getting us into the mess and the Democrats for failing to find a solution. A third party emerges in the 2016 election year. The National Progressives (NPs), as they call themselves, are fed up with both parties, the stagnation, the ineffectiveness, the partisan bickering. It's immoral, in their view, for Congress to fiddle while the nation is going up in flames. Why can't Congress, and the White House as well, put aside partisanship and just do what's right for the country? The National Progressives elucidate a clear platform that borrows from the philosophy of both the Left and the Right:

1. Wage a "real war" against terrorism. In concert with a new coalition of Asian and Western nations, the Middle East problem is to be resolved once and for all. The growing number of Islamic theocracies, including Iraq, Iran, Afghanistan, and Pakistan, will be replaced through military and economic warfare. The coalition will include most of Europe and Russia, all pestered by Muslim troubles of their own.
2. Strategically default on American bonds sold to foreign governments and investors. For too long, say the NPs, Americans have allowed their country to be mortgaged to foreigners. Besides, the country's credit

can't get any worse anyway. Trillions of dollars of debt now held by foreign banks will be erased, except in the case of allied nations willing to endorse the NPs' new plan to save the world from terrorism.

3. Root out corporate interests in the conduct of national policy. The National Progressives promise to remove the influence of oil companies, military contractors, and other commercial interests in awarding contracts connected to the war against terrorism. Their loud criticism of these interests throughout the campaign plays heroically against the Republican and Democratic candidates, who are largely funded by precisely those interests. Defense contractors are nationalized, as are the major oil companies, large financial concerns and other strategically important industries.

4. Nationalize health care, education, and welfare. The NPs say the states have been forced into a "race to the bottom," providing fewer and fewer public benefits so as not to attract those citizens who need them the most. This conduct has degraded the quality of American life and cheated Americans of their due while more and more of their wealth has been sent abroad. Americans finally get a national health care system.

5. Pursue antiglobalization policies. All free trade treaties are to be abrogated, since they reduce the power of the state and give it to multinational corporations. This power shift tends to dissolve national boundaries and national identities, threatening Americans with a loss of their own cultural identity. Globalization has also unfairly punished American workers, reducing their wages or sending their jobs abroad.

6. Take control of the media. The airwaves have become a cesspool of violence, sex, and crass commercialism. Worse, they are controlled by giant corporations that have become so international that they have no loyalty to the American people anymore. The media arms of these corporations are to be bought by the government—or else their broadcast rights will simply be withdrawn—and run as different channels of a greatly expanded but more closely controlled Public Broadcasting System.

7. Intern or deport all Muslims. Several government-funded studies find that virtually all large-scale terrorist acts have been committed by Muslims in the name of Islamic fundamentalism. The time has come for Americans to unite behind a final solution to our problem and to endorse the internment, investigation, and deportation of all Muslims.

In 2016 the NPs gain six seats in the Senate and thirty in the House. By 2020 they have assembled a strong organization in most of the fifty states and make a challenge for the presidency. Their leader is a fiery orator, a political outsider free from the taint of any experience in elected office. At this point, either the Democrats or Republicans—it doesn't matter which—might adopt the party's platform as a means to capturing the third party's votes. This tactic worked in the 1896 election, when the Democrats nominated William Jennings Bryan, thus outmaneuvering the surging People's Party and forcing it to endorse the Democratic ticket. Or perhaps the NPs would split the vote, preventing either party from winning. The election would then go to Congress, which would likely be deadlocked until the NPs could broker a deal to give their candidate the presidency.

The National Progressives' platform steals a page from the Nazis themselves in appealing to both the Left and the Right. For the Left, it includes national health care and assistance for both education and welfare. It includes labor protection and curbing corporate interests through the antiglobalization efforts. For the Right, there is the heady nationalism afforded by the abrogation of various treaties and the defaulting on bonds held by foreigners. It takes on the moral cleansing of the media through nationalization and, finally, the cultural cleansing accomplished by getting rid of the expanding anti-Christian threat of Islam. For all, there is the economic remedy of erasing debt and of military conquest for securing strategic oil resources.

It's not hard to imagine a scenario in which the United States lurches by progressive steps into fascism. But, of course, that is not the same as saying that it will do so. For even if the circumstances described above should come to pass, we are still left with the question of how the public would respond to each of the political steps taken. Would the public really tolerate repression of Muslims? Would it endorse abrogation of international treaties and a realignment of alliances? Would it permit nationalization of the airwaves? In short, would the National Progressives really win many votes? What kind of people would we have to be—that is, what kind of culture would we have to live by—to go along with such initiatives and grant power to such a party?

The question is a simple one: in what ways do American beliefs, values, and aspirations make us prone to fascism, should events create the conditions described above? The chapters that follow examine the five cultural traits described above, first, as they shaped the Germans' thoughts and actions in the early twentieth century and, second, as they might be found in America today. To the extent that they can be found in contemporary American culture—in short, the extent to which Americans are romantic, nationalist, populist, racist, and authoritarian—we will be open to the same sorts of appeals that the Germans were nearly a century ago.

—3—

ROMANTICISM

WHAT HAPPENS TO DEMOCRACY when people take leave of their reason?

The idea of the enlightened voter, educated and practical enough to apply reason and wisdom to political life, was a cornerstone of the political structure laid down by America's Founding Fathers. It was assumed that candidates for office would appeal to the interests of these enlightened voters, and those who proposed policies aligned with the interests of the most people would win the day. But the American electorate does not typically act on reasoned judgment, and the successful modern campaign strategist recognizes this fact.

Consequently, national election campaigns are not usually waged on concrete issues or principles or even interests. Instead, successful politicians appeal to symbolic pseudo-issues that serve as markers of identity and solidarity—abortion, religion in the schools, family values—or to fears of foreign attack, crime, or racial mixing; or to representations of a candidate's character that the voters well know are brewed up in the boardrooms of media consultants. Are Americans satisfied with this state of affairs? Are we happy with the Swift Boat Veterans discrediting an actual decorated veteran? Or the whisper campaign against John McCain in the 2000 South Carolina primary that implied he had fathered an illegitimate black child? Or the Willie Horton affair of 1988, in which Michael Dukakis was branded as soft on crime? Or, for that matter, Lyndon Johnson's exploitation of nuclear fears to defeat Barry Goldwater in 1964?

We are not satisfied, but there's little sense in blaming the political operatives. We voters abandon our reason time and again during most election campaigns; consequently, such campaigns are effective. Most of the time that doesn't do too much harm. Whether one candidate or the other is elected to the presidency, a congressional seat, or the state house may shift policy one way or another, but it usually doesn't threaten the institution of democratic government itself.

But once in a while it matters a great deal—when, for example, the country is in crisis and the executive reaches for power beyond that granted by the Constitution. During periods of economic instability, war, and internal unrest or threat, the people's taste for democracy is at greatest risk, and this seems as true of Americans as of anyone else. In such times, we tend to seek strong leadership, which usually amounts to single-party dominance and executive rule. We acquiesce in the abridgement of freedoms, trading liberty for safety. We abandon faith in reason and judgment and in prudence and caution. We are prone to rash, uncompromising solutions to complex and subtle problems, because thinking about them is too unpleasant.

Americans found themselves in this state immediately following 9/11. The sense of crisis created by the attacks and by the war on terrorism did not shake the public into caution and sensibility; to the contrary, it sharpened the public's appetite for daring action. Congress responded to the clamor a month later by handing the administration extraordinary powers to address the threats, as the Patriot Act was approved with a single dissenting Senate vote. This ceding of power only helped to reinforce the crisis atmosphere, which was redoubled with the onset of the war in Iraq and Afghanistan. Later Congress granted legitimacy to the Iraq War, with all of the Democratic senators who would later contend for the presidency voting yea. By the 2004 election campaign, it had become difficult for any candidate to articulate an opposition viewpoint without appearing weak, even disloyal.

In these circumstances, the use of reason and of thoughtful discussion and debate was not politically effective in America. It had been replaced by a more hubristic vision of how to govern, as Ron Suskind related:

> [A White House aide] said that guys like me were "in what we call the reality-based community," which he defined as people who "believe that solutions emerge from your judicious study of discernable reality. ... That's not the way the world really works anymore," he continued. "We're an empire now, and when we act, we create our own reality. And while you're studying that reality—judiciously, as you will—we'll

act again, creating other new realities, which you can study too, and that's how things will sort out. We're history's actors . . . and you, all of you, will be left to just study what we do."[1]

The George W. Bush administration capitalized on the public's preference for bold leadership over reality-based policy, but there's little point in blaming the administration. The simple fact is that every day the president railed against the "evil dictator" Saddam Hussein, "those who hate freedom," European "appeasers," "people who want to kill your family," or other of America's "enemies," he had a pretty good day. On those occasions when he strayed into considered discussion of foreign policy options, his political base vilified or ignored him altogether.

––––––––––

The United States is a product of the Age of Reason, but that is the United States on paper, the parchment nation set forth in the Constitution. We Americans actually value reason fairly lightly; fine for engineers and corporate executives, but no basis for national policy, ethics, or even education. There are more votes to be gained by a vaguely articulated bold vision than by reams of well-considered policy; dreams are more important than plans; and Ronald Reagan's "It's Morning in America" campaign will trump Walter Mondale's call for a nuclear freeze and passage of the Equal Rights Amendment every time. In short, we are a nation of romantics.

The Germans were like that, too. When in the 1920s crisis begat more crisis, from defeat in war to runaway inflation to moral and artistic upheaval, the Germans' romantic side led them to a series of political choices that ultimately brought their nation's utter destruction, along with that of a good part of the rest of the world. Today we generally view the Germans as the archetype of a rational and clearheaded people. Germans historically have been leaders in science, philosophy, the arts, and much of what we consider modern thought. But in the early twentieth century this sober and conservative people simply went mad with enthusiasm for a heroic and revolutionary new order. Drunk with a sort of hopeful ecstasy, they abandoned their reason as they acquiesced, step by step, in the policies of a regime that became the most notorious in modern history.

It was passion, not reason, that the National Socialists exploited in their political campaigns and later used to keep the German populace to heel. Perhaps the defining feature of German fascism was its appeal to the emotional side of German thought, with its basis in pageantry and agitation rather than in reasonable thought or even self-interest. National Socialism as a political movement fed on a rich diet of emotional energy, of symbols and ritual, of anti-Semitic stereotypes, and of revolutionary fervor. Possibly the clearest example of this emotionalism in German life of the period is the following description of the 1936 Nazi Party Rally in Nuremberg:

Twilight covers the Zeppelin Meadow as we enter the grandstand. It is only on the outer limits of the field that a sea of light envelops the walls formed by the flags of the movement, which extend and shine for miles into the dark evening. Twenty straight columns cut across the square of the Zeppelin Field; they are the 140,000 political wardens, who have formed ranks in rows of twelve. Innumerable swastika flags flutter in the light evening breeze, torn from the darkness by the floodlights, and providing a sharp contrast to the pitch black nocturnal sky. The Zeppelin Field proves to be too small. The stands will not hold the vast stream of people who are moving without pause. . . .

A distant roar becomes stronger and comes ever closer. The Führer is there! Reich Organizational Leader Dr. Ley gives him the report on the men who are standing in parade formation. And then, a great surprise, one among many. As Adolf Hitler is entering the Zeppelin Field, 150 floodlights of the Air Force blaze up. They are distributed around the entire square, and cut into the night, erecting a canopy of light in the midst of darkness. For a moment, all is deathly quiet. The surprise still is too great. Nothing like it has ever been seen before. The wide field resembles a powerful Gothic cathedral made of light. Bluish-violet shine the floodlights, and between their cone of light hangs the dark cloth of night. One hundred and forty thousand people—for it must be that many who are assembled here—cannot tear their eyes away from the sight. Are we dreaming, or is it real? Is it possible to imagine a thing like that? A cathedral of light? They do not have the time to pursue such thoughts, for a new spectacle is awaiting them. It is perhaps even more beautiful and compelling for those whose senses can embrace it.

Dr. Ley reports the march-in of the colors. Nothing is to be seen yet. But then they emerge from the black night—over there, on the southern edge. Seven columns of flags pour into the spaces between the ranks. You cannot see the people, you do not recognize the bearers of the flags. All you can see is an undulating stream, red and broad, its surface sparkling with gold and silver, which slowly comes closer like fiery lava.[2]

Such hyperbole might be expected where the media are state controlled. But whether newspaper readers found such accounts persuasive or comical, there is little doubt that the attendees of these rallies were completely taken in by the sheer appeal of ecstatic communion. One participant admitted, "It was a definite struggle to remain rational in a horde so surcharged with tense emotionalism."[3] Even foreigners invited to attend the rallies were impressed. British ambassador Nevile Henderson called the 1937 rally "both solemn and beautiful."[4]

One of the factors that allowed the Nazis to come to power in Germany was the way the German people had become used to thinking and making judgments. They had come to view thoughtfulness, tolerance, and prudence as wrongheaded and cowardly, as signs of a lack of conviction, and as unpatriotic. They had come to devalue reason as a way of judging policy and turned to boldness of vision and righteous faith as better guides. They had come to see the world as a mysterious, chaotic place, governed by forces that could not be comprehended except by recourse to ideas about what *must* be true. They too had come to disparage reality-based thinking, and the Nazis were only too happy to indulge them.

These two faces of the German character—the cool reason of the sciences on the one hand and the deep attachment to the mystical and the emotional on the other—reflect a historical contradiction in German culture. It is the contradiction between two great cultural movements: the Enlightenment, during which the West threw off the shackles of church orthodoxy and sought a new, rational understanding of the world; and the romantic era that followed, during which much of the West rebelled against the Enlightenment's sterile reason.

ENLIGHTENMENT AND ITS DISCONTENTS

As most Europeans, the German people had in the seventeenth and eighteenth centuries found themselves in a period of transformation. For centuries, Europe had been climbing out of the darkness of the Middle Ages through global exploration, trade with the Far East and the New World, the rediscovery of the Greek and Roman ideals, and a spirit of technological innovation led by the harnessing of nonanimal power and the construction of great cathedrals. All these changes, encapsulated in the ideals of the Renaissance, had gradually led the way out of the stagnation of the past. They culminated in the cultural revolution called the Enlightenment, so described because it had swept away the darkness of theocracy and superstition in a blaze of clarity. It was as if someone had turned on the lights and everyone, finally, could see.

And there was much to discover. Scientists like Isaac Newton, Robert Hooke, Carolus Linnaeus, and Joseph Priestly bathed the world in the light of empiricism, and rapid advances ensued in medicine, physics, astronomy, and biology. The social sciences, too, were born during this period, as society was "discovered" as an object for analysis.[5] The new social thinkers came to believe that the social and political world could be understood by applying logic and careful observation to its analysis and not simply taken for granted as the creation of God or the king.

Enlightenment Principles
This new, scientific way of thinking exemplified the Enlightenment's basic tenets. First among them was the belief in order in every sphere of life. Enlightenment thinkers took as a fundamental assumption that the world was characterized by regularities at every level and that these regularities could be understood. The new thinkers' overriding goal was to discover them and to express them in the simplest possible generalizations, or "laws." This search applied not only to the laws of nature but also to principles of beauty and ethics. Good art was orderly, balanced, understandable. Music was too, with a clearly established key and a melody that a listener could follow. Meanwhile, social and political theorists looked for order and regularity in the social world. Human action was, at least in principle, also governed by forces that could be understood and measured in the same way that gravity or inertia was.[6]

The second basic tenet of the Enlightenment was the belief that reason provided the best way for understanding the world's inherent order. The ancient Greeks had established the principles of logic; fortunately, they had been preserved through the Middle Ages. These principles were perfectly adapted to the work of the Enlightenment thinker; the assumption of an orderly world made explanations based on mysticism, divine intervention, or other magical devices unnecessary. It is only in a random, chaotic universe that one has to resort to unfathomable forces to explain events.

Not all Enlightenment thinkers abandoned religion. The French, to be sure, elevated reason above all religious thought as the only legitimate means of understanding; in fact, one could say that reason became the religion of the French Enlightenment. But the English and American varieties acknowledged God not as an unfathomable or capricious tinkerer but as the ultimate designer of the universe. For these thinkers, scientific methods were viewed not as an antidote to religion but as a way of understanding God's orderly system. God or no God, simplistic recourses to scripture or tradition were questioned at every turn. The certainty of faith had become a jumble of disreputable superstitions and preconceptions that could only mislead one from the truth. In short, the Enlightenment elevated reason and observation above emotion and authority, if not above faith.

The third principal tenet of the Enlightenment was universalism, the belief that humanity could and should engage in the pursuit of universally accepted truths and universally recognized notions of beauty and goodness. What was true must be true for everyone; further, what was beautiful and what was good must also be the same for everyone. All of the civilized world, it was assumed, would naturally embrace the Greco-Roman ideals of the past; thus classical music, classical sculpture, classical architecture, and classical philosophy ruled the day. In social thought, the universalist ideal translated into the search for an essential human nature by which a universal moral system might be developed; thus the ethnographic reports of travelers in the new empires emphasized the similarities among cultures.[7]

These principles—order, reason, and universalism—most clearly distinguished the Enlightenment thinkers from their forebears, and their application could be seen in all three of the classical categories of thought: questions of truth, of beauty, and of goodness. Enlightenment principles were of the most immediate use in the first of these questions, as they founded the idea of scientific observation. One apocryphal Enlightenment anecdote has two philosophers engaged in a debate over the number of teeth a horse has, upon which one of the new thinkers suggests they simply look in the beast's mouth and count them.

If this story seems improbable, consider that seventeenth-century medical faculty were still lecturing from the anatomy text of Galen, a second-century Greek follower of Hippocrates. As church law had forbidden the dissection of cadavers, Galen's text remained widely used, even after fifteen hundred years. By contrast, during the Enlightenment physicians were encouraged to perform dissections as a part of their research and teaching activities. This practice not only gave faculty and students a better sense of how the body actually worked, it also modeled the process of observation-based inquiry. Physicians began diagnosing their patients by actually examining them rather than resorting to philosophical tracts, and they began using trial-and-error methods to find treatments. Medicine became a practical art rather than a branch of abstract philosophy.

As for beauty, the Enlightenment values of order and universalism became guiding principles in the arts. Architecture harkened back to the Greeks and Romans in a neoclassical style that is still seen across Europe and the New World today. Greek colonnades and pediments lent dignity to public buildings from the Brandenburg Gate to the United States Capitol and proclaimed a prince's or a nation's membership in a universal world order. Sculpture and painting both exemplified order and extolled its virtue, much of it portraying Greek or Roman myth or alluding to ancient works of art. Music especially was rooted in the ideal of order. J. S. Bach, who came to be called the father of harmony, stood at the pinnacle of ordered and rational music in the early eighteenth century.

It was in the realm of moral philosophy—questions of goodness—that the Enlightenment had its most revolutionary effect, for the universalist and rational ideals implied a new view of the individual's place in society. Moral philosophy became the study of economic and political behavior, as Enlightenment thinkers began to understand that rational individuals shaped and were shaped by forces beyond their immediate control. This realization led to surprisingly varied ideas about desired political systems. The French, who valued reason above all else, favored the enlightened monarch as the most perfect form of government. Since not everyone could be sufficiently educated to apply reason and since ordinary people would always be blinded by their own interests anyway, only the king would be able to rise above the muddle and make reasoned decisions for the good of all. He would, of course, be assisted in this task by a corps of Enlightenment philosophes.[8]

But the British and American thinkers came to quite a different conclusion. Rather than being simply a prince's or sovereign's subject, the individual was thought to play a substantive role as a *constituent* of the political system. Adam Smith, Herbert Spencer, and others focused also on the economic role of ordinary people in constituting the social order. Even some French thinkers took this view. Henri de Saint-Simon made the bold suggestion that people who contributed to the economy were more important to society than the aristocracy.[9] This proposition was quite a new, and dangerous, idea in Bourbon France. (Saint-Simon did not, by the way, abandon the idea of the philosophical elite actually running things.)

These ideas spilled into the New World, where a new sort of republic was about to be born. The American republic was to be based not on tradition or on aristocratic power but on a clearly Enlightenment argument that governments formed by rational people pursuing their own interests would be inherently reasonable. The Constitution of this new government was even documented on paper—a distinctly rational approach—such that anyone could track the republic's performance against the ideals that had been proclaimed. The French ultimately did the same, though, as we know, with much greater difficulty.

This idea of self-government through rational pursuit of self-interest is called liberalism. This belief system maintains that when everyone's interests are pooled in reasonable discourse and hammered out by democratic means, the best ideas are bound to rise to the top or, at least, that the resulting policy must afford the fairest compromise. The value of compromise is an essential component of liberalism. Since each individual is of equal worth and since, further, individuals have differing and even competing interests, the government's role is largely to balance those interests against one another, ensuring that none are ignored and that none dominate. An additional virtue is that liberalism discourages radicalism, as compromise usually leads to incremental and evolutionary change.*

This "marketplace of ideas" approach could be seen at work not only in the halls of Congress or Parliament but also in public discourse, as citizens of all stripes pooled their individual interests and evaluations of candidates at election time. Through public exposure in election campaigns, the best candidates or policies could be expected to prevail as the fanatics and cranks failed for lack of support from the educated and literate populace. Thus these two elements were thought essential to the functioning of the process: free speech because an idea cannot be judged good or bad without public exposure and equal rights because all interests have to be represented in order to evaluate them.

---

*   This philosophical definition of the term "liberalism" should not be confused with the liberal Left of the American political spectrum. Both liberals and conservatives subscribe to the philosophical idea of liberalism—that people can govern themselves without need of an aristocracy.

The German Strain

The German version of the Enlightenment was the *Aufklärung*, or "clearing up." Among the Germans, too, the spirit of reason and order gave birth to a torrent of discovery in the sciences, particularly in mathematics, chemistry, and medicine. This progress was mirrored in artistic innovation, most importantly in music, which was called the most German of the arts. By 1800 Berlin was the "capital of the Aufklärung," a center of international trade in goods and ideas.[10] But just as the French, English, and American Enlightenments varied in significant ways, the Germans also had their own version. Like the English, and perhaps partly out of contempt for the French, the German Enlightenment did not cast religion aside. In fact, as the stewards of both the Holy Roman Empire and the Protestant Reformation, the Germans retained a strong attachment to both the old and new Christianity.

But unlike the British and Americans, the Germans remained wary of liberal democracy. The Aufklärung did not liberate the individual from authority; rather, it viewed the objective truth revealed by Enlightenment thinking to be itself authoritative. Neither did it liberate the individual from the state; instead, the individual's newfound wisdom made him better suited to his natural role as a servant of the state.[11] It seems the spirit of the Enlightenment never completely took root in German culture after all. It was maintained in Prussia "only by dint of constant effort" by the aristocracy, largely by constant attention to education. Enlightenment thinking did not come naturally to people, at least not to the Germans, in everyday life.[12] In any event, the Prussian royal house's efforts to maintain the Enlightenment were not enough. Later the Germans led a reaction against it.

THE ALLURE OF DARKNESS

The light began to dim toward the end of the eighteenth century. The French Revolution, that paragon of Enlightenment virtues rooted in reason and equality, metamorphosed into a nightmare of terror. Other social and economic crises around Europe periodically threatened the Enlightenment's ideals of freedom and tolerance. Finally, Napoleon's reign of conquest made the universal ideal less and less appealing to many Europeans, to the Germans least of all. Paris had become the cultural capital of Europe, supplanting Berlin, and the Germans felt that the ideals of universalism had failed to give due weight to German thought and ideas.[13] In reaction to all these misfortunes, the Germans came to lead a cultural movement called romanticism.

The one thing on which virtually all scholars agree is that romanticism is hard to define. One early twentieth-century writer offered a list of some thirty-one definitions of the concept, most of them running a paragraph long.[14] Another of the same period took apparent delight in demonstrating the many paradoxes, contradictions, and ambiguities in the idea.[15] Nonetheless, there are a few central characteristics of romanticism on which most agree.

First and foremost, the romantic movement was a reaction against the Enlightenment's supposition that the reality of the world—truth, in all its forms—could be understood by the intellect. Romantic thought rested instead on the premise that nothing could be perceived or understood except through the lens of an already established set of ideas. It followed that all of what passed for knowledge only existed in the eye of the beholder and that the underlying reality of the world could never be really understood by reason or logic.

This presupposition led to the complete rejection of the three fundamental principles of order, reason, and universalism in all spheres of endeavor. The Enlightenment's supposed orderly world was a figment of the human imagination, an imposed order that helped humans cope with what was an inherently chaotic and unfathomable world. And since this order was only imaginary, reason was nothing more than a set of conventions for understanding the logic that humans had themselves imposed on things. Finally, it also followed that such conventions were culture bound: a Frenchman's reason was very likely peculiar to French culture, and a German's could be different. In short, the universal worldview, whether in science, art, literature, or ethics, was a chimera.

The Enlightenment's principles were rejected most clearly in the arts. Music, for example, had in the classical era been an enjoyable logical exercise for the audience, a puzzle to be figured out in real time. A quartet or symphonic movement was intended to engage the listener in a sort of game in which a simple melody was stated clearly, then varied and bent in a variety of ways, and then returned to the "home key" whence it had started. The listener's task was to learn the melody the first time through, then try to hang on to it as the composer twisted it around, and finally to foresee its return just before it was restated at the end. There was an aesthetic delight in figuring out where the composer was going, even as he tried to lose the listener in a thicket of key and melody changes. It was a distinctly rational problem that involved a good application of Enlightenment rules of order and reason.

Romantic music asked the listener to take an entirely different orientation. Music was no longer an intellectual exercise but an emotional one —a journey meant to use, in today's vernacular, the other side of the brain. To engage deep emotions, romantic composers had to overthrow the rules of order. Rules were for cowards, not men; moreover, they were confining to the artist, whose own inner feelings yearned to be expressed. The listener was encouraged to let go of the tendency to figure out the music and instead to feel it deeply and with abandon. And these feelings were often not the usual ordinary human superficialities—sadness, fear, agitation—but rather deep yearning for things unattainable, forbidden, or inexpressible in words.

Thus Richard Wagner's operas, for example, are not just stories about people but myths about humankind and often entirely allegorical. His music was savagely chaotic to listeners of the day. Wagner intentionally made it difficult for listeners to figure out his melodies so that they would abandon themselves to deeper, mystical feelings. His *Tristan und Isolde*, for example, actually deprives the audience of the simple fulfillment of completing a melody for nearly five hours! It does so only in the final chord of the opera, a final note of serene resolution following a crescendo that can only be called orgasmic. Professional musicians, among the best in Europe, found the whole thing completely incomprehensible. An attempted premiere in Vienna "was abandoned after no less than seventy-seven rehearsals, the work then being pronounced unperformable."[16]

Painting and sculpture also portrayed a less orderly world. Romantic paintings often showed impossibly wild landscapes—dark, primeval forests and craggy cliffs—of the sort that hadn't existed in Europe since the Middle Ages and in many cases had never existed. They depicted chaotic places, where humans were small and few and where the forces of nature were impossible to understand, let alone control. Romantic paintings offered the viewer "neither clarity nor even intelligibility," and thus they were inaccessible to understanding through the application of reason.[17] The subjects didn't look like anything in real experience, so the works had to be appreciated on a visceral, not a cerebral, level. Romantic art was meant to evoke awe, fear, and wonder. It did not represent a world that really existed but one that might exist only in the artist's mind or even in his soul.

Even the sciences began to devalue reason and order. The empirical, trial-and-error methods that medicine had adopted during the Enlightenment gave way to mystical theories about the essence of life, of spirit, and of "animal magnetism." To the romantic mind, the steady accretion of scientific knowledge was too slow and cautious. Surely a heroic or visionary doctor could cut through the underbrush of plodding science to deeper insights about life and disease. Theories of miracle cures thus gained hold over people, as did all sorts of quacks and charlatans who ped-dled them.[18] At the same time, scientific medical theory gave way to a more holistic sort, concerning not only the body but the mind and spirit as well.

In addition to the reaction against order and reason, the romantics disparaged the ideal of universalism. In W. A. Mozart's time, at the height of the Aufklärung, there had been a right and a wrong way to write a symphony, concerto, or quartet; in fact, music scholars still write articles about "Mozart's error" in this or that work. Painting was the same way. Everybody knew what paintings should look like, how to interpret what they meant, and what themes and subjects were appropriate. A good piece of music, or a good painting or poem, was most of all a finely crafted one that was an excellent example of its type. Art was more akin to what we might call craft today. Making a good painting was similar to building an excellent house or cobbling a fine pair of shoes.

The romantics saw these universal ideals of orderly beauty as so many constraints against individual expression. Rather than hew to standards of beauty and taste, the romantic artists and writers expressed their own innermost thoughts, feelings, and spirit. In doing so, they took the great risk of personal rejection but retained their all-important personal vision and integrity. This emphasis led to the new elevation of difference, uniqueness, and creativity as the highest of artistic goals. It was the beginning of the time when artists of all kinds began to be thought unique and interesting personalities who expressed themselves—their joy, their pain, their personal insight—in their work. During the romantic era, the term "genius," defined as an innate capability to communicate feeling along with intellect, came to be applied to these personalities.[19] This romantic idea of artistic expression still lingers in American culture today in the popular (if inaccurate) image of the artist as a loner, a nonconformist possessed of a solitary vision that few can understand.

With the elevation of originality and personal style came the elevation of individual, even idiosyncratic, variety as an aesthetic virtue. Many different kinds of music and art developed; in fact, originality came to be the predominant virtue in the arts; to be like another artist was regarded as the kiss of death. According to George Boas, writing early in the twentieth century:

> Two hundred years ago few critics, if any, would have judged a picture good because of its originality, its internal variety, its revelation of a human personality—the artist's, its difference. Whereas a few generations ago it was obvious that conformity to a universal rule was a mark of greatness, to-day most people call such conformity "unoriginality."[20]

These ideas applied not only to the aesthetic world but to the social and moral realms as well. If the value of a painting or musical work lay in the vision of its creator rather than in its conformity to universal standards, then the very idea of standards was dubious. Human institutions thus became suspect, inasmuch as they tended to squelch the spirit of the artist and, by extension, the human spirit in general. Thus in art, literature, and philosophy, the community came to be cast as the villain against which the lone human was pitted in a struggle for identity, redemption, and fulfillment of his destiny.

Ordinary people had to submit to this dehumanizing trend, but a few gave themselves to the struggle against it. They were romantic heroes who came to be lionized in the arts and in philosophy. Heroes were not merely people who were better, stronger, or wiser than others; they were people who could escape the bonds of convention and get away with it. Heroes were people who, by virtue of genius or other unfathomable powers, had a *right* to flout convention. They advanced human progress because they could think things and do things that ordinary people were not allowed to think or do, thus showing the way for the mortal masses to follow. Of course, sometimes they failed, and sometimes they were crucified by the very masses they sought to redeem.

The elevation of the heroic individual reflected a suspicion of social progress. The social thinkers of the Enlightenment had looked forward to incremental improvement in the human condition through the expansion of individual rights and the exercise of humane public policy.[21] But the romantic thinkers looked to heroes and saviors—Jesus, Frederick the Great, and the fictional Dr. Frankenstein were diverse examples—for great leaps of human progress. To these heroes, social conventions were hindrances, often tragically so. All human institutions—conventional religion, family, the economy, and morality—were barriers to improving the human condition. A more naturalistic way of life was the answer to human misery, especially the misery of the soul. Human institutions were, in short, the problem rather than the solution.

Romanticism and Fascism
We can see that through much of the nineteenth century, German culture was bathed in reaction against Enlightenment values in every sphere. The Enlightenment was thought to have robbed the arts of feeling and emotional intensity. Science and philosophy had degenerated into a sterile universalism that dissolved both individual and collective—that is, national, cultural, and racial—differences. Liberal political systems had created self-interested and small-minded citizens. Humankind had become materialistic and shallow and would be dragged lower and lower by the pernicious creep of the Enlightenment's modernism.

But as the Enlightenment had never completely won the German mind, neither did the romantic movement. Kaisers Wilhelm I and Wilhelm II ruled by managing a tricky balance of Enlightenment values in the romantic age. The sciences were nourished by government subsidies. Social and legal reforms brought increasing equality to Jews, albeit in a two-steps-forward, one-step-back fashion. Labor reform protected women and children.[22] Germany was even among the first nations to establish a national health care system. Germany sought to play a role on the world stage, inserting itself into the universalistic community of nations even as it reveled in a parochial nationalism. It was a strain between the enlightened elite and the romantic populace, symbolized best of all by the blood ties among Europe's rulers. These ties seemed especially vexing to Kaiser Wilhelm II, whose massive arms race with England and Russia gave no end of annoyance to his grandmother, Queen Victoria, and his cousin, "Dear Nicky" Czar Nicholas II.[23]

World War I unwound the spring. Between the massive bloodletting, the disastrous defeat, the punitive Treaty of Versailles, and the practical end of the age of monarchy, Germany was undone. The old nationalists were routed, and a new republic was born of a brief revolution in the winter of 1918–19. Wilhelm fled to Holland. With a national election in January, the Weimar Republic was born.

The republic was weak from the start. Though led by moderates, the government coalition included both mainstream and minor extremist parties of many stripes. Worse, even the major parties were beset with rifts: the nationalists were an amalgam of parties left over from the prewar era, the liberals were divided into leftist and centrist factions, the Communists vexed everyone. Moreover, party identification and party structures were quite rigid, with each party maintaining its own newspaper, its own clubs and associations, and its own mutual aid societies. The constant roiling of multiparty politics resulted in an inherently weak government, "since all they could settle on was the lowest common denominator and the line of least resistance."[24]

The postwar economic climate didn't help, either. While there were periods of stability and growth, the republic tended to lurch from one crisis to the next, brought on by the debt resulting from a total war, by the destruction of two million men, by the loss of the Rhineland, and by the Versailles Treaty's punitive reparations. Between the political weaknesses inherent in its fractious electorate and these economic infirmities, it is little wonder that no fewer than twenty different governments led the republic in its fourteen-year life.[25]

Perhaps more significant than government instability was the cultural upheaval that Weimar represented. Artistic expression fairly exploded in a blur of modernism, admired today but considered jarring then by many of the German elites. Expressionist painting brought forth the likes of Wassily Kandinsky, Max Beckmann, and Paul Klee. Robert Wiene made the expressionist film *The Cabinet of Dr. Caligari* while Fritz Lang made *Metropolis*. And architecture! The architects of the Bauhaus established a style far removed from the familiar neo-classical conventions. It featured bold geometric forms with a minimum of decoration. Aggressively un-German, it was even called International Style to press the point. And that was not the worst. In nearby Potsdam, home of the imperial palace itself, Erich Mendelsohn erected the Einstein Tower, an observatory facility of futuristic boldness and noticeably phallic. He also built the Columbus Haus in the center of Berlin, a curvaceous and spare edifice; the SS later used it as a prison.[26] In music, the richly textured work of Ludwig van Beethoven, Wagner, and others gave way to the thin, edgy compositions of Kurt Weill; meanwhile, Alban Berg and others experimented with twelve-tone and atonal music. In theater, Berthold Brecht became part of a movement called the *Neue Sächlichkeit* (new objectivity), a realistic view of life that tended toward cynicism and resignation and was a direct reaction against the romantic. At the time one journalist contrasted it with the earlier romanticism: "now after the exorbitant, gushing ecstasies, the tendency toward a new reality and objectivity—sächlichkeit—is becoming palpable in all areas of life."[27]

The new republic was a utopia for scientists, too. The kaiser had supported Albert Einstein, Paul Ehrlich, Fritz Haber—all Jews, by the way—and many others with government funding for the sciences. They were, if anything, more prominent and more celebrated under the Weimar regime.[28] The prestige of these thinkers, as well as of those in the arts and letters, hurtled Germany into the vanguard of Western thought. In short, Weimar either gave birth to or nursed a large part of what we think of as modern culture today, from art to music to architecture to science to government. In Eric Weitz's view, the artists, thinkers, and reformers of the Weimar era:

> created new forms of cultural expression, worked valiantly to build a more humane society, and pondered deeply the meaning of modernity. They planned new housing developments that alleviated the miserable conditions in which so many Germans lived. They wrote and lectured about sex and established counseling clinics, convinced that every woman and man deserved a fulfilling sex life. They reduced the length of the inhuman workday that had prevailed in industry before the war. They composed music, wrote novels and philosophical tracts, took photographs, made photomontages, and staged theater productions with riveting creativity and profound contemplation about the meaning of modern times.[29]

But, of course, this new world stood in direct contrast with the one so many Germans held dear. While the new art and music delighted the avant-garde of the large cities, many ordinary Germans as well as the conservative elites found it unfathomable and unpleasant. And as for moral thought and moral life, these elites took an alternative view of the new sexual freedom:

> Berlin transformed itself into the Babel of the world. Bars, amusement parks, pubs shot up like mushrooms. What we had seen in Austria proved to be merely a mild and timid prelude to this witches'

sabbath, for the Germans brought to perversion all their vehemence and love of system. Made-up boys with artificial waistlines promenaded along the Kurfürstendamm—and not professionals alone: every high school student wanted to make some money, and in the darkened bars one could see high public officials and high financiers courting drunken sailors without shame. Even the Rome of Suetonius had not known orgies like the Berlin transvestite balls, where hundreds of men in women's clothes and women in men's clothes danced under the benevolent eyes of the police. Amid the general collapse of values, a kind of insanity took hold of precisely those middle-class circles which had hitherto been unshakable in their order. Young ladies proudly boasted that they were perverted; to be suspected of virginity at sixteen would have been considered a disgrace in every school in Berlin.[30]

The strain between Enlightenment and romantic values had been suddenly released, but had it been resolved? To be sure, liberal elements in Weimar culture—free expression, equal rights, individualism, and democratic policy—encouraged a return to the Enlightenment. Tradition was overthrown as a cultural or moral guide, and reason and freethinking came to the fore. There was also a large move toward universalism in cultural values, with a consequent repudiation of German identity. Many fretted over the creeping "Americanism" of German life.[31] Though artists were no longer constrained by the rules of classicism, they reached out to an artistic community that was not German or even European in its identity, but global. The republic's government desperately wanted to rejoin the global community of nations, so it did its best to pay the war reparations of the Versailles Treaty while it negotiated a better settlement. Weimar society invited foreigners in the arts, sciences, and all forms of thought to take part in German life, and it included Jews as well.

It could have gone either way. The ideals of the Enlightenment might have won the day, as Germans might have prized their new cultural freedoms and diversity. They might have discovered a new German spirit in their newfound participatory democracy. They might easily have seized upon a sense of belonging to the community of nations and upon their place as citizens of the world first, Europe second, and Germany third. Their politicians might well have campaigned for office on a platform of thoughtful, democratic discourse and responsibility to this world community. They might have based their appeals on a belief in a world order that Germans would embrace.

But we know that didn't happen. In Germany in the 1920s, as now in twenty-first-century America, appeals to enlightened reason and universal values were no way to get votes in times of strain. Much more effective were appeals to the wounded pride of the German people. A politician could attract more votes by criticizing the government than by praising it; by calling it ineffective at best, villainous at worst; by blaming it for the economic ruin in which Germany found itself; and by labeling it a band of "November criminals" responsible for capitulating in the face of the enemy. One of the problems of democracy is that voters aren't always rational, and appeals like these can be very effective.

It may be that Hitler and the National Socialists astutely recognized the cultural strains and confusion of the Weimar era, or perhaps they only stumbled into electoral success by being in the right place at the right time. Either way, the Nazis' appeal was largely an appeal to romantic values. In the first place, democracy was anathema: the policies of a democracy were, by definition, always half wrong because they were born of compromise among diverse views, some of which must be wrong. This tendency to average out the views and opinions of everyone, to "embrace diversity" in today's usage, could only mean that the true will of the people would always be compromised. And the will of the genuine German people— once outsiders, Communists, and Jews were excluded—would by definition be united, coherent, and rooted in German racial and cultural unity. National Socialism was, if nothing else, antiliberal in the sense that it rejected completely the idea that a marketplace of ideas could bring forth good policy.

Moreover, extremism itself was encouraged by a deeply cherished romantic ideal. Cowardly halfway policies of accommodation, of compromise, and of give-and-take, either in domestic or foreign affairs, were for weak-willed peoples like the French or the Americans. If Germans needed more territory—lebensraum—then they must seize it. If they were to be militarily strong, then they could not be bound by arms limitation treaties, least of all those that had been signed by leaders of questionable loyalty. If there was a "Jewish problem," then Germany must be rid of Jews. The notion of a unified government taking bold action was a powerful comfort to a German public wracked by assassinations, political chaos, currency instability, and international condemnation. Ernst Röhm, an early founder of the party, "used words like 'prudent,' 'compromise,' 'intellectual,' 'bourgeois,' or 'middle-class' almost invariably in a pejorative sense; his positive, admiring expressions included 'strapping,' 'daredevil,' 'ruthless,' and 'faithful.'"[32]

The Nazis' program could not have been advanced using Enlightenment arguments based on reason and coolheaded observation. The sense of German destiny, the intense feelings of injustice visited on the German people by the world, the suspicion of democracy, the deification of a heroic leader, and most of all, the fear of and contempt for the Jews—these ideas could not easily take root in the Enlightenment mind. The Nazis appealed instead to the romantic leanings of the German populace, grounding their political discourse not in reason and clarity but in emotion and mystery. Rousing speeches and candlelight marches were the party's stock in trade from the beginning; later they were institutionalized when the party became the government.

More than anything else, the rise of Nazism was fueled by the rejection of reason as a basis for government and for social and political discourse. Romantic art and music accustomed Germans to let go of their logical faculties, romantic social thought encouraged them to yearn for a world steeped in mystery and led by heroic individuals, and romantic science legitimated racial policy. These cultural elements helped create the romantic politics of National Socialism, which were characterized by appeals to emotion, adulation of a leader, and scorn for democracy and the rule of law. Ultimately, romantic thought led Germans to their own destruction, foreshadowed by Albert Guérard: "Better a tragic and magnificent *Götterdämmerung* than a thousand years of peace."[33]

The Germans took to Hitler in part because he promised a miraculous solution to problems that seemed intractable and an escape from the realities of conventional economic, political, and social thinking—an escape from objectivity, from sächlichkeit. To make Germany great again would require faith, will, and ecstatic commitment. With Hitler's encouragement, Germans became a people for whom resolve was valued more highly than thoughtfulness, destiny more than diligence, daring more than prudence, and righteousness more than doubt. In many ways, they were a people not so different from today's Americans.

ROMANTICISM IN AMERICA

The United States was, as we know, born of the Enlightenment. The new colonies were mostly English, after all, and the steady importation of

English goods, migrants, and ideas had its effect on the colonists. When the Revolution came, its authors were Enlightenment figures through and through: Benjamin Franklin, John Adams, Thomas Paine, Thomas Jefferson, and a host of other philosophers, scholars, scientists, inventors, essayists, and architects. These men believed in the power of reason not only as an intellectual tool but also as the basis on which to found a society.[34] And that they did. The Declaration of Independence and the Constitution are as clear statements of Enlightenment principles as can be imagined. The new United States of America was to be a democracy of educated, enlightened, and engaged citizens. Unlike the French but very much like the British, they acknowledged God as the creator of the orderly universe, and they sought to reflect its order in the political system they built.

But it wasn't long before that ideal began to show limitations. Expansion westward, first across the Appalachians to the Mississippi and then across the plains, isolated increasing numbers of Americans. The education so necessary to maintaining an enlightened populace was slow in coming to many regions, and in the West, even the rudiments of law and order were makeshift. The pioneers lived in a world that was exuberant, rowdy, undisciplined. In the absence of much control from without, justice often became dispensed on the barrelhead and by the immediate consensus of the townsmen.[35] Confronted with territory that was by all accounts more wild and unfathomable than anyone had imagined, the sober reason of the Enlightenment was of little use to the isolated migrants. True, Enlightenment science and engineering made the railroads run and the telegraph sing, but these achievements depended on more than technological prowess. The main resource in settling the West was cultural—that is, the sense that taming the land was a moral struggle, a test of will and fortitude that could break a man who didn't have the courage, wiles, or ruthlessness required.

Like the Germans, these Americans looked to their hearts and their souls for understanding their circumstances. Instead of thoughtful essays and scientific experiments, this new wave created a lore of tall tales of heroes and untamed nature: Paul Bunyan of Northwoods fame; Pecos Bill, who could ride a cyclone and rope an entire herd at once; and Mike Fink, king of the Mississippi boatmen.[36] Some of the tall tales were even more or less true. Wild Bill Hickok and Calamity Jane, Davy Crockett, Billy the Kid, the Donner Party, and dozens of now-forgotten mountain men and cowpokes figured large in people's thoughts of the restless West. In most of these tales, fictional as well as historical, the protagonists were common folk, addressing nature not by educated reflection but by daring heroics and sheer will.

In the rural parts of the East, too, local communities were left to their own cultural devices as people found themselves struggling against an untamed wilderness. They too needed the wherewithal to face the struggle and to make sense of it, and the cool reason of the established institutions in the cities was too far away to help. Here the tall tales of the West were translated as evangelical religion, with the testimony of sinners providing the drama of struggle and redemption that gave meaning to their battle against nature.[37] Faith healers cured the sick. Preachers told of heathen peoples across the oceans as well as across the river. Religion was dramatic, heroic, and fraught with Sturm und Drang. Between the westward migration and the immigration of various evangelical sects from Europe, religion in rural and western America diverged more and more from the Enlightenment's brand of English and Scottish Protestantism practiced by the established easterners.

But the romantic ideal did not stay confined to America's backwaters. Over time it became a principal orientation of the body politic, as the cross-cutting streams of Manifest Destiny and abolition took on increasingly messianic tones and cast America as God's instrument on Earth. The United States was a "redeemer nation" in the words of George Bancroft, the most prominent historian of the time.[38] In fact, one historian has called July 4, 1826—coincidentally, the day Thomas Jefferson and John Adams both died—the date on which romantic America was born. It was ushered in by Bancroft's first major speech, a Fourth of July oration in Massachusetts. He borrowed from German romantic philosophy of the day to elucidate the view that there was a source of knowledge beyond the senses. Furthermore, this source could bind people together in a general will: "The popular voice is all powerful within us; this is our oracle; this, we acknowledge, is the voice of God."[39]

The American romantic spirit was, as in Germany, partly a reaction to the new Industrial Revolution and the destruction of meaning it portended. Even as the nineteenth century began to bring large-scale innovation, its consequent industrialization and urbanization had fostered a strong thread of suspicion. This strain simmered for a hundred years, until in 1925 it came to a boil with the trial of John Scopes, a Tennessee schoolteacher put on trial for teaching the theory of evolution. The prosecuting attorney was William Jennings Bryan, the personification of the romantic way of thinking: colorful, emotional, persuasive. His opponent was Clarence Darrow, who appealed to reason and the logic of law. It was a titanic clash between the two strains of American culture. Fought to a draw—Scopes was convicted of teaching evolution but without putting evolution itself on trial—in many ways the case has been continuing ever since.[40] In a debate among Republican presidential hopefuls in 2007, three of the ten present said they simply didn't believe in it. This admission was hardly surprising, since a CBS poll in 2004 showed that a majority of Americans believe humans were "formed by God in their present state."[41]

The distinction between the romantic vigor of expansion and the enlightened reason of settled institutions remains a visible divide in American culture today. It has been expressed in a thousand disputes between suburbanites and ranchers, between effete environmentalists and strapping timbermen, between bureaucrats and rugged individualists, between the courts and the church. It is, in fact, at the heart of many of the most divisive and heated debates in American life.

American Romantic Themes in the Arts

While American romanticism was not identical to the German variety, it was consistent with the principal strains of German thought. In the arts, the romantic movement tended to focus on two themes: the mystic power of nature and the individual hero. Like the Germans, American romantics considered nature as embodying something essentially unfathomable. American landscape painters celebrated their continent's grandeur, wildness, and vastness. From the forests of the Hudson River School's paintings to the western mountains and deserts of George Catlin and Frederic Remington, the American landscape emulated nothing as much as the Teutonic primeval depictions from German painters. Howard Mumford Jones encapsulated the western landscape in five descriptive nouns: astonishment, plenitude, vastness, incongruity, and melancholy.[42] These descriptors almost exactly parallel the values of the romantic movement itself.

The second great theme of American romanticism extolled the essential value of the individual above the community, the American version of the hero. Escape from social convention was a high ideal, and it was better still if it involved a connection with nature. Herman Melville brought these two themes together in *Moby Dick*, which included not only the tragic figure of Ahab stepping outside the conventions and commercial pragmatism of the whaling life but also the vivid and romantic descriptions of the sea and weather, of the mystical nature of the whale, and of the meaning of whiteness itself. Much later, the western movie again combined the heroic individual with the majesty of nature, setting tall tales of America's destiny amid vast and forbidding landscapes. The central theme of many westerns is the contrast between the wilderness and civilization—"between the open land and the town, between the illusion of freedom and the necessity of compromise, between a relaxed association with nature and a tense accommodation to society."[43]—or, in other words, between the romantic and rational ways of thought.

One familiar thematic device is the individual hero who pursues the righteous path in contradiction to the rules. One example is Clint Eastwood's *Unforgiven*, in which the hero exacts the community's revenge on a killer when the corrupt sheriff refuses to act. Perhaps more explicit in their disdain for rules and procedures are the myriad movies featuring the police versus criminals. Virtually every one pits the independent-minded detective against a police bureaucracy (usually represented by the precinct captain) that wants to tangle his investigation in the red tape of due process. Eastwood figures again here, in his portrayal of the character Dirty Harry, who has to be a renegade cop because the police hierarchy, the criminal justice system, and the community overall are too gutless to do the right thing. Overall, one might say the abiding theme of American popular culture is that the individual is good while the system is bad.

As for music, it might be said that the Enlightenment's classical styles never existed in America. Virtually all serious music of that period was imported from Europe, and besides, the romantic era began not long after the founding of the republic. American music was popular music, and romanticism eventually came to pervade this music as well. In most eras, popular music had relied on a fairly strong sense of order, with a melody that can be hummed and easily remembered and a rhythm that sets the foot tapping and makes good dance music. But popular music in the modern age began to overthrow convention in favor of a more raw emotionalism with the birth of rock 'n' roll out of country music and blues. The early rock of Elvis Presley, Jerry Lee Lewis, Little Richard, Chuck Berry, and others brought a level of emotional abandon that pop music had not generally seen before, to the consternation of parents everywhere. Later the psychedelic and heavy metal styles stretched the relevance of melody and rhythm to the limit; Jimi Hendrix's Woodstock rendition of

"The Star-Spangled Banner" is a prime example. Rock thus embodies essentially romantic values: "originality, primal order, energy, honesty, and integrity."[44]

Romantic Academic Thought

American intellectual life has always been grounded in the university. The American aristocracy, such as it is, never really served as the arbiter of intellectual thought, at least not since Jefferson's day. The world of ideas has been largely ceded to the faculties of universities, starting with the traditional colleges at Harvard, William and Mary, Columbia, and a handful of others, and then greatly expanding with the land grant colleges of the mid-nineteenth century and the private endowments of the great industrialists.

For much of their history, most of these institutions have taken their role to be the elevation of Enlightenment and pragmatic values, first for the gentlemen and clergy of America's gentry and then to generations of teachers, professionals, technicians, and others of the emerging middle class.[45] Through most of this time, students attended universities to acquire what was considered universally recognized knowledge through the application of the methods of science and reason. The American college was a homogenizing institution; indeed, everyone who went to college had similar experiences and came to know the world in pretty much the same terms, namely, the terms of the Enlightenment. Since they were thought to be universal, they excluded and disparaged other ways of understanding.

Things began to change after World War II. The GI Bill offered access to an unprecedented number and variety of students, many from families that had migrated to America only a generation or so previously. Almost all of them were the first in their families to ever go to college. Colleges and universities swelled with the new enrollments, but after the veterans had passed through the system, around the 1950s and 1960s, the universities that had grown to accommodate them were faced with the problem of filling empty seats. This need for new students fit well with the growing technical needs of the country and, at the same time, with increasing demands for social equality. Women, African Americans, immigrants, and foreign students populated classrooms in growing numbers through the sixties and seventies, and with them came increased chafing at the constraints of the curriculum's embedded universal values. The women's movement was especially astute in identifying those constraints, and at the same time it began to model alternative approaches to knowledge. It turned out that knowledge wasn't universal at all but was rooted in the preconceptions and biases of the old European Enlightenment.[46]

Until this time, there had been only a few in the classroom who didn't get those values, and they could easily be ignored or weeded out. But by the seventies there was a critical mass of disaffected students, many of them students of color and women, and they could no longer be dismissed. The old ideal of education as a means of assimilation into Enlightenment ideals yielded to the idea of education as a means of liberation from their tyranny. Thus feminist scholars today speak of challenging the "controlling strategies of neo-liberalism" and making the academy "at once intellectual and emotional."[47]

The result was the erosion of Enlightenment values, to the point today of near discreditation. It is most complete in such departments as English literature and sociology, where gender and ethnicity were either already incorporated into the curriculum or easily could be. Even the natural sciences have come to terms with the diversity of knowledge, first by developing new teaching methods and then by embracing new points of view in the discipline. Thus Carol Gilligan challenged much of psychological research by noting its overreliance on males as subjects, and biology students were assigned readings like "The Aggressive Egg" and *Woman in the Body: A Cultural Analysis of Reproduction,* which take a more female-centered view of the natural world.[48]

The word of the day is "deconstruction," the recognition that much of what we call knowledge is a social construction based on taken-for-granted ways of seeing the world. By taking those constructions apart, we might better recognize alternate views, such as those of different cultural groups and of women, and some that are perhaps entirely novel. The deconstructionist view, like the romantic one, challenges the "tyranny of reason" as well as the notion that neutrality and objectivity are possible.[49] Today few academics dare use words like "objective" or "logical" anymore and certainly not "truth."

The academic goal today is to render the world of knowledge more reflective of differing points of view and, more profoundly, of various methods of establishing a point of view. Thus many of these non-Western approaches embrace biography, personal experience, and sharing as ways of making claims to knowledge and put them on a par with empirical rigor and logical reasoning.[50] This effort creates a more inclusive and livelier academy. But a less positive effect of rejecting reason is the loss of a standard that everyone can use to evaluate ideas. Without universal or at least agreed-upon standards of knowledge, the truth of a statement comes to depend on the speaker's identity, persuasiveness, or charisma. These appeals, under the old Enlightenment rules of logic, define fallacy—the ad hominem argument—and their use makes plausible any declaration that can be stated with conviction: for example, that white America drugs the water supply in African American communities, that the White House orchestrated the 9/11 attacks, that the Holocaust never happened, or that Janet Reno was Hillary Clinton's secret lover. It also lends legitimacy to the religiously based attack on evolution. Nearly a century after the Scopes trial and despite a wealth of empirical confirmation, a majority of Americans still consider Charles Darwin's useful and powerful generalization about the order of nature "just a theory." Two-thirds believe it should be complemented in the public schools by the idea that God created all the species at once or at least commanded the changes in species that Darwin described.[51] To many Americans, scientific knowledge—that sort of knowledge that is gained by observation and tempered by inviting the critical review of others—has become just another set of opinions promulgated by a privileged elite and is therefore suspect.

Romantic Political Discourse
Since the deaths of Jefferson and Adams, Americans have viewed the political world with a romantic eye. The fundamental romantic idea that there is a reality behind that which we can see, a world of truths than can't be inferred from observation or reason, has played out in some of the most persistent and fractious strains in the American political fabric. It underlies the continued influence of religion in politics, for religion is after all a system of thought that seeks to access a different plane of reality, where the ultimate truths lie inaccessible by reason and logic.

Clearly religion has provided much of the driving force behind the most important political movements in American history. The abolition movement was born in the pulpits of Protestant America and in the messianic visions of John Brown and others like him. Prohibition was the child of righteous fervor as well, both as an antidote to the sinful excesses of demon rum and as a way to control the papist hordes of Irish and southern European immigrants.[52] Much of the anticommunist zeal of the past century was motivated by the godlessness of the Marxist-Leninist world. The civil rights movement was led and organized by preachers and their churches throughout the South, and its strongest voices echoed the voices of Christian scripture. And today religion cleaves the body politic over prayer in the schools, abortion, and, still, evolution.

This is not to say that religion has been the only motivator of political opinion or that it has not been used as a tool by baser interests. Certainly anticommunism was as much a movement of American indust-rialists as of American pastors, and the contemporary use of religion as a wedge issue is in large part a calculated electoral tactic. Nor have all political movements been religious ones, at least in the usual sense of the term. Neither the antiwar movement nor the women's movement, for two examples, were founded on scripture, though both took the "no com-promise" attitude of religion-based movements. Both saw the evil of war and the oppression of women as moral absolutes.

The religious and, in the larger sense, the romantic have waxed and waned in importance to the American body politic. It may be that religion's influence varies with the degree of threat the public feels. In times of war, economic recession, or other fearful episodes, citizens might tend to cling to certainty and the dogmas of their various political, regional, ethnic, or other communities. Whatever the cause, the romantic spirit is at a peak today in political discourse. The Enlightenment values of compromise, of accommodation and pluralism—those very ideals that are the hallmark of democracy itself—are suspect. In fact, one analyst of the electoral process makes the frank assertions that Americans are just not very well suited for voting because of our "strong hatred for the inevitable 'give-and-take' of politics," and that the average voter "hates the very process of democratic debate."[53]

This contempt for partisanship has ironically made inexperience in public office a virtue in an election campaign, since it suggests freedom from the taint of politics. Jimmy Carter campaigned as a Washington outsider in 1976 and won; however, after a term in office he had become the insider, responsible for the country's economic ills. Ronald Reagan defeated him by taking on the same outsider persona, though he had been involved in national politics behind the scenes since the Goldwater campaign and had been a two-term governor of California. The quadrennial spectacle of the presidential election campaign always yields a bounty of contrived outsiders vying for the nominations of the two major parties, sometimes comically, with candidates standing on hay bales, wearing plaid flannel shirts, and munching pork rinds. In 2008 John McCain, a twenty-two-year veteran of the Senate, even ran as a maverick.

On occasion even a genuine outsider will emerge, as, for example, Jesse Ventura did in his third-party victory in the 1998 Minnesota gubernatorial race. His principal campaign theme was a rejection of party politics and a pledge to do the right thing for Minnesotans even if (perhaps especially if) the Republicans and Democrats objected. One of the most visible communication devices of his campaign was a TV ad featuring a toy Jesse Ventura action figure, in the style of G.I. Joe, that would presumably take on the establishment through feats of political daring. The figure was so popular that it was mass-produced and sold as a fund-raising gewgaw. This implied promise of bold action, without compromise or accommodation, appealed to the romantic sensibilities of voters, or to enough of them anyway to divide the two major parties' votes to Ventura's advantage.

If voters don't actually hate the democratic process, they at least find it unsatisfying, especially when political issues are couched in moral terms. According to a recent newspaper article, "the public seems to see more and more bickering among politicians, and asks 'Why can't they just get along and do what's right?'" This is a cornerstone of romantic social and political discourse: suspicion of the open competition of ideas that is the legislative process and the desire for bold action by a heroic leader representing the "people's will." It should be no surprise that this article appeared in the "Faith and Values" section of the paper's Saturday edition.[54]

A second cornerstone is the rejection of reason as a basis for judging political policy or promises. Political campaigns have always been rough-and-tumble affairs and seldom rise to the intellectual level of great debate. But there are reasons to think that election communication, largely via the mass media, is more devoid of useful information than ever. For one thing, modern mass media have a bias—not to the Left or to the Right but toward the negative on both sides. A whiff of scandal or even an unfortunate comment caught on an open microphone will often get far more attention than a well-delivered speech. Even the long tradition of the "honeymoon" given to a newly elected president is dead. In his first two months in office, 57 percent of Bill Clinton's media coverage was negative.[55] Coverage of Congress is even worse, probably owing to the additional criticism coming from the White House as well as to the usual partisan bickering. All of this scorn both fosters mistrust in politics and disenchantment with democracy and validates the notion that all politicians are crooks looking to advance their own interests or, at best, those of some narrow constituency.[56]

Moreover, political discourse has become more extremist and less tolerant over the past few decades. One cause is the sheer number of people and groups getting involved in political campaigning. In the past, the candidate, with the help of a few advisers, was responsible for all speeches and media ads, whereas today dozens of activist and lobbyist groups are involved. In the 2002 congressional races, such groups sponsored almost half of the 1,249 campaign messages studied. As these are typically single-issue groups and by definition are highly committed to a "no compromise" point of view, they tend to run extreme ads.[57]

For that matter, the number and strength of groups like the National Rifle Association (NRA) or NARAL Pro-Choice America or Focus on the Family actually make the American two-party system function more like a multiparty parliamentary arrangement. The two major parties vie for the support of these groups or, in some cases, are held hostage by them. Witness in 2008 the McCain campaign's compromises, including his choice of running mate, which were made to shore up the party's political base of fundamentalist Protestants, antiabortion Catholics, the military, and veterans. Each national election becomes, in effect, an attempt to form a coalition government of many of these single-issue groups. It is reminiscent of the Weimar Republic's babel of narrowly defined parties.

PROSPECTS FOR AMERICAN FASCISM

For the past two centuries, American culture has vibrated with the strain between Enlightenment and romantic values. It can be seen in the arts, where originality of the individual artist's vision is the principal criterion of artistic value and where conventions of form are disdained, even while much of the public is puzzled or offended by modern art and avoids new orchestral music. It can be seen in the popular arts too, where the struggle of the heroic individual against convention is a staple theme of films and bestsellers, even as television's soap operas and sitcoms offer morality plays that indulge the viewers' yearning for the comfort of convention. In the academy, faculty have largely discredited Enlightenment values. College freshmen still must learn about Melville, Newton, and Socrates but often as examples of an outdated canon.

Most important, the strain plays out in the realm of politics. Americans revere democracy and freedom in the abstract, but they become frustrated when the government fails to act decisively to advance moral causes. At such times, antigovernment action has often been used to overcome democracy's natural inertia. For example, abolition, Prohibition, and the civil rights and antiwar movements were all powered by civil disobedience, rioting, and even the occasional armed insurrection. In other cases, the strains simmer for generations, as the antievolution and antiabortion movements have. Such zero-tolerance movements simply can't live with the accommodations that are the usual outcome of the democratic process.

In an effort to overcome democracy's tendency to find compromise, Americans are often drawn to leaders of a heroic bent or at least to those who can cast themselves in that vein. Such leaders, it is hoped, will cut through bureaucracy and red tape, perhaps purely by the strength of their character, and forge single-minded policy that even the bickering partisans will support. Most candidates for high office find it necessary to foster such an image, either by demonstrating past heroism (as a war veteran, for example) or by casting themselves as political outsiders untainted by the stink of compromise.

We don't always elect such leaders or demand uncompromising action. In ordinary times, free of dire emergencies, we accept the ebb and flow of the democratic process, and we place a smaller premium on boldness of vision and freedom from influence. But during times of strain, the romantic elements of American culture are likely to overwhelm our Enlightenment traditions. At these times, the old guard can more easily be blamed for our troubles and the old solutions more easily discredited as ineffective. Unorthodox and revolutionary approaches, pursued by steadfast leadership, can promise astonishing solutions beyond the imagination of ordinary politicians.

Such actions reinforce the further abandonment of reason. In World War I, President Wilson actively and successfully campaigned for public hysteria as the United States mobilized for war.[58] Franklin Roosevelt's response to the Great Depression was to sidestep any number of legal barriers to solving the country's economic problems, and most Americans were glad he did. World War II saw the internment of Japanese Americans by Roosevelt's executive order, widely applauded at the time by a hysterical populace. The 9/11 attacks of 2001 have since brought forth the internment of ill-defined illegal enemy combatants without charge or representation, surveillance of citizens on an unprecedented scale (owing to the efficiency of today's technology), and the costly invasion of a foreign country that was not the source of the attack.

These actions are not so different from what happened in Germany in the early twentieth century. The political Right had no use for the Enlightenment values of universalism, reason, and order. Instead, it felt these things had robbed Germans of their Germanness and polluted their ideals in a stew of democratic compromise and accommodation. The Right viewed the Enlightenment's faith in order as a thin disguise for cowardice, for business as usual, and for orderly process even when disorder was necessary. At the same time, the Left saw liberalism as reactionary and a tool of the capitalist, since the ruling class could easily control the democratic process and shape the political discourse. Both sides disdained the law as a body of abstract principles, because neither side believed in the ideal of objectivity. The National Socialists promised to sweep it all away and to substitute for the stodgy principles of law the righteous activism of a government unafraid to do the right thing.

Americans were headed in the same direction in 2008. The election's issues were being drawn in the same terms that had become common practice, focusing on who would be the strongest commander in chief, who was ready to answer the White House phone at three o'clock in the morning, who could talk the toughest, who was the most outside of the outsiders, and who would win the war. Then the focus was changed by events that could not be ignored while the candidates postured: a decline in the housing market triggered a worldwide collapse of capital and a consequent recession that seemed about to spin out of control. At the same time, Barack Obama emerged as a genuine outsider, having not even been in the Senate when it approved the Patriot Act and the Iraq War, let alone not having been born white. He also possessed the sort of magical persona that made voters believe that he really could unite the nation into one people and that he had the confidence and boldness to lead America out of the morass into which it had wandered. Obama's once-a-generation gift was that he could ignite romantic passions even as he applied Enlightenment principles to governing. If his administration is successful at solving the economic crisis and bringing some resolution to foreign policy, those Enlightenment values may hold sway for some time. But whatever change Obama brings to American political life, it will not soon erase our romantic values.

Nor will the reemergence of romantic ideals in American culture some-day inevitably bring about a fascist political regime. That change would require continued and severe crisis, far beyond one terrorist attack or an economic recession. Our romantic predilections will, however, shape how we will face such new crises if they come—that is, how we will interpret their meaning, how we will identify their causes, how we will respond to our leaders as they enact responses to them, and how we will view our own national identity in the process. Our cultural history suggests that such responses will not be measured and reasoned. The public will reward dramatic and revolutionary action rather than incremental remedies, we will demand strong leadership rather than extended debate, and we will respond to emotional calls to action rather than to considered analysis of the problems. We will be quick to demonize enemies and to crush dissent at home. We will give the government powers disallowed by the Constitution. And in the process, we will deny to ourselves that we have done any of these things.

__4__

POPULISM

IN THE YEARS FOLLOWING WORLD WAR I, Munich roiled with political instability and intrigue. The home of lederhosen and Oktoberfest, of Catholic
piety and agrarian yeomanry, Munich had variously been the capital of the
Bavarian monarchy, an independent communist city-state, and finally part
of the unloved Weimar Republic. Fringe political parties held a bedlam of
meetings, speeches, and rallies in the city's celebrated beer halls. There
were communist, socialist, Christian, and a gaggle of nationalist and anti-
Semitic parties. There were parties against anything one cared to be against,
and compromise was a rare occurrence.

On January 5, 1919, a new party held its first organizational meeting
in the upper story of the Hofbräuhaus, which today is still a cheerful must-
visit for tourists. Above the oompah and *weisswurst* of the main beer hall,
a small group of disaffected workers and veterans of World War I met to
establish the Deutsche Arbeiterpartei (DAP, the German Workers' Party).
The DAP championed the value of honest labor as opposed to the oppression of unearned wealth and profit. But they were not communists; on the
contrary, the DAP despised the universalism and internationalism of the
communist movement and what it perceived to be its Jewishness. Instead,
the DAP offered "socialism with a nationalistic twist," aimed at wresting
the loyalty of workers from the communists by elevating German workers
above all others.[1]

The DAP was just a part of the babble until one of its members began
to show a stunning talent for galvanizing a crowd by emotional rhetoric.
He was Adolf Hitler, one of those disaffected war veterans, whose deepest

conviction was that the sophisticates, the urbane city dwellers of the north, the capitalists and industrialists and aristocrats, the centrists, and especially the Jews had betrayed the fatherland in signing the treaty of Versailles. In so doing they had shamed the German military, burdened Germany with debt, and brought about the cowardly, democratic, modernist Weimar Republic. In signing the treaty, these self-interested and unprincipled moguls had, in a phrase Hitler used incessantly, "stabbed Germany in the back," robbing Germany of its honor and dignity. As this appeal caught on, the DAP gained enough strength to absorb some of the weaker nationalist parties and became in 1920 the Nationalsozialistiche Deutsche Arbeiterpartei (NSDAP). Its familiar name was Nationalsozialist, Nazi for short.

The name was significant. The Nazis were not only a nationalist party but also a socialist party and a workers' party. Their target demographic, at least early on, was the rural working class, the farmers and petty merchants who had not received the Enlightenment education of their sophisticated urban betters. But their consistent goal, from their inception until their ultimate political victory in 1933, was to unite the socialists of the Left with the nationalists of the far Right under a twenty-five-point platform.[2] For the nationalists, they promised the union of all Germans (that is, including Austrians, Alsatians, and Sudeten Czechs), revocation of the Versailles Treaty, territorial expansion, an end to immigration, and revocation of citizenship for Jews. For the socialists, they also included sweeping reforms in public education, pensioners' benefits, and public health. Most of all, they sought an end to the rigid class boundaries of German tradition and especially the elevation of manual labor to greater prestige.[3] This revolutionary new combination of agendas transcended the old Left–Right continuum. Indeed, it had been referred to as the "Third Way" by Arthur Moeller van den Bruck, who later coined the term "Third Reich."[4] Consequently, the National Socialists viewed their party as a revolutionary movement that transcended politics itself.[5]

In November 1922 the Nazis believed themselves ready to take the reins of government, so, in accordance with what was becoming something of a custom, they staged a coup d'état—a putsch in German—to seize control of Bavaria and, they hoped, the entire country. Meeting them in a beer hall called the Bürgerbräukeller, they tricked the local government officials into a back room, where Hitler threatened them with a pistol unless they agreed to back his seizure of power. He had organized a small army of his own and also coopted some of the regular army generals—most notably

Erich Ludendorff, hero of World War I—and had arranged for key military units to march on Berlin the next day. When the assembled ministers refused to join him, he strode into the main hall, where he staged a classic bluff: he announced that the ministers had in fact joined him and warned that everyone ought to get on board:

> The Bavarian Ministry is removed. . . . The government of the November criminals and the Reich President are declared to be removed. A new national government will be named this very day here in Munich. . . . I propose that, until accounts have been finally settled with the November criminals, the direction of policy in the National Government be taken over by me. . . . The task of the provisional German National Government is to organize the march on that sinful Babel, Berlin, and save the German people. . . . Tomorrow will find either a National Government in Germany or us dead![6]

Even in this speech, given under the greatest duress, Hitler was able to convey two of the essential foundations of the Nazi Party's platform. First, he made the "November criminals"—those who had stabbed Germany in the back by capitulating at Versailles and by implication the existing Weimar government—a target of all Germans' wrath. Second, he reemphasized the gulf between Munich and Berlin, the one a city of decent and right-minded folk who could see the truth without a monocle, the other a den of sin—sexual license, jazz, modern art—and worst of all, a babel of cultural and racial mixing. He played to the crowd as a preacher might play to a Tennessee revival, railing against the moral cesspool of New York or Los Angeles.

In the end, the bluff didn't work. The crowd was galvanized by the speech and marched into the center of town, but the local officials slipped away. The marching throng was met by police loyal to the government, several party members were killed (later made martyrs in the Nazis' annual commemoration of the putsch), Hermann Göring was wounded, and Hitler was imprisoned. But, of course, that was not the end of Hitler and the Nazis. Their appeal was simply too strong, and a large part of that appeal came from a distinctly German form of populism.

In the general sense, populism refers to a political philosophy that seeks the empowerment of ordinary people against political, economic, and cultural elites. It is partly a product of the modern age, an age characterized by changes not only in economic relationships but also in all social institutions: church, family, art, sexuality. To the Germans, it was an age during which the agrarian world's old values and old aristocracies were replaced by the modern elites of capital, nouveau wealth, raw political power, and bureaucracy. These new elites were worse than the aristocrats of the past because they were impersonal, anonymous, and single minded. The National Socialists, and especially Hitler himself, sensed this fundamental change in values and exploited it successfully through Hitler's oratory.

But the story of populism is best begun on the American prairie.

PRAIRIE FIRE

The People's Party was the voice of a short-lived American political move-ment of the late nineteenth century, though its roots reach deeply into the founding of the nation itself. The United States had been established largely by, and for the benefit of, independent farmers. They had forged a nation based on the Enlightenment ideal of a fairly loose confederation of landholders governed as little as possible by a distant central government. But just as the nineteenth century challenged the Enlightenment ideals discussed in chapter 3, it also threatened the agrarian roots of economic, political, and social life.

Again, migration and westward expansion played a central role. The conquest of the West made available vast tracts of land, and in the agrarian society that America took itself to be, land meant wealth, security, and respect. People living on ever-smaller farms or in insular towns or stinking cities in the East were offered the opportunity to live the American ideal: a piece of land larger than could ever be available in the East could be had cheaply in the West, with some parcels even free for the tilling. Any man with ambition and the right virtues could become that exemplar of American values, the independent yeoman farmer.

The trouble was, America was changing. The myth of a nation of independent farmers was receding further into the past as the towns and cities in the East and then the Great Lakes states swelled with new immigrant populations. Some were drawn by the promise of western land, but many came for employment in the new industrial society America was becoming. This burgeoning demand in the cities encouraged farmers to aspire beyond self-sufficiency to profitability and growth. Instead of raising a mixture of foods and a few animals solely for his family's consumption, the growing mass markets of the big cities enticed the farmer to develop cash crops for sale afar.

There were four growing economic institutions that encouraged this change in the farmer's orientation. The first was the railroad, as without mass transport none of the farmer's product could reliably get to market. In a spiraling symbiosis, railroads drew farmers to distant regions while the westward expansion of the farmers simultaneously fed the railroads, giving them products to ship and ways to generate revenues. The railroads had also been granted land along their rights of way that they were free to sell off; in fact, for many decades selling the real estate was their main source of income. Thus there was a clear incentive for the railroads to encourage maximum development, and as the most reliably arable land was taken, they encouraged latecomers to settle ever farther westward.[7] By the 1870s railroads were touting western Nebraska as the land of milk and honey, using rainfall data of the most recent years (a period of unusually wet weather in the region) to show that there was plenty of water to raise crops. Scientific thinking of the time also asserted that plowing the land itself increased rainfall, or in the slogan of the time, "the rain follows the plow."[8] When that theory wasn't credible, dry farming techniques were touted, forcing farmers to specialize in a few drought-resistant crops on huge tracts of land. In the event, the 1870s saw 190 million new acres come into cultivation.[9]

The second institution was the rapidly changing technology of farming itself. The invention of the mechanical reaper, the steam tractor, and a host of other laborsaving devices had the effect of vastly increasing the farmer's productivity by increasing the number of acres a family could work.[10] But they also had the accompanying effect of reducing crop prices: as yields grew higher, supply overtook demand and prices sank ever lower. Moreover, the economics of this increased productivity were such that farmers had to increase the size of their holdings to stay afloat, and the small family plot became simply unprofitable. Farmers worked more acres and reaped better yields, but they got no richer for it. In fact, purchasing machinery and other technological improvements only added to the farmer's debt.

This situation increased the influence of a third institution in the farmer's life—the bank. As farms grew and more land became accessible by railroad, it made sense for farmers to borrow in order to expand as rapidly as they could. They mortgaged their existing holdings to buy the parcels held by neighbors who had been enticed farther west; if nothing was available, they moved west themselves. Rather than be tied to their land as in the old days, farmers became restless speculators, leveraging their holdings to acquire more or selling their holdings to reinvest elsewhere. By 1890 there were "more mortgages than families" in the western states of Kansas, Nebraska, and the Dakotas.[11]

The fourth institution was the commodity market, where the price of the farmer's crop was set. Individual farmers could not negotiate directly with buyers in distant cities to sell their wheat or cattle. The whole process of buying and selling large quantities of crops from large numbers of independent farmers was made possible by the development of speculative markets, where middlemen negotiated the price of agricultural goods daily.

American farmers were thus dependent on four human but impersonal forces that they could not control. They were dependent on the railroads to ship their product to distant markets, and they had no say over the rates charged. Shipping costs could consume a fair portion of their profit, and with little competition among railroads (especially since they tended to merge when they served the same area), these costs could rise suddenly and unpredictably. They also depended on the banks to make or renew mortgages on acquired land. Finally, they were dependent on the speculative mood of traders in far-off cities, men who often cared little about farming or even the commodities they traded other than their cash value, and whose hopes, fears, and greed could make or break a farmer's year. Farmers had been accustomed since the dawn of agriculture to uncontrollable forces; after all, the vagaries of weather were the visible manifestation of the farmer's reliance on the grace of God. But these new institutional forces were far from godlike. Though equally inscrutable, they were perceived, often rightly, to be actively working against the farmers' interests. These four institutions could in combination bring terrible crisis to the farm. A period of drought might raise prices on the expectation of a small crop, but if rains suddenly came prices could collapse. An actual crop failure could ruin a farmer with loans to pay, and if he tried to sell off part of his holdings he likely did so at a depressed price. The local railroad might raise tariffs or gain a monopoly by merging with a larger line, or it might abandon a route altogether. In all, the person actually producing the crop seemed to have the least control over it. Farmers increasingly became speculators, financiers, and mostly, debtors—all roles to which they were disinclined and ill suited.

But the bankers and the traders flourished even as many farmers failed, and this inequity did not escape the notice of those at the bottom of the food chain. "What was more natural than to fix the blame for this situation upon the manufacturers, the railroads, the money-lenders, the middlemen—plutocrats all. . . ?"[12] Seeing that their problems were under human and not divine control, farmers became increasingly political. They had learned early on to form collective associations—financial cooperatives, mutual-aid associations, and granges—and they now began to turn them to political action.

The Populists, as the movement was called, made strong political gains during periods of crisis in the farming regions of the West and South. They did so largely through a strategy of fusion, by which they allied themselves with the weaker of the two major parties in various state political races.[13] By throwing their support to, say, an underdog state Democratic Party member challenging a Republican incumbent in a state legislature or congressional race, they could dictate the nomination of the candidate as well as the party's platform. By these methods, in 1890 they took the majority of House seats in Kansas and Nebraska as well as one Senate seat and scored similar victories in several southern states. By 1892 they had formed a genuine third party in national politics, the People's Party, and ran their own candidate for president, James B. Weaver. On the strength of an extensive national campaign, Weaver polled more than a million votes and twenty-two electoral votes. In 1896 they lost their momentum when the Democrats outflanked them by nominating William Jennings Bryan for president. As Bryan espoused many of the Populists' pet themes, notably the free silver issue, they had no choice but to support him and the Democratic Party in the election. The resulting infighting and distrust within the People's Party spelled the end of their strength; although they elected thirty-one candidates to Congress that year, they never showed much clout again.[14]

Populists and Populism

Although the People's Party failed to become a permanent force in American electoral politics, populism as a political philosophy ran too strong and too deep in American thinking to go away. Hence, populism was not merely a short-lived movement that sprouted and died on the prairie; on the contrary, it was a manifestation of deeply held American values and "endemic in American culture."[15] According to George McKenna,

> True, historic populism lasted no more than a decade, but the soil that nourished it was rich enough to support other strains of populism,

and these have cropped up with seasonal regularity down to our present time. Populism, then, is not a sometime thing which puts in an occasional appearance in America. It is the perennial American "ism," with its roots extended at least as far back as the American Revolution.[16]

These other strains of populist thought have cropped up regularly in American politics. Populist sentiment had a large influence on Theodore Roosevelt's presidency, as he moved to rein in the robber barons of the new industrial state. Populism energized the labor movement in its long struggle against exploitation by capital. Later, populism was the philosophical basis for Franklin Roosevelt's New Deal, by which government power was again brought to bear on what had become glaring flaws of unfettered capitalism. And a generation later, Lyndon Johnson harnessed once again the populist spirit in American politics to pass a series of measures that added up to the Great Society program: sweeping civil rights legislation, infrastructure improvements, and additional support for the old and the poor. In each of these cases, Populism was a powerful tool for the political Left, embodying a claim as old as the republic itself that the government was constituted to serve the interests of the general citizenry.[17]

But there were other aspects of populist thought that, if not official components of the People's Party platform, fed on less noble currents in American political thinking. In the South, the Populists had since the early days tended to ally themselves with the Democrats, whose principal platform was the protection of poor and working-class whites against advances made by blacks. This stance, of course, aligned them with Jim Crow racism, even if their own predilections were to unite workers of all races against the Eastern elites. And as we have seen, Theodore Roosevelt's brand of populism included not only trust-busting but also a turgid nationalism that could be xenophobic and racist.

Like the progressive and egalitarian rendition of populism, this re-actionary version also projected right through the twentieth century. Notable Populists included Father Coughlin, whose racist and anti-Semitic diatribes electrified radio listeners in the 1930s, and Huey Long, whose own Louisiana-based political machine was as legally questionable as any in Chicago or New York had been. In the South, populist politicians continued to capture votes by resisting integration and civil rights; after losing to an explicitly segregationist candidate for governor of Alabama in 1958, populist George Wallace declared he would never be "out-niggered" again.[18] Senator Joe McCarthy had also carried the banner of populist ideology, rising above the tenets of either party to cast suspicion on suspected Communists who had, he was certain, infiltrated a variety of American elites by use of foreign and domestic agents. For many critics, this darker side of populism looked a lot like fascism.[19]

How is it possible that a single political philosophy could motivate such different political figures and spawn such divergent policies? How could politicians of the Far Left and the Far Right both claim populist sentiments and galvanize populist passion? The short answer is that populism as a political philosophy transcends the usual distinctions between Left and Right, liberal and conservative, and Democrat and Republican. But though populism has embraced a broad range of particular policies, both virtuous and odious, a few common denominators of populist thought remain that trace all the way back to the founding of the nation.

The most pervasive and deeply held of all American populist values is contempt for elites of all kinds. Americans from the beginning have resented the conferral of status on any group, class, or estate beyond practical worth or functional utility. By this I don't mean that Americans have thought themselves an egalitarian community of brothers and sisters without distinctions. Rather, Americans accord prestige and status on fairly limited bases, such as wealth, race, and certain areas of practical accomplishment. They don't recognize taste, sophistication, intellect, or birthright as legitimate symbols of status. Americans use few titles or honorifics beyond Doctor, Reverend, and Your Honor. Even the president is addressed simply as Mr. President, thanks to the precedent set by George Washington.

In the populist era, elitism was found in the growing exclusivity of the social world of the robber barons, of the financiers and industrialists, and of the urbane culture that promoted the establishment of museums, symphony orchestras, opera houses, and other assets of high culture that the new elite self-consciously pursued. The suave urbanite, debarking from his carriage in high collar and swallow-tailed coat at the concert hall, represented to the populist mentality all that was wrong with American society. This perception did not change in the twentieth century. Indeed, the latter-day inheritors of the Gilded Age became objects of scorn by both the labor movement in the twenties and thirties and the legions of Hooverville denizens during the Depression. Ivy League bureaucrats and the Hollywood glitterati of the 1950s were singled out by McCarthyites as disloyal threats to American democracy. The chieftains of the military-industrial complex of the 1950s through the Vietnam era were the targets of first the anti-bomb and then the antiwar movements.

One particular group that has always been suspect in America is the intellectual elite. True, from the beginning Americans valued education as a precondition to democracy. After all, how could the citizenry participate intelligently in the republic without being literate or without some training in reason and rhetoric? Moreover, education in the practical arts of agriculture and other skills and trades was an economic necessity. But at least since the Populists, a strong current in American thought has viewed learning and knowledge for its own sake with a jaundiced eye. William Jennings Bryan himself had made the romantic appeal against the intellectual by declaring, "What this country needs is not more brains but more heart."[20] Anti-intellectualism has appeared in cycles according to the nation's political and technological needs. It reappeared in a particularly virulent form in the 1954 army-McCarthy hearings, when Senator McCarthy's followers seemed especially to relish his attacks on academics. These people had critical minds, were more likely than others to seriously consider unpopular or unorthodox points of view, and could be readily made to look suspicious. McCarthy particularly despised the academic diplomats of the State Department and most especially the suave Averell Harriman.[21] But McCarthy and his followers didn't need to focus too sharply. Instead, he gained a passionate following simply by associating communism with "fancy manners, Anglophilism, Harvard, pretensions to high culture . . . the Eastern Establishment."[22] In a brilliant reversal of logic, he managed to associate Marxist sentiments not with the unwashed masses but with the privileged classes.

Earlier the Eisenhower-Stephenson election of 1952 had shown the political benefits of an anti-intellectual stance, when Adlai Stephenson played the role of the egghead to Eisenhower's simple country soldier. Even Eisenhower didn't shrink from the occasional barb at the intelligentsia. In 1954 he amused a meeting of Republicans with his definition of an intellectual: "a man who takes more words than are necessary to tell more than he knows." This witticism had followed a complaint about the many "wise-cracking intellectuals" who were bent on showing how wrong other people were, especially those who made policy.[23] Stephenson, too, had recognized the political baggage he was carrying. When a woman on the campaign trail shouted to Stephenson that he "had the vote of every thinking person," the candidate was heard to quip, "That's not enough—we need a majority!" In all, intellectuals had become the scapegoats for America's anxieties, and professors became targets of "a constant barrage from Oklahoma fundamentalists, Midwestern rural congressmen, and small-town newspapers, for their supposed left-wing sympathies, their godlessness, their immorality. . . ."[24] The Right, especially, had a "folkish dislike for the educated classes."[25]

A second principal element of populist thought is distrust of the city, born of the prairie farmers' enslavement to urban interests. Since many of the farmers' tormentors were urban and eastern people, populist anger came to be focused on the cities themselves and their parasitical and polyglot inhabitants. The movement appealed to the suspicions of rural folk who had no use for, and maybe never saw, the big city. The cities, in their view, were the home of the railroad barons, of the commodity traders and big banks, and of immigrants of every stripe. They were the homes of machine politics, where self-serving politicians bought the votes of exploited workers to advance their own and their corporate sponsors' interests. Worse, they were home to foreign cultures and practices, which corroded American traditions. The cities were the antithesis of the Jeffersonian republic that they admired and yearned for; in fact, Jefferson himself had warned that urbanization was inimical to democracy.

By the 1920s, all the Populists' suspicions seemed to have come to pass. American cities were not much different from Berlin in the 1920s. Centers of Jazz Age culture, they were teeming with immigrants and other transients, choked with people and smoke, and the likely source for whatever guilty pleasures one desired. The cities' rich were fabulously wealthy while the poor were destitute and seemed to do all the work. Many of the latter were the strange and disease-ridden foreigners whom the moneyed interests had brought in to depress the ordinary Americans' wages. But the Populists' worries about the city were not just the fears of a reactionary fringe. The newly emerging social scientists also viewed the cities as the breeding ground of America's problems, although they couched the problems in terms of alienation, status seeking, and dehumanization. Using empirical data and a variety of statistical and mapping techniques, they began to quantify the cities, their people, and their troubles, thus founding the American tradition of urban sociology.[26]

The crash of 1929 and the ensuing Depression did nothing to ease America's wariness of the cities. The poor were still there, of course, only in much greater numbers and in even worse straits. It was small consolation that there were so few members of the idle rich left to lord it over them and smaller comfort still in the knowledge that rural life had also taken a severe turn for the worse. Yet everyone's financial ruin was easy to attribute to the bubble of the Roaring Twenties, when Chicago gangsters, New York flappers, Detroit flagpole sitters, Hollywood movie stars, Boston college boys, and Harlem jazzmen had ridden a wave of gin-infused urban euphoria even while, as all decent folk could see, society's foundations crumbled.

The third basic tenet of populism was a distrust of modernism itself. Most of these suspicions—of the new elites, of the intellectuals, of the cities—could be summed up as the result of the new modern age. Art was unintelligible. Cubism, Dada, and worse were the darlings of the new elites looking to give a patina to their wealth. The new popular music was, if nothing else, at least better than what these moguls were listening to in the concert halls. The latter was all so foreign anyway, the work of polished Germans and Frenchmen. To the populist mind, moral values were in steep decline, largely because financial speculation and conspicuous consumption had replaced hard work and frugality as the firm foundations of the good life. Worse yet, this change in values had been inflicted on the majority by a small, effete minority of moneyed interests.

The common decent folk felt not just exploited but also bypassed and humiliated by the new industrial society. Farmers had simply become less important in American society, their contribution to the gross domestic product (GDP) having declined from 36 percent in 1870 to just 22 percent in 1900.[27] And here is where a curious thing happened: it turned out that the old upper class felt the same way, as they too had become less important. The Lodges, the Cabots, the Astors, and all the others had similarly been made to seem obsolete and silly by the aggressive upstarts of mass production and high finance. They still had wealth, but they had forfeited a great deal of their influence to this new industrial class, many of them newcomers, immigrants, and Jews. In the end, the oppressed suddenly found themselves in league with their oppressors against the new cultural wave, though as might be expected, the old aristocrats maintained the upper hand and held their noses as they encouraged the Populists to rouse the rabble.[28] And this instance was not the only case of the Right and the Left joining forces to resist the depredations of the modern age. The National Socialists were also making electoral gains from just such a coalition in Germany.

GERMAN POPULISM

It's generally understood that populism in America was at bottom a response to the changing economic basis of society.[29] As one of the most rapidly industrializing countries in the world, the United States was replacing the small yeoman farmer with the large-scale mechanized agribusinessman. This trend was self-reinforcing, as the farm's greater size and productivity both made possible and depended on the burgeoning city of industrial workers, immigrants, and financiers. And as anthropologists have long understood, changes in a society's economic basis inevitably bring changes in its values and beliefs. The more fundamental the change in a society's economy, the more fundamental are its cultural changes as well, and the change from an agrarian to an industrial basis is as fundamental as it gets. As anyone in what we today call the developing world can attest, the forces of modernization, industrialization, and urbanization really do wrench apart a people's traditions and beliefs.

As it happened, Germany was undergoing the same sort of change, only more rapidly. A latecomer to industrialization, owing partly to its late unification as a state, the Germans had a lot of ground to make up. From a country that was two-thirds rural when it became unified in 1871, Germany became two-thirds urban by 1939. The proportion of Germans who worked on farms declined from 50 percent to 10 percent in the same period.[30] Like all industrializing societies, Germany also experienced other profound demographic changes: an aging population owing to longer life spans, lower infant mortality, a lower birthrate, smaller families, and fewer extended families. Women consequently were freed from much of the pressure to reproduce and found their traditional roles reduced. Adding to this the surplus of women after World War I, it is easy to see how the traditional women's role of *Kinder, Küche, und Kirche* (children, kitchen, and church) was becoming obsolete.[31]

Economic and demographic changes also disrupted the status hierarchy that Germans were accustomed to, and the political crises of the Weimar Republic only brought them all into sharper focus. People with little status acquired great wealth while many respected aristocratic families saw their fortunes decline. As some sectors of the middle class gained, some lost; it all seemed so unpredictable and arbitrary. A profiteering ethic arose by which everyone was cast in the uncomfortably equal position of trying to wrest a living from everyone else, and with it came a general sense of moral relativism. Sexual taboos were called into question, raised largely by rational considerations: what exactly was wrong with sexual freedom? What practical problems did it introduce, and how could they be avoided or solved? With the decline of ordinary prudery, Germans entered a "sexual enlightenment," by which they sought to approach sex scientifically. Objective information and scientific thinking were to replace old superstitions and guilt, health considerations took precedence over moral threats, and sin was replaced by illness.[32] These problems of modernization and industrialization were not new discoveries; indeed, a great deal of German social thought had focused on just these sorts of things through much of the previous century.

The Modern Specter

Social thinking along these lines was exemplified by the writings of Karl Marx and Max Weber, two of the greatest social thinkers in Western history and both Germans. Marx is well known for his condemnation of capitalism, expressed most forcefully in the manifesto he and Friedrich Engels wrote for the emerging Communist movement in Paris. But Marx's critique of capitalism was just part of a grand theory of how the economic, political, and social world worked. In his view, all of human activity, evil and benign—from the formation of families to religious faith, to the institution of law, to the production of art—could be characterized as a struggle among classes for material gain.

Capitalism was only the most recent manifestation of this struggle, but at the same time it was one of the most pernicious because it tended to dehumanize people in ways that earlier forms of economic organization did not. For example, social relationships that in earlier times had been based on kinship or obligation tended to become based on money, or what he called the "crass cash nexus." Where people had once worked because they owed their labor to the lord of the manor, or because it was a part of who they were, they now worked purely for money. Worse, their relationship to the product of their labor was destroyed by capitalism's tendency toward industrialization. Factory workers no longer had any personal attachment to what they produced because they did not produce the whole product themselves but only a part of it. Cobblers or weavers or coopers or smiths were no longer responsible for the quality of their work; instead, workers became interchangeable and anonymous slaves to machines and organizational processes, and their only interest was in getting paid. In short, labor was no longer a humanizing activity but a dehumanizing one without inherent meaning. People worked not because it was what made them human but because they could get money to do other things that might make them human. Unfortunately, they seldom got enough money from their labor to do much more than stay alive.

The laborer's overlord, the bourgeois capitalist, was likewise dehumanized. The nature of capitalism was such that no capitalist could stay in business unless he continually exploited labor by paying workers less than the value of what they produced. This arrangement degraded the relationship between employer and worker, reducing it to a constant struggle of each to get the most out of the other while giving the least. Capitalism and its attendant industrialism thus dehumanized what had been a more human world. Even slavery was better in some ways; at least the master knew his slaves' names.

This dehumanization extended beyond the relations between employers and workers. Because capitalists had wealth, education, and organization, they were able to appropriate the various institutions of society —government, the church, the press, and in our time, the electronic media—and use them to control the lower classes. The church promulgated doctrines that encouraged obedience, hard work, and conformity while governments passed laws that favored the upper classes and criminalized the workers. These institutions had always served the ruling class, but this was a new ruling class, one which lacked the old legitimacy of noble birth and benign intent. In the modern capitalist society, all relations were based on wealth and power, and all human values were suspicious at best, cynically false at worst.

Max Weber picked up the thread, spending the better part of his career worrying about the modern age, which he too considered a threat to genuine human values. In Weber's view, the history of the West over the past several centuries could be described as a massive trend toward the increasing "disenchantment" of life. This was caused, fundamentally, by an increasing emphasis on rationalization in every sphere of life, with the traditional or spiritual bases for human action replaced by instrumental, calculating ones. Where people once had acted morally because it was simply the right thing to do, it now made sense to ask *why* one should obey the rules. Where in the past they had married, worked, raised children, and undergone all of life's experiences guided by the certainties and obligations of tradition, all of these activities had become ruled by reason, efficiency, and self-interest.

One clear and pervasive manifestation of this change was the growth of modern bureaucracy. In government, in commerce, in education, and in any number of other realms, the organization and management of tasks had become increasingly driven by the need for greater efficiency, greater control, and greater predictability and order. This was endemic in the industrial age, just as Marx had shown: the fundamental imperative of capitalism's competitive reality was the continual reduction of labor costs. This trend could be accomplished only by reducing workers' skill levels, which in turn required ever-tighter coordination of their behavior. This step meant that their superiors' judgment and authority were replaced by the book, the manual of policies, rules, and standards. Thus the essence of bureaucracy is the replacement of good judgment with laws and regulations. Division of labor becomes rampant as the individual's role in the organization is very tightly circumscribed; the worker or officeholder participates not as a whole person but as a function or part of a machine. One's contribution is quantified according to a set of standards, one's advancement proceeds according to highly specified criteria, and one's individual traits are irrelevant.

We can see that this arrangement had the effect not only of reducing individual variability on the job but also of bringing greater justice—at least in our modern definition—to it. In a bureaucracy, promotions are granted on the basis of objectively measured merit, reducing the effect of whim or favoritism. Individuals are hired or retained according to their performance or qualifications and not their race or age or identity. The whole thing is a wonderful edifice in control and predictability. But we know, as Weber did, that bureaucracy has a downside. The elimination of human whim from organizational decisions can also be read as the elimination of human judgment and wisdom. Decisions made out of slavish adherence to the letter of the law frequently violate the spirit of the law. Promotions go to the people who have jumped through the correct hoops while more genuinely worthy candidates are passed over. Everything is judged and evaluated on the basis of its contribution to something else rather than its own intrinsic worth. Ends become means and means become ends in themselves.

As bureaucracies evolve and grow, rules and policies are devised to cover every conceivable circumstance; meanwhile, each rule and policy creates both its own loophole as well as the desire to exploit it. Of course, more rules and policies can be enacted to close the loopholes created by the existing policies, but this process becomes an infinite spiral into ever-growing snarls of red tape. Bureaucracies are thus notorious for their irrationality and inefficiency, even as they strive for greater rationality and efficiency. Even more troubling is the tendency for bureaucratic rule to suck the meaning and value out of the organizational task. Working precisely to the standard while ignoring quality, teaching to the test, and career ticket punching devalue and displace the actual purpose of the activity. Bureaucratic life is inherently prone to cynicism, to alienation, and to a lack of human caring for the task. In Weber's view, the inexorable march of rationalization and bureaucracy would ultimately imprison humanity in an "iron cage" of serfdom to impersonal masters.[33]

The problems of bureaucracy were but one manifestation of a more fundamental malaise of the modern age. To Weber, the drive toward greater rationalization crept into all areas of life, replacing tradition with calculation. Authority—of the state, the church, the family, or any institution—was now to be constantly challenged on rational and self-interested grounds. Social values now had worth only if they worked toward some other end; expediency replaced principle. Morals were situational. Life was becoming, in his phrase, disenchanted—that is, characterized by a loss of inherent belief and meaning.

Weber and Marx both seem to have wished for some sort of return to an era of genuine human values and meanings and to a world in which a person knew right from wrong and knew from deep immersion in a genuine community what was true and what was false. For both Germans and Americans, this time is embodied in much the same agrarian idyll, where moral virtues and eternal realities were clearly understood by all. Never mind, of course, whether such an age ever existed.

The ideas of Marx and Weber are, at bottom, romantic ones. Both were suspicious of the idea of an inherently orderly world: Marx because all perceptions of order were promulgated and maintained at the behest of the ruling class and Weber because the modern age's desire for order had created bureaucracy and disenchantment. The old days—whether a century or a millennium ago, or even existing only in myth—were better days because beliefs and values were rooted in tradition, in the sacred, in faith. These principles gave meaning to life while reason and logic killed meaning in favor of efficiency and predictability. If life in the modern age was not nasty, brutish, and short, one might say that it was vacuous, impersonal, and cheap.

In short, the modern age was essentially un-German. For one thing, modernism tended to homogenize cultures by nationalizing and even globalizing their economies. Mass communication and transportation across national and ethnic boundaries eroded the distinctions among peoples and thus eroded cultural traditions and beliefs. The efflorescence of Weimar culture in all its modern decadence was evidence enough to many that Germany was headed down the wrong path. Fulfillment of the human spirit—the re-enchantment of life, one might say—could be achieved by retreating from this dehumanized existence, by returning to simpler values and honest labor, and especially by reaffirming one's attachment to the land instead of to organizations or governments or things. Like the Americans, the Germans yearned for the better days of the past, though Germany had experienced such rapid change that most Germans could actually remember those better times, when values were more certain, hopes more realistic, and people better behaved.[34] Though there were, of course, diverse views with some welcoming the changes and others condemning them, Germany had become a nation of "unmodern men in a modern world."[35]

Also like their American counterparts, the Germans clung to an agrarian romanticism that glorified country life as healthful and vital and that denigrated the new, urban world in which they found themselves. The new urban age collided head-on with the growing folkish sentiment that the Germans had adopted over the course of the nineteenth century. Folkism elevated the farmer and the small townsman to an iconic status as the genuine German, unpolluted by the eroding influences of the modern city. The real German was, most of all, a child of nature and not of the city; he used common sense rather than sophisticated reasoning and lived simply, in tune with his natural surroundings.

What the Germans did not have was a long-held disdain for elites. In this they differed from the American Populists, as the Germans had long respected, more or less, the monarchs and princes under whose rule they had lived. For millennia German aristocracy had symbolized much that was excellent in German culture: the Rhine castles, the hunt, the faith, the arts. The Prussian military tradition supported by the Junker nobility, that bygone glory that the new egalitarian republic had destroyed, was after all the foundation on which the German state had been unified.

But how could a populist ethos flourish in a society that had no despised elite? The ultimate triumph of National Socialism was the manufacture of just such an elite—a shadowy cabal that was powerful; embraced heartily the new culture of modernism; and was essentially un-German. With the increasing integration of Jews into German society during the kaisers' reign and their attendant gains in wealth and status, the Germans had begun to perceive an elite they could blame for their troubles.

National Socialist Populism
In December 1924 Hitler gained his release from prison after the putsch, having served a scant nine months for what was normally a capital crime. The leniency of the courts and prison system attests to the depth of sympathy for the Nazis' views. Moreover, Hitler had successfully used the court to put the republic itself on trial and had made himself a figure of national importance in the process. Though the party was banned in some of the German states and Hitler personally was barred from speaking, he began to rebuild the party organization around a push for parliamentary power.

Although the Nazis' popularity had early on been strongest in rural Bavaria and Franconia, by 1925 they had calculated that the way to national prominence would be via appeals to the disaffected, urban, industrial working class. Hitler reorganized the party after his release from prison to correspond to the Reichstag's parliamentary districts and set up a system by which the most active and ruthless revolutionary leaders were installed as regional leaders.[36] Then they set out to win the north by stealing away the support of the other far-right parties and, at the same time, of the urban, industrial workers loyal to the Communists.

It didn't work. By 1927 the party's membership had only grown to seventy-five thousand from the fifty-five thousand of four years earlier.[37] What surprised the Nazis, however, was that they had shown more strength in the rural areas despite their efforts in the urban enclaves. What had happened was that the urban workers' economic situation had gotten marginally better while the farmers' plight had gotten worse. Realizing that they were not going to penetrate the industrial working class, they recast their approach, both ideologically and structurally. The urban plan was dead.[38]

Refocusing on the rural districts in northern Germany, they backed away from the twentieth-century version of socialism they had initially adopted. They removed the promise of the state's appropriation of land from their twenty-five-point platform while promising a ban on food imports and the establishment of a high-level government office dedicated to farm issues. Although they actually lost ground in the elections of May 1928, they showed even more strength in the rural districts: gaining only 1.4 percent of the vote in Berlin, they polled up to 18 percent in areas of Schleswig-Holstein.[39] For the remainder of their electoral life, the Nazis worked the folkish line.

In most ways, folkism had been originally an elitist view, elevating as it did the landholder above factory workers and others who occupied the lowest classes in the German economy.[40] It was the Nazis who recast the landsman as the common denominator who could represent all real Germans, urban and rural, north and south, Catholic and Protestant. This was accomplished by representing the farmer as the German within all Germans—that is, the original German from which the newer varieties descended. Anyone taking the Nazis' propaganda films as representative of German society would conclude that all Germans were either soldiers or village folk, in peasant garb or stark uniform, and that only Jews wore suits.

The peasant was to be "the core of the new national identity," according to the new appeal.[41] Hitler refined his themes continually, toning down the rabid anti-Semitism when necessary while extolling the virtues of family, moral cleanliness, the volk, and *Vaterland*.[42] But while emphasizing folkish themes, the Nazis could not afford to give up completely their efforts to penetrate the urban working class. Ultimately, by linking the industrial worker as best they could with the rural peasant and equating the Communists to the Jewish and foreign interests, they made progress. By the elections of 1930, the National Socialists had become "a catch-all party of social protest," appealing to a wide variety of demographic groups.[43] The strongest appeal of all was the constant drumbeat of social and cultural unity that would be achieved by repressing foreign elements and eliminating social classes. All Germans were now to be considered workers, whether workers who used their hands or their minds.

This appeal did not change after Hitler was made chancellor and the Nazis consolidated their power. One of the strongest themes of Leni Riefenstahl's *Triumph of the Will* is its portrayal of the populist and working-class focus of the 1934 party rally. These enormous spectacles were week-long festivals in which party officials down to the level of block wardens, various guilds and workers' associations, youth and arts groups, and the military celebrated the party's accomplishments and focused its agenda for the coming year. One memorable and early scene featured the communal housing of participants in campgrounds, where they lived collectively and rurally, slept on straw, and dined together. The camaraderie, the rough accommodations, and the sheer joy of life in the open are clearly portrayed. Hitler Youth spent the days hiking and participating in athletic competitions, the League of German Maidens in open-air exercise and dance. Both groups formed up for the torchlight parades around Nuremberg's medieval city walls in the evening.

A later scene depicts a ritual of consecration of labor, in which men with shovels join with men wielding sledgehammers in chanting their solidarity with the party, with all of Germany, and with each other. Most of all, they declare their mutual importance to the cause of German greatness. Most Germans might live in the city, but their roots were in the soil of the ancient land. If they were not farmers themselves, they were descended from farmers and continued to depend on them not only for their subsistence but also for their dignity.

There can be little doubt that the National Socialists were essentially a populist movement. It's true that Hitler was not averse to courting the industrial elite for funding or for votes, but these alliances were couched in the language of German nationalism and industrial superiority, anti-communism, anti-Semitism, or militarism. It's also true that the Nazis' support for the industrial worker fluctuated wildly from 1925 to 1933, but this oscillation was largely the result of intra-party conflict or more often, electoral expediency.[44] In the end, the Nazis were at bottom a party of anger—anger about the war, anger toward the Weimar Republic, anger over the economy, anger about the decline of morals, anger at the Jews—and they capitalized on whatever made Germans most angry at the moment.

Their populist appeal was not very different from that of their American counterparts. They sought a fair shake for the little guy in his struggle against the secretive and powerful financial interests. The farmer was the most aggrieved by these interests and at the same time was the most noble of citizens, and so the farmer was, if not the principal constituent of the movement, then certainly the icon of it. The Nazis relentlessly attacked elites of all sorts, but like the Americans they did so not to replace them or banish them from society but to incorporate them into a utopian, classless, and unified national community. In both societies, for example, the problem was not that the banks were considered a bad thing, and no one seriously proposed abolishing credit or finance. It was just that the bankers, as the result of both their inherent greed (being labeled as foreigners and Jews) and the collusion of a corrupt or slothful government, had enjoyed unfettered control of an economy that ought to serve all citizens.

The Nazis and Americans both included intellectuals among the elites they despised. Too much education was thought to make people artificial, unproductive, and thus less useful to the Reich.[45] Hitler himself said in a 1938 speech, "What we suffer from is an excess of education. . . . The wiseacres, however, are the enemies of action. What we require is instinct and will."[46] The parallel to William Jennings Bryan's call for less brains and more heart is striking but no less so than the parallel to Eisenhower's complaint about wise-cracking intellectuals or to Senator McCarthy's outbursts. Hitler had also cultivated his anti-intellectual character from the start. In *Mein Kampf* he had described himself as "an anti-intellectual whose ideology was shaped, not through formal study but through personal experience and self-education."[47] The party propagandists used Hitler's very mediocrity in this and other areas as symbolic of his deeper greatness.[48] Of course, the Nazis made careful distinctions between those with too much education and those with just the right amount at least partly as a matter of political strategy: the Nazis' appeal worked best not on the totally ignorant nor on the highly educated but on those with just enough knowledge to buy the Nazis' arguments about conspiracy in high places, their half-baked theories of genetics, and their infected version of history.

The Nazis also played on antiurban sentiments, and these efforts were not much different from the Populists' moralizing about the sin and crime of the American city. They exploited the Germans' desire to return to basic values and to a simpler time when everyone understood the rules and shared them deeply. They called for a strong, traditional family, which women were encouraged to manage and guide. "The archenemies were liberalism and its economic system, capitalism; both were expressions of hated 'modernity' and grasping materialism."[49]

And they called for fundamental economic reform. Though this exhortation varied in intensity and sincerity throughout the party's history, the National Socialists never abandoned their original twenty-five-point platform, by which a classless society would be fashioned from all workers of both hand and mind. The state would manage the economy for the benefit of all and get Germany out of the economic mess that the war, the treaty, and the Depression had caused. In effect, Hitler promised a New Deal to the Germans that was not so different from the one Franklin Roosevelt used in the United States.[50] The parallels between the National Socialist platform and those of various populist reformers in the United States of the same general period are many. It should not be too surprising, inasmuch as both nations faced similar crises: economic depression, growing class conflict, fear of a Communist infiltration of the labor force, and a sense of moral decay brought on by rapid industrialization and urbanization. Both nations had an ample supply of scapegoats: Jews and foreigners for the Germans; Jews, blacks, and foreigners for the Americans. In a 1941 speech in Des Moines, Charles A. Lindbergh, son of a Minnesota populist politician, named the British, the Jews, and the Roosevelt administration as the greatest threats to American peace, and his wife praised National Socialism as the "wave of the future."[51] As far as can be known today, it was solely the Japanese attack on Pearl Harbor that silenced Lindbergh's isolationist and pro-Nazi movement, as it had been making clear gains among the populace.

AMERICAN POPULISM TODAY

Populism remains a central tenet of American social and political ideology. When American scholar George McKenna called it *the* American ideology, he was writing in 1974, at the height of the antiwar movement, the civil rights movement, and the downfall of the Nixon presidency. What McKenna saw then was an ideology that both the civil rights and antiwar activists of the Left and the "silent majority" of the Right embraced fully: the idea that the people who mattered in America were the ordinary people, who had been deprived of their rightful power by an elite of know-it-alls who thought they should dictate what was best for the country. Of course, these groups all railed against different elites: for the antiwar movement, the enemy was the military-industrial complex; for the civil rights marchers, it was local, white political machines and community groups; and for Nixon's hard hats and silent majority, it was the intellectuals, the Harvard types, and other "nattering nabobs of negativism." The secret to populism's longevity is that in many ways it is a tabula rasa onto which any enemy can be projected and through which any policy can be promoted. The problem—and the beauty—of using phrases like "power to the people" is that almost any group can think of themselves as the beneficiaries.

Populism has not faded away since Nixon's time. Jimmy Carter came to Washington almost entirely on the appeal of his outsider status as a small-time peanut farmer (an image carefully crafted and convincing, if not entirely accurate). Ronald Reagan called for a new morning in which Americans would turn away from the Washington insiders and modernist ways to regain America's simpler past. Reagan loved to be photographed chopping brush or riding a horse on his ranch; never mind that he made his fortune as a Hollywood movie star. George H. W. Bush worked hard to cultivate his Texan side even though he was the son of a U.S. senator from Connecticut, was a prep school boy, and was a Yale graduate who summered on the ancestral estate on the Maine coast. But Bush's populist image was no match for Bill Clinton's, who after all was the real article, more or less. He really did come from a meager rural existence, replete with family troubles and an absent father. Later he became a Rhodes Scholar, but that was forgiven as he had kept his Southern accent and played the saxophone. His vice president and successor-apparent, Al Gore, simply didn't have the populist credentials. Another senator's son, Gore had no claim to hardscrabble roots nor could he act the part. When polled, voters called him schoolmarmish and simply too smart for the job.

Gore ran against a more convincing populist candidate, George W. Bush, who was certainly convincing as an intellectually mediocre but earnest country boy. But Gore's bigger problem was that the country had taken up a new populist revolution, one that rivaled the civil rights movement of the 1960s, the McCarthy witch hunts of the 1950s, the temperance movement of the 1920s, and even the original farmers' revolt of the 1890s. This wave of populism had all the earmarks of the old-fashioned little man's revolt, with its yearning for a simpler time and the elevation of folkish values, its idea that a shadowy elite was in charge of things, its distrust of the city, and its contempt for the modern. There was also the disdain for European influence (Bush had never been to Europe until after he became president) and no small degree of anti-intellectualism.

America, Real and Other
Populist themes continued to prevail in the 2004 election. The Democrats' nomination of John Kerry gave the Bush campaign a ready foil for populist contempt. A longtime New Englander, well educated and philosophical, well married to old wealth, and an avowed internationalist, Kerry was everything the Right could want in an opponent. Bush repeatedly drew distinctions between the cultures of the East Coast and that of the heartland, and Vice President Cheney made the distinction a staple of his stump speeches. "I'm much more comfortable with the values that I find

in the middle of the United States than I do in Massachusetts," he told an audience in North Dakota, against a background of stuffed and mounted game. In the same speech, the former congressman, defense secretary, and millionaire government contractor managed, remarkably, to distance himself from the insider culture of Washington.[52] As for Kerry, he was just lucky that no one had videotaped him speaking to foreign reporters in the fluent French he had learned from his childhood vacations on the continent—a practice he had enjoyed before the presidential bid.[53]

By 2008 the populist rift had become a chasm dividing the country into the "real" America and the urban, or eastern, or Californian, or generally liberal America, which vice presidential candidate Sarah Palin described to a crowd in North Carolina. If the remarks had been a gaffe or simple ineloquence, they were not very far from what Cheney and Bush—and Democratic candidates, as best they could—had said four years earlier.

What Kerry, Gore, and the Democrats found most distressing about this new populism was that it somehow had managed to steal a good many of their target voters and at the same time demonize the rest. American populism had become the property of what used to be called the political Right. But these new populists had managed to transcend the traditional continuum of the Left and the Right by reconfiguring the social class hierarchy in America. No longer was class a socioeconomic matter as the old Marxists saw it; rather, class had become a matter of culture, of status, of respect. Today the elite is not the industrialist, the banker, the military, or those who use wealth to amass power so as to get more wealth. Today the elite is cast in terms of culture: a cabal of influence, which uses the media, the schools and universities, the arts, and the out-of-control government bureaucracy to tear us away from our bedrock values and erase our memory of America's Golden Age. Its members are overeducated and urbane. They love the city because it offers snobbish diversions such as degenerate art, sexual license, and worse, contact with foreign cultural influences. The new elite is thought to be irreligious and without core beliefs at all other than contempt for traditional American values. This elite cynically exploits African Americans and other ethnic groups for electoral power, all the while using the crushing alienation of welfare and government handouts to keep these groups powerless.

The principal tool of this new elite is thought to be the government itself. Through its power of taxation and its enormous civil service, the elite controls information, ideology, and resources. The state apparatus is controlled by this elite lock, stock, and barrel, and for this reason the ordinary citizen is humiliated and marginalized day in and day out. For the new populists, big government isn't just expensive and wasteful; it actively works to debase the culture, just as Weber had said bureaucracy would. Big government's rational imperative, with its crushing burden of rules, policies, entitlements, and its guarantees of trivial rights to trivial people, works tirelessly to disenchant American life. This bureaucracy embraces rules prohibiting prayer in the school, encourages welfare fraud, and hurts small business by imposing minimum wages and big business by demanding workplace safety. It hands out grants to perverted artists and anti-American historians. It gives jobs to unqualified minorities over better-qualified white people. And it pursues this course with the hard-earned tax dollars of ordinary Americans who want none of it.

This new populism sounds similar to the usual lament of the conservative Right, but just as it did at the beginning of the twentieth century, a strange thing has happened: the ruling class and the working class have united in their outrage against the new liberal elite. In his excellent study of contemporary Kansas politics, Thomas Frank observed that the more working-class people a county had, the more likely it was to vote for George W. Bush in 2004 and thus endorse tax cuts for the wealthy, rollbacks of government benefits, and a foreign war.[54] These populists are not fiscally conservative, however; while they agitate constantly for smaller government, for example, they expand its size. Ronald Reagan's federal budget grew much faster than that of his predecessor, and George H. W. Bush's budget did as well. George W. Bush and his "conservative" government abandoned all restraint, bloating the budget to several trillion dollars.

Moreover, the new populists' complaints against the government's power sound awfully similar to the complaints of the radical Left; that is, the ruling class uses the government to control the people as a means of advancing their own interests. Sociologist C. Wright Mills made the leftist argument effectively and early: the state was solidly in the hands of the power elite—an alliance of industrialists, military leaders, and government leaders—who used it to control education, the arts, the academy, and every other important institution in increasing its power and influence.[55] Today the Far Left and the Far Right both agree that the government is controlled by the elite, but each faction construes the elite differently.

These new American populists are often called neoconservatives, pseudoconservatives, radical conservatives, or abbreviations of these names. But they are not conservatives. Moreover, they have accomplished what the National Socialists accomplished in Weimar Germany: they have united factions of the Left and the Right by transcending the usual continuum of liberalism and conservatism. The new populists are neither progressives, in the sense of wanting to move the country incrementally forward into the modern age, nor conservatives seeking to hold on to the values and policies of today or the recent past. Instead, they are generically radical. They wish to leap into a future that harkens back to a mythic past, with a classless society in which owner and worker are united in their morals, their faith, and their aspirations for the country. It all has a curious "back to the future" flavor.

In the 1960s and 1970s, a spirited academic debate swirled about the true character of American populism. It ultimately came down to a simple question of whether the Populists were Marxists or fascists, but this discussion turned on a mistaken understanding of fascism. Fascism is the wedding of both Left and Right and a radicalization of discourse itself fueled by a romantic contempt for moderation and compromise. In joining the Left and Right, fascism reconfigures the class struggle as an alliance of workers and owners against thinkers and snobs, producers against consumers, and common folk against city slickers. This argument is how the Far Right has enlisted the working class once again to do its bidding.[56]

At the start of the new century these new populists seized control of political discourse, using the very media upon which they heap contempt. They took control of the White House, both houses of Congress, a sizable proportion of statehouses, and the judiciary. They made no secret of their intention to control debate, to stifle and demonize opposition, and to relentlessly pursue righteousness in the face of a cowardly, bureaucratic, and compromising political system.

It worked fine for a while, but then things began to unravel. More and more of the new populists were found to be manipulating the very wheels of government and commerce they railed against. Corporate scandals were followed by cases of personal fraud, which were followed by even bigger corporate scandals. Those common folk whom the new populists adored were hurt the most by the politics they themselves had supported. In the 2008 election, the populist mantra fizzled for the Republicans. Even Joe the Plumber failed to show up for his introduction on the stump.

For their part, the Democrats began to win back their claim to represent the little guy. Hillary Clinton found electoral magic by drinking shots and beers and delivering her stump speech from the bed of a pickup truck in Pennsylvania while Barack Obama repeatedly used the term "middle class" in his speeches. The latter may have been the more remarkable of the two, if less comical, for the very recognition of class differences and interests had for a long time been poison for any serious candidate. But this time the speeches were not denounced among charges of class warfare, as had happened in the past. Instead, the populist ideal was recast to its original form, with the moneyed interests as the villains. Voters ignored Obama's education and erudition, his exotic origins in Hawaii, and his refined tastes. Even his remark that those Pennsylvanians who voted for Clinton were embittered by recent economic and social policies, turning them to guns and religion, were forgiven. Once again, Obama's message of change was couched in the deep and permanent sentiments of American political culture, and it worked.

Populism continues to reverberate with Americans, perhaps constituting the most essential of American values. For now it has been redirected as the nation recovers from economic and diplomatic difficulties. The very elites the neocons so despise are now in charge. Obama's cabinet and staff may be one of the most highly educated and best-connected administrations in more than a generation. But should the new elite fail to repair the damage done by the recent populist revolt, the anti-intellectual, anti-urban, antimodern brand of populism will reemerge stronger than ever. If our crises deepen and if Americans become more disenchanted, populism will be the rallying point of a bold and angry visionary who will unite the Left and the Right against that other America, claiming louder than ever that "Washington is broken" and that the democratic process is too easily dominated by people who think they are better than average working-class Americans. If America turns to fascism, populism will be at its heart.

__5__

NATIONALISM

A FEW DAYS AFTER THE SEPTEMBER 11 attacks I happened to be driving through the upper Midwest, through what's called America's Heartland, the mythical home of genuine American values and morals. In those early days of real fear that more attacks might be imminent, the outburst of nationalist sentiment was obvious: displays of Old Glory more conspicuous than usual, fire station doors draped in black, flags at half-staff, and messages on nearly every signboard that could display one. Where a church sign might normally display a biblical verse, there was Pray for Our Country or Thy Will Be Done; where gas station signboards had said Free Car Wash with Fill Up, many then vented national sorrow and anger. One, near Hannibal, Missouri, kept it simple: Bomb Them.

Such spontaneous outpourings were not limited to the heartland, however. Congress assembled on the Capitol's steps to sing "God Bless America," and one might guess that at least a few members felt a bit coerced. Media analysts praised President Bush's distinctly awkward speech before Congress on September 20, 2001, as one of the great orations of the times. David Letterman and other entertainers, lacking the audience or the stomach for the usual light fare, gave somber discourses on the state of the world and their hopes for the country.

Later Congress, the media, and the citizenry conspicuously failed to apply any critical thought to the decision to invade Iraq. The ill-focused "bomb them" sentiment came to fruition in March 2003, as the display of shock and awe visited on Iraqis gave to many Americans a certain militarist pride and to others a fatalistic sense that there was no point in objecting.

Media outlets read the public sentiment and gave Americans what they wanted, a wave of sentimental patriotism and national pride. They had been advised to do so by paid consulting agencies, who specialize in reading listeners' and viewers' tastes. One widely used consultant advised its client radio stations to go on a war footing: "Get the following production pieces in the studio NOW. . . . Patriotic music that makes you cry, salute, get cold chills! Go for the emotion. . . . Air the National Anthem at a specified time each day as long as the USA is at war."[1] And when France declined to join the coalition of the willing, patriotic restaurateurs poured French wine into gutters and French fries became Freedom Fries on the House of Representatives' lunchroom menu.

Few objected when, via the Patriot Act and other legal, half-legal, and illegal measures, the government assumed extraordinary powers to monitor communications, to authorize secret and warrantless searches, to declare anyone an enemy combatant, and to imprison suspects without trial or even a hearing to determine if the authorities had the right person. Congress was unable to act effectively to curb this expansion of executive power—but not because the majority of members themselves agreed with these policies or because powerful lobbyists blocked their efforts. Congress couldn't act because too many members were afraid of being labeled soft on terrorism, weak on national defense, or simply un-American. In short, they feared the voters' reprisals. It was just too easy for political opponents to focus Americans' patriotic wrath on anyone daring to criticize the government.

This sort of nationalism worries people, and in a decade or two many will likely look back with puzzlement at how we could have lost our calm, the way we look back today at the Red Scare or the internment of Japanese Americans during World War II. But do our episodes of national hysteria represent a deeper element of the American character that could, under sustained national stress, entice us down the path to a more permanent hysteria and more extreme actions? Does the flyby of B-2 bombers and the display of a giant flag at halftime engender a truly different sense of pride than the Nazis' torchlight marches, the black-and-red banners, and the "Horst Wessel Song"? It may be impossible to say whether contemporary Americans are as nationalistic as the Germans of the 1920s and 1930s were because national sentiment has varied widely from time to time in both countries. Still, we can't help making wary comparisons between the two political cultures and asking whether there is any similarity between the nationalism these two peoples felt toward their respective countries.

The answer is not simple. The problem is that there are many different kinds of nationalism. When we speak of German nationalism under the National Socialists, do we mean feelings of attachment to German culture? Or to the German land? Or to its people? Or to the party or even to the führer himself? Similar questions can be asked of American nationalism and often are: are Americans bound to the land, the Constitution, the flag, a cultural tradition, or the policies of the current administration—or to none of these things?

Nationalism poses a paradox for Americans, as it does for the peoples of all democracies, for it tends to undermine the democratic principles of individual freedom and the give-and-take of partisan debate.[2] Because feelings for the nation are supposed to transcend partisan or personal interests, nationalist fervor is taken to be a nonpartisan position; thus any views diverging from the resulting consensus are easily labeled as disloyal. The paradox is most acutely seen in times of national threat or perceived threat, as illustrated in post-9/11 America. The ubiquitous Support Our Troops yard signs, the yellow ribbon stickers, the replacement of "Take Me Out to the Ballgame" with "God Bless America" at the seventh-inning stretch, the newfound tolerance of encroachments on personal freedoms in the name of security—all of these, by a ratcheting incrementalism, moved Americans toward the sort of xenophobic nationalism that was far from our consciousness a generation ago. Those who disagreed with the war, with the Patriot Act, with tax reductions, with privatization of Social Security, with torturing prisoners, with creationism or intelligent design, or with anything the national leadership proposed ran the risk of seeming not fully American. Or as Ann Coulter's book title had it, it was simply "treason."

But surely these are aberrations from the norm in American political life. American nationalism is different in kind and degree from that felt by the Germans in the early twentieth century, isn't it?

———

The beginnings of nationalism can be traced as far back as the thirteenth century, though a familiar early example is posed by the French Revolution, in which people "turned from loyalty and identification with *le roi* to loyalty and identification with *la patrie*."[3] People had become capable of recognizing and acknowledging their connection to an abstract concept—the nation—that was independent of the more concrete idea of a ruling clan or person. Today we so take for granted the state system, in which the world's area is divided by borders delineating political organizations to which people are bound, that it is hard to imagine that at one time such borders did not exist. In fact, it's hard for many to realize that even today there are places in the world—parts of the Middle East, Africa, and western Asia—where such boundaries are nonexistent, ambiguous, or irrelevant. Such arbitrariness and ambiguity of borders is behind much of the civil warfare we see in the developing world today. To what extent do tribesmen of the Khyber Pass think of themselves as Afghans, or the Mesopotamian Kurds as Iraqis?

Nonetheless, the state system has encompassed all of these people, at least in the abstract. They have been included within one nation or another on the map whether or not they like it, feel bound to fellow countrymen, or even know it. Such varied circumstances suggest that nationalism, the union of people's identity with the abstraction we call the nation, must vary in many ways. Nations composed mainly of a homogeneous cultural group are likely to feel strong bonds of ethnic nationalism, or that deep sense of shared moral, spiritual, aesthetic, and linguistic understandings about the world.[4] The Japanese, various Scandinavian peoples, and the Serbs provide current examples while emerging Islamic states like Iran seek to forge new *ethnic* ties.

For nations composed mostly of immigrants—Canada and the United States, for example—national identity might be entirely separate from ethnic or other personal identification. These nations might be held together by *civic* bonds, the collective awareness of the political and legal contracts of which the nation is formed (though in the Canadian case, ethnic bonds among French-speaking citizens have at times strained the national union). Other national bonds might be forged by the sense of *economic* interdependency among peoples of diverse cultural or religious identities. The European Community might be viewed as an emerging nation in this way, as the removal of trade and customs barriers and the use of a common currency make French, Italian, and German people, for instance, begin to feel more like Europeans. *Religious* bonds, too, can enhance a sense of nationalism. On the one hand, few nations are more ethnically diverse than Israel, for example, which is composed of immigrants from all over the globe and of widely disparate cultures and yet their deeper religious roots serve to attach them to one another and to the Jewish state. On the other hand, differences between Shiite and Sunni Muslims have so far proven more important than bonds to the Iraqi state.

In short, there are many kinds of nationalism, and each may be present in varying strength. What we do know is that nationalism was a bedrock of German culture, if for no other reason than the tremendous difficulty the Germans had in forging a nation in the first place.[5] Until after the Napoleonic wars the Germans occupied about three hundred kingdoms, duchies, principalities, and free towns. These were reduced to thirty-nine by the Congress of Vienna in 1814–15, but this was still a far cry from nationhood. It was not until 1871 that King Wilhelm of Prussia and his chancellor, Otto von Bismarck, created a unified Germany. Even this arrangement failed to include Austria and the German parts of Bohemia, omissions that would later become starkly significant.

GERMANNESS AND ETHNIC NATIONALISM

For the Germans, the foundation of nationalism was their cultural identity, the idea of Germanness itself, which transcended political or class boundaries. Their yearning for a national identity had been further aroused by Napoleon, whose attempt to create a Pan-European empire came just as the German romantics viewed pan-anything with contempt. His defeat at Waterloo, aided significantly by the Prussian army, struck a powerful chord with the Germans and set in motion a vigorous effort by scholars, artists, and the general public to find the roots of German culture and identity. The question was, what *is* German? Emerging in the eighteenth and nineteenth centuries several philosophers led the search for an answer. One of the most influential was Johann Herder, who used the term *das Volk* in the late eighteenth century to identify an essential Germanness. He is considered the father of what is now called ethnic nationalism.

In Herder's time, the state was a contrivance of princes and monarchs who, through warfare, marriage, and mutual agreement, divided up the land according to their own interests and often without much regard for the ethnicity or culture of those who lived on it. In many cases, nations and empires, through territorial expansion, came to include people of diverse ethnicities. An English family (of German descent) ruled the Scots and Irish, the Russian czars ruled dozens of ethnic groups, and the French at times had some ethnic Germans or Dutch within their realm, not to mention the Bretons, who spoke a language derived from Celtic roots.

Herder took language to be the central cultural bond. He posited that people who shared a common language tended to think in the same ways and thus would naturally form the most vigorous and most governable nation. The idea was extended beyond language per se to include folklore, literature, music, and art as the means of genuine nation building and national identification. In short, nations ought to be formed by people who shared the same culture; political boundaries should follow ethnic ones.

But in that romantic age, concepts like ethnicity and culture were inadequate to express the deep, even mystical essence of a people, and Herder sought a more profound concept. The notion of volk fit the bill for it was an idea beyond mere culture, embodying the ethnic, geographic, racial, religious, and other inexpressible ties that bound a people of common destiny. Johann Gottlieb Fichte called the volk a "powerful German spirit as well as a permanent German national character which had to be kept clean" of foreign influence.[6]

The romantic movement, as we have seen, gave impetus to the idea that art, as well as other forms of thought and expression, ought to reflect the peculiar character of the culture that produces it rather than attempt to appeal to universal tastes. For the Germans, this quality was naturally most pronounced in their music, the most German of the arts. By 1800 German music had eclipsed the Italian and French styles, and German themes and locations had begun to permeate opera and other programmatic music. Richard Wagner was perhaps the most forceful proponent of a distinctly German music. His aim was to invent a completely new and distinctly German musical form in his music dramas.

Wagner wrote extensively about what made music German and how he intended to advance the form in that direction. His most notorious writing along these lines was an essay in which he described Germanness in the negative, by describing what it was not—Jewish. In "Jewishness in Music," Wagner argued that Jews were incapable of deep musical expression because only a volk deeply grounded in a geographic home could express true passion. He held up Felix Mendelssohn as the bad example: he was highly skilled but lacking in "soul-depth."[7]

But Germanness in music went beyond the musings of Wagner and other thinkers. More than other cultural groups, ordinary Germans also made music themselves as a participatory community activity. From 1800 on, amateur music making in the form of community orchestras, chamber ensembles, and especially choruses became ubiquitous throughout Germany in both the cities and rural areas. Community music groups were thought to be both cohesion-building activities and a cure for social dissent, which explains why the government encouraged their growth, especially when the country was under duress. Thus by 1929, as the Weimar Republic headed for crisis, there were more than thirteen thousand choirs alone, with 1.3 million members; by 1931, as the republic approached its breaking point, the movement had grown to nineteen thousand groups with more than 2 million members.[8]

Moreover, these groups sang and played music that focused increasingly on Germanness itself. The German *lied* genre grew rapidly in popularity, and a large number of these songs focused on distinctly German themes. The Rhine was a favorite subject and was featured in more than four hundred lieder published by the middle of the nineteenth century. The Rhine image had become embedded, as Cecilia Hopkins Porter observed, "deeply within the German Romantics' heart and soul."[9] It's no wonder, then, that Wagner's effort to forge a uniquely German musical form through the *Ring* cycle began and ended at the Rhine.

The Rhine as a natural geographical representation of Germanness is critical. The Germans' ethnic nationalism mingled with Romantic myths about the natural rootedness of people to form what came to be called the *blut und boden* (blood and soil) ideal. Germans were, according to this view, a people rooted to the German soil just as Arabs naturally belonged to the desert and the English were attached to the British Isles. The blut und boden ideal made it clear that culture and territory were linked: by virtue of their ecological circumstances, Germanic and Norse peoples were hardy and ambitious and possessed numerous other qualities. Peoples of the tropics, the plains, the jungle, and other environments were naturally endowed with different cultural traits, most of them less esteemed. It was the Germans' attachment to the fatherland's soil that made them German; therefore, immigrants, Gypsies, and Jews could never share that identity. Jews were especially disqualified for Germanness because they were considered an inherently rootless people, having wandered around the desert for centuries and then scattered over Europe.

Literature also became a part of the search for Germanness. Wilhelm and Jakob Grimm, most notably, developed an entire genre of distinctly German literature derived from careful research of local folk tales. Their meticulous scholarship took them from village to village all over the German world, collecting legends and wives' tales from anyone who could remember them. They then shaped them with little modification into a body of work that anyone who grew up in the Western world will recognize. "Hansel and Gretel," "Cinderella," "Rapunzel," "Rumplestiltskin," and "The

Golden Goose" are the more notable tales familiar not only to children but also to film audiences, music lovers, and operagoers. One of the Grimms' lesser-known yarns, "The Story of a Youth Who Went Forth to Learn What Fear Was," found its way into Wagner's *Ring* cycle in the character of Siegfried.

Though the Grimm folk tales are among the most beloved and enduring children's stories, they also functioned to express and promote German ethnic nationalism through a variety of recurring themes. The stories' locales are consistently romantic, rural, and German: the farm, the village, the small town, the forest. The characters are familiar stereotypes, divided clearly by class and by ethnicity, that reflect German social structure of the time. Most of all, the stories promote fear of outsiders through the characterization of city folk, Jews, and interlopers into the family. The evil stepmother often fulfills this role, representing both the intruder in the German family and the foreigner in the German state. As for Jews, wherever they appeared in a story they were assumed to be the cause of whatever trouble occurred.[10]

The stories are also extraordinarily violent and grisly, involving all sorts of imaginative punishments visited on the evildoers in the final scene. Burning alive, baking in ovens, cutting off of hands, and gouging out eyes are all standard fare. In one story, a Jew is forced to dance in a briar patch until his clothes are stripped from his body. Louis Snyder suggests that these punishments paved the way in some small measure for the punishments visited on the Jews in the twentieth century. After all, these elements of hysterical fear and revenge had been largely toned down in editions published in the early twentieth century but were reinstated after the Nazis took power.[11]

The Search for Germanness Intensifies
Through philosophy, music, and literature—those pillars of German culture—the volkish ideal was thus deeply embedded in the German mind. And while these themes had permeated German thought for centuries, to most Germans they were not a conscious preoccupation. As most cultural ideas, they were below the surface, taken for granted, subtle, and the sort of understood reality that nobody thought much about; but as unification approached in the nineteenth century, volkism became a more explicit and intense pursuit. Increasing numbers of academics, independent scholars, mystics, and cranks found audiences and readers in a society seeking the definitive answer to the question of what was German.

This search for the roots of the natural German life took some strange turns. All sorts of cults and beliefs arose to answer the question of what was true Germanness by tracing the culture to its aboriginal roots. Wagner's reinterpretation of the Nordic myths was only the beginning: the late nineteenth and early twentieth century saw solar cults, Wotan cults, and cults that revered ancient symbols, including the swastika. Many came to view the first historical account of the Germans, Tacitus's *Germania*, as an authoritative record of how the Germanic Goths saved civilization as decrepit Rome crumbled. Ancient religions came into vogue as scholars and amateurs alike recounted the origins of the German people in the World Ash tree. This powerful symbol's roots represented nicely the rootedness of the German volk while its crown "aspired toward the cosmos and the spirit."[12] It is no coincidence that Wagner's operas refer to the ash tree often: Tannhäuser's walking stick is made from one; in the final scene it sprouts a green leaf signifying his redemption. Siegmund's sword is embedded in one; he draws it from the trunk in a dramatic Arthurian allusion. Wotan's lordly spear is fashioned from the World Ash itself.

Guido von List was one of many private scholars of the day who rejected the Enlightenment's academic collaboration in favor of romantic personal revelation. He claimed to have deciphered a lost Teutonic language by reinterpreting ancient runes, thus rediscovering the origins of the true German. Other amateur scholars advocated a rejection of Christianity in favor of Teutonic pantheism or advanced the wildest racial theories to prove the Germans' preeminence. All based their claims on deep insights by various methods, largely nonrational; what they had in common was that they rejected traditional scholarship in favor of an "inner correspondence with Germanic antiquity."[13] These methods were widely accepted in the romantic spirit of the times, according to George Mosse: "We say today that such beliefs verged on the magical, the irrational, the insane. What is important, however, is that at that time these viewpoints were acclaimed precisely *because* they were magical."[14]

The universities themselves became incubators for the development of German nationalism. In addition to the romantic scholars' work, university students took up the nationalist banner and established a variety of clubs and societies. In the early nineteenth century, Friedrich Ludwig Jahn had promoted physical culture through the establishment of the first gymnasiums. This movement was intended to promote the betterment of the German volk through the rigors of exercise, and it caught on rapidly.

Student associations called *Burschenschaften* also came into being about this time and were explicitly nationalist groups. The burschenschaften celebrated the three hundredth anniversary of Martin Luther's revolt during the Wartburg Festival of 1817 by, among other practices, burning books antithetical to his teachings.[15]

In this distinctly romantic sort of nationalism, the people were thought bound by spiritual ties that could not be explained or understood by reason or self-interest. There was also a mystical element to nationhood: because the state was "too miraculous" to be the work of humans, it had to be the work of forces beyond the control or ken of humans.[16] Nationhood gave the German people a sense of destiny that could only be captured in the collective will and the volkish sense of belonging to a higher mission—that is, advancing the German race and culture.

In these and other ways, the idea of Germanness was pursued vigorously throughout the nineteenth century. Through intellectuals like Herder and others, through the music of the great German composers and the singing of lieder by citizens throughout the German world, through the cultivation of blut und boden ideology, through the rise of youth groups and the university fraternity, and not least through the development of scientific racial theory, Germans worked toward an overall notion that there was such a thing as Germanness. This abstraction could in itself bind all German people into a single unified and cohesive reich.

Other Forms of Nationalism
While the bedrock foundation of German nationalism was this profound sense of shared ethnicity, the Germans embraced other kinds of nationalism as well. Some were derived from ethnic nationalism while others sprang from different roots altogether. As it happens, Germans were receptive to all of them at the time of the emergence of National Socialism.

One form of nationalism easily overlooked is economic nationalism. This sense of mutual and collective identification with the nation is rooted in feelings of economic interdependence, the sense that one's own economic well-being depends on that of one's fellow citizens and the nation as a whole. Economic interdependence was the principal tool that Bismarck used to forge the German nation in the first place. Until the early nineteenth century, the thirty-nine German states had been divided by customs boundaries that hindered transport from one to another with a complex system of tariffs and tolls. These restrictions had kept German industry from developing fully, and British products flooded German markets to a troubling extent. Throughout the century Prussian leaders had gathered various states into a free-trade coalition, called the *Zollverein*, within which goods could be easily transported. In addition to a proportional sharing system for revenues, it also created standard toll rates, weights and measures, and coinage.[17] Bismarck accelerated the completion of the Zollverein when he became chancellor, partly by encouraging railroad development across the states' many boundaries. These powerful symbols served as concrete manifestations of the shared economic fate of the people within the Zollverein.

Religious nationalism was strong in Germany as well. As custodians of the Holy Roman Empire as well as the heirs of Martin Luther, Germans felt themselves uniquely placed in the history of Christianity. They also had become accustomed to the close linkage between church and state, for both the Roman and the Protestant churches had been at one time or another coterminous with the state apparatus.[18] Moreover, Johannes Gutenberg had produced the first printed Bibles.

The Germans had a long history of militarism, too. This sort of nationalism, derived from the view that military power is what ultimately defines and maintains the nation, was deeply felt among the Germans and especially by the Prussians, who had nourished a strong military ideal even before the Napoleonic wars. The Prussian military had provided the political and social foundation for the Junker aristocracy, and its traditions had become synonymous with German authoritarianism. The military had also set the stage for Germany's unification with the Franco-Prussian War. The Hessians, the Saxons, and the armies of the other German kingdoms were no slouches either.

But the Germans felt something else about their nation. On the surface it appeared as the ordinary belief that they were simply better than other peoples. This chauvinism was evidenced in their art, their literature, their philosophy, their science, and most of all their music, unparalleled in depth and beauty. But there was also an aspect that differed from the usual ethnocentrism most peoples felt. The Germans had an acute sense that Germany was truly unique among nations, because it had been formed in a manner different from others' founding and on a different basis. Because the nation was founded on a mystical cultural bond, its people shared a deeper sense of identity and destiny. And because it had been formed so late, it had mostly escaped the age of popular revolts that had pitted the people against the state, as had happened in England and France. Thus while other nations had had to choose between a strong state and political freedoms, Germany could be both authoritarian *and* progressive. They even had a name for this uniqueness—*Sonderweg*, or "special path." Because of their unique path to nationhood, the Germans believed themselves favored by history and destined to protect the world (that is, Europe) from the defilement of other cultures. Fichte put the challenge clearly enough: "Should the German not assume world government through philosophy, the Turks, the Negroes, the North American tribes, will finally take it over and put an end to the present civilization."[19]

The Germans embraced every kind of nationalism, and they all converged in sharp focus in 1914. German politics had stabilized, overseen by an authoritarian but benevolent government, and political rights had steadily been extended. The new nation had excelled in science and technology with the help of the kaisers, and its industry had grown rapidly once the Zollverein had removed the barriers to trade. Germany had acquired an empire, if a small one, that included several territories in Africa, scattered islands in the Pacific and Atlantic, and Tsingtao, a port in China (a vestige of the brief German presence is a brand of Chinese beer of the same name). The German army was unsurpassed, and its navy had leaped ahead of Britain in technology. Every German city of any size could boast a good orchestra and opera house; moreover, a large proportion of the new nation's citizens actively participated in making German music. They had every reason to want to call themselves Germans rather than Swabians, Westphalians, or Saxons.

Nationalism to National Socialism
It's no wonder that their defeat in World War I was such a crushing blow to German sensibilities. How could such a thing have happened? How could a nation of such vigor, discipline, intellect, vision, and military prowess be defeated in war? Many Germans posed this question as the Weimar Republic struggled for legitimacy, but there were not many acceptable answers. The nationalist political parties that arose and prospered tended to focus on the few that were acceptable: that Germany had been betrayed, that the international community had ganged up on it, that the German volk had lost its way by liberalizing social policy during the economic good times, that the Jewish conspiracy was at the bottom of it all.

Enter the National Socialists. They were, as their name announced, a nationalist party in every sense of the word. They were able to exploit every variety of nationalist sentiment the German people felt. Some varieties were deeply grounded in Nazi ideology, since Hitler had written *Mein Kampf,* while others they simply incorporated into their campaigns as political necessity arose.

First, the Nazis were ethnic nationalists who claimed legitimacy by promoting the maintenance and purification of German culture. Hitler had taken this duty as his personal mission since he first saw Wagner's *Rienzi* as a youth; indeed, the German people's unification and advancement became the bread and butter of National Socialist ideology. This focus on the culture was, of course, grounded in a deeply romantic sense of the mystical bonds that existed between the individual German and the volk.

As we shall see in chapter 6, the volkish ideal motivated the Nazis' racism as well. Obsession with maintaining the purity of the volk underlay the long campaign to marginalize and then eliminate Jews and other "non-German" influences. The Nazis made their concern concrete by committing substantial resources to studying and illuminating the volk's cultural and racial heritage. They commissioned an organization called the Society for Research into the Spiritual Roots of Germany's Ancestral Heritage, or *Ahnenerbe,* to study ancient German history and mythology. This group included teams of archaeologists who scoured the world in search of evidence linking the German race to the Aryans, to ancient Christians, and to the original Europeans. They collected skulls from ancient gravesites and, later, from death camp victims and Russian POWs to prove the distinctions between Germans, Jews and Slavs. They even went in search of the holy grail, convinced by their own charlatans that Christ was a sort of proto-German and the grail he drank from was a pre Christian Teutonic artifact. Steven Spielberg caricatured the Ahnenerbe in *Raiders of the Lost Ark,* with Indiana Jones racing against it to find the ark of the covenant.

The Nazis' ethnic nationalism also motivated them to control every aspect of German culture, from the academy to the print and broadcast media and from the film studios to the literary and artistic guilds. They established the Reich Chamber of Culture and connected it to the Ministry of Propaganda so that all cultural production would serve to clarify and purify the volk. Its seven sub-chambers—in literature, music, cinema, radio, theater, fine arts, and press—became gatekeepers to funding, production, and public airing of all cultural work, as the chamber took control of key finance and production companies. The government bought outright Germany's largest film studio, Universum Film AG (UFA), in 1937 in order to produce not only serious propaganda films but also light entertainment of an appropriate nature.[20] These included such titles as *Jew Süss,* which was immensely popular; *The Wandering Jew,* which wasn't; and later a host of home front films designed to soften the impact of the war.[21]

The Nazis' ethnic nationalism included the blut und boden ideal as well. They even went so far as to develop a National Socialist style of landscape design, and this project was no minor sidelight of the administration. In his capacity as "Reich Commissioner for the Strengthening of Germandom," Heinrich Himmler created a planning board whose responsibility was to ensure that the German people lived among landscapes that were befitting of their culture—that is, naturalistic, rustic, romantic. It would require an especially large effort in the conquered lands like Poland, where the inferior Easterners had not yet "formed" the land. The reich envisioned legions of landscape architects reshaping the environment there to accommodate the German settlers' need for "close union with the soil."[22]

The Nazis did not confine their appeal to ethnic nationalism. They capitalized on the pervasive German militarism through the infamous marches, rallies, martial music, and festivals. Militarism had been an essential part of the Nazi brand of nationalism from the start, since much of their membership had originally been composed of angry and unemployed veterans of World War I. Some became members of the Sturmabteilung (SA), the party's own paramilitary organization, which was familiarly known as the Brownshirts. Since the party's early days, the SA marched in uniform under the swastika and the torch during party demonstrations, patrolled and guarded party meetings, beat up opponents and Jews, and performed other duties as needed.

But as we know, for the Nazis, militarism was not only symbolic. Once in power, they wasted little time in abrogating the Versailles Treaty by rebuilding the German military, at first stealthily and then in open defiance. As Siegfried had reforged Wotan's mighty sword, Hitler reforged the German military. New aircraft designs purported to be airliners later became bombers and transports. German shipyards designed and built a class of giant battleships and cruisers, which, as in World War I, failed to influence the coming war's outcome. Thousands of tanks, artillery, and U-boats were built and displayed proudly at every opportunity. The Nazis offered the promise—fulfilled at first—of glorious military victory.

They could also be religious nationalists when it was convenient. Of course, they indulged the romantic pantheism and tribal faiths through symbol and myth. Still, God—the German, Christian God—was invoked frequently as the one who had given the German people their führer, who had ordained the Germans as the master race, who had made them the Chosen People, who had planted them on German soil, and so on. This appeal fit nicely with the sonderweg myth, as it emphasized Germany's God-ordained historical destiny—that is, to save European culture against the depredations of the French, the Slavs, the Russians, and the Jews. The sense of divine origin made belief in a special destiny all the more plausible. Later it helped the Germans rationalize the rush to war for Germany was to control Europe not for selfish purposes but to carry out God's own plan.

By appealing to every sense of nationalism, the Nazis were able to capture support from a variety of demographic and political strata. Of course, not every citizen or group of citizens responded to every sort of nationalism. Some were old-line militarists who were angry about the army's humiliation in World War I, others were racists who blamed Jews for the country's economic ills, and still others were intellectuals who yearned for a clearly defined German cultural ideal. Some just couldn't resist a good parade. The Nazis could weave all of these themes into their propaganda as leitmotifs, sometimes emphasizing one above the other and sometimes combining several to synthesize a deeply emotional attachment to the reich. Like successful political parties everywhere, they were skillful opportunists who could cover their inconsistencies with propagandistic fig leaves and misdirection. It's little wonder that the German public was able to maintain its attachment to the Third Reich, even to the very end.

AMERICAN NATIONALISM

There is little doubt that nationalism was a central foundation of German culture. The German people had recognized their common national bond before they forged a political union, and the best German minds had pondered for a century and longer what made that bond. They shared, and understood that they shared, deep volkish sentiments and religious, economic, and militarist bonds as well. Americans seem to share strong nationalist sentiments too, but the histories of the two peoples suggest that American nationalism is of a different sort.

No American Volk

A principal difference is that Americans do not share a common volkish bond rooted in land or art or a cultural heritage. In the first place, the United States was born of very different circumstances than was Germany. For nearly two hundred years, American colonists lived and thrived as subjects of the British crown, for much of that time with little complaint. Even as late as 1776 most Americans viewed themselves as Englishmen; their revolutionary fervor was directed against the king and his policies rather than against England itself. The New World was a land of plenty, a limitless wilderness to be exploited and ultimately civilized, and the colonial system seemed well suited to the task. The colonies served as a vast source of raw materials for the mother country, and the Americans could trade them in return for what they could not produce for themselves. The problem was that as the colonists gradually became increasingly self-sufficient, the crown imposed increasingly arbitrary and restrictive tariffs on goods flowing in both directions. Moreover, they suffered the simple failures of British leadership: "There was arrogance, and arrogance bred mistakes, and obstinacy meant that they were persisted in to the point of idiocy." A contemporary minister of parliament "found the government 'so perversely, so inflexibly persisting in error on every occasion . . . that they never deviate into sense nor stumble into propriety by downright accident.'"[23] Annoyance with the crown's economic policies nourished ideological differences in turn. The colonials chafed at the denial of direct representation in Parliament, of meaningful self-government, and of the normal rights and privileges that Englishmen enjoyed. Thus it was the growing annoyance with economic controls that fed the colonials' revolutionary spirit of the colonials, and not a desire to form a nation around a cultural identity, as in the German case.

In fact, some historians have marveled that the Americans formed a nation at all. In 1760 Benjamin Franklin noted the lack of any commonality at all among the colonies and predicted that "a union amongst them for such a purpose is not merely improbable, it is impossible."[24] America had none of the usual facilities for the formation of nationhood: no common history, no ancestral land, no official religion, no shared destiny, not even shared economic interests.[25] Most of all, it did not endure a thousand years of struggle; rather, the United States was born seemingly all at once. According to Daniel Boorstin,

> Elsewhere the making of a political nation had commonly been the work of a strong province—a Prussia, a Savoy, or an Ile-de-France—imposing its will on others; or of an invader—a William

the Conqueror or a Napoleon—imposing his administration on a disorganized people. But the United States somehow became a nation spontaneously, strengthened by the very forces of diffusion.[26]

There was little sense of Americanness among the colonists. Indeed, what was distinctly American was foreign, wild, and primitive, the sort of thing the colonists had come to tame or eliminate. And when the nation was formed, the word "nation" was purposely excised from the Declaration of Independence at the insistence of the southern states; it is also absent from the Constitution.[27] There were few everyday symbols of American unity, cultural or otherwise. The national flag and national anthem were not adopted until much later. There was no national paper currency, either; for half a century banks issued their own notes, which could be exchanged for those of other banks in the way foreign currencies are exchanged today. The states were politically disparate in many ways as well. Until a constitutional amendment standardized the electoral process in 1913, the various states employed different methods to elect U.S. senators, some by popular vote and others by vote of their state legislatures.

Regarding attachment to the land, Americans were as far from the blut und boden mentality as could be imagined. The Americans' rootless character was obvious and widespread. Their westward migration began when New England farms could no longer support the growing families that worked them, and they quickly populated the western territories of Pennsylvania and Ohio. The Cumberland Gap facilitated the movement of southerners, too. Jefferson's purchase of the Louisiana Territory opened the transportation capabilities of the Mississippi and Missouri rivers, providing further incentive to go west.

The beginnings of industrialization needed the raw materials available in the hinterlands; thus, coal, iron, lead, and any number of other commodities were sought beyond the frontier. Industrialization also brought European immigrants, many of whom soon discovered that life could be better on a piece of land in the West than in a mill in New England or New York. The establishment of canals and then the railroad and telegraph hastened this migration, especially as the western railroads actively encouraged migrants to settle the prairie and create demand for shipping. Many European immigrants barely slowed down on arrival in New York or Philadelphia, boarding immigrant trains for Minnesota or Nebraska or Kansas immediately.

The 1848 victory over Mexico brought the Pacific coast into the American sphere, and the great migration, that mythic exodus that still dominates America's historical heritage, began in earnest. People went west for land, for gold, or simply for a new start. The Mormons were pushed westward for more than a generation, finally settling around the Great Salt Lake. And the end of slavery saw the movement of African Americans north and west, first in a trickle and then, after 1900, in a torrent.

The westward expansion is one of the central events of American history and constitutes the source of many of the country's early crises, triumphs, failures, and tragedies. The plow on the prairie, the railroads, the gold rush, and the prairie schooner are emblematic of the Americans' restless and curious character. They also represent the American penchant for rapacious exploitation, for conquest and elimination of other peoples, and for opportunistic profit from cheap foreign labor. The move west continues to this day, as evidenced by the gradual westward creep of the country's population center, which is now located west of the Mississippi in rural Missouri. Americans are anything but rooted, and the virtue of moving on has remained a bedrock of American belief. If they did not move westward, then they went northward in the great black migration, or from the farm to the city as part of the urbanization of American life, or perhaps even from the city to the suburb in the second half of the twentieth century. All are evidence of the American readiness to pull up and move when opportunity beckons or misfortune threatens.

If the land doesn't provide the national identity of Americans, neither does a common ancestry. More than any other country, the United States has been from the beginning a nation of immigrants. From the start, the English were not the only colonists in North America. Parts of the Northeast, the Great Lakes, and the Mississippi Valley were explored by the French; California, the Southwest, and Florida were occupied by the Spanish; and yet the continent was already long inhabited by natives when these Europeans arrived. Africans were an early presence, which increased through forced immigration and population growth to a substantial proportion of the southern populace by the mid-nineteenth century. The Mexican War, as noted above, also brought a significant Hispanic presence. Finally, the deluge of European immigrants to eastern ports and Asian immigrants to the West reduced the original English population to just 15 percent of those who called themselves Americans.[28]

American Civic Nationalism

The absence of a common ethnic heritage retarded the formation of national sentiment among Americans for some time. The early republic could not claim much loyalty of its citizens, consisting as it did of a loose confederation of independent states. In any case, the local basis of the agrarian economy made people feel more bound to their town or county than to a national union. In fact, it was not until 1834 that the first distinctly American history was written by George Bancroft, it being assumed until then that "a history of the United States would consist of a history in turn of each of the states."[29]

The first truly national bonds were economic and militarist ones. The War of 1812, ending in what seemed a miraculous victory over the vaunted English military, stunned Americans into the view that the United States had a rightful claim to the top tier of the world's nations.[30] But more profound in its effects was the transition of the American economy from local, barter-based, subsistence commerce to one in which farmers and other producers could trade at long distances, aided by new roads and canals as well as by the national government's increased power. Beginning with Andrew Jackson's administration, the government imposed and manipulated tariffs on foreign trade, using them to raise revenues and at the same time to stimulate or protect domestic industries. Later it sanctioned timber and mining claims as well as the homesteading of new farmland. It dispossessed Indians of their land and subsidized the development of railroads to bring goods to market. It stimulated regional economies and raised the labor force's capabilities through the establishment of land grant colleges in each state.[31]

By the 1830s citizens had begun to feel more like Americans and less like New Yorkers or Virginians, but something was missing. While there were pragmatic reasons for identifying with the nation as a whole, Americans lacked an ideology that could provide the emotional and symbolic bonds they were seeking. What would make them love their nation? One such ideology was a quasi-religious faith in democracy and its institutions.

Hector St. John de Crèvecoeur, an early immigrant from France and among the first to comment on American culture, wrote in his *Letters from an American Farmer* that the lack of a cultural tradition was itself the essence of the American character. The task of every American was to throw off one's previous European identity and develop a new and unique one: "The American is a new man, who acts upon new principles. . . . Here individuals of all nations are melted into a new race of men."[32] This new man, in his view, was not formed out of cultural tradition but out of the circumstances of his surroundings and his livelihood, not out of birth or background but out of necessity. The sentiments Crèvecoeur and others expressed gave origin to the ideology of civic nationalism, or the sense of connection to the nation via its political and legal institutions. This bond was nicely contrasted with the blut and boden ideal by Charles McKay as early as 1837: "Give the American his institutions, and he cares but little where you place him."[33]

Civic nationalism, like other forms, is expressed and renewed by traditions and symbols. In America's early years, these symbols tended to focus on the myths and biographies of great exemplars of American virtue. It's often difficult to distinguish between the myths and the biographies, as the founding fathers, explorers, and revolutionary heroes were lionized sometimes beyond recognition.[34] Fabulously embellished stories of Christopher Columbus, Patrick Henry, Capt. John Smith, and most of all, George Washington became the national mythology; indeed, most could still be recited by elementary schoolkids late into the twentieth century. The cherry tree, the discovery of America, and the phrase "Give me liberty or give me death" all made up the historical caricature of America that provided some sense of shared heritage, and in some ways they still do.

Our most cherished symbols of genuine civic identity—the Declaration of Independence, the Constitution, and the Bill of Rights—are all kept permanently available for public viewing on what can only be called an altar at the National Archives. Few Americans who see them fail to be at least a little awed by their gravity, and for even the most alienated they undoubtedly generate some sense of connection to what the United States is supposed to be. Arthur M. Schlesinger is probably right in his claim that they engender feelings of "fidelity to the unifying principles that hold us together" and promote a "common adherence to ideals of democracy and human rights," even among those who acknowledge the nation's failure to realize these ideals completely.[35]

But these documents did not emerge as important unifying symbols all at once; rather, various interests appropriated them over the course of a century to advance any number of causes. The declaration, for example, was the focus of the first ritual of American identity. The fourth of July, the date on which most of the original states' representatives at the Continental Congress approved the document, became a national fete in which groups of all sorts paraded, orated, posted slogans, and otherwise competed with one another for control over what the declaration, and the nation itself, represented. It was commandeered by Federalists and Democrats, by slaveholders and abolitionists, by imperialists and isolationists, later by labor and capitalists, and by peaceniks and militarists. It was not until after the War of 1812 that Federalists and Democrats even celebrated the date together; prior to that, each party had typically held separate commemorations.[36] And the myth of the Liberty Bell—that it was rung on July 4, 1776, to proclaim the new nation's birth—is a total fabrication, partly advanced by the abolition movement, which also gave it its name.[37]

Other symbols of civic unity emerged slowly. American flags could be seen in baffling diversity for more than a century after the Constitution was ratified. Even after the overall idea of stars and stripes had become something of a standard, their number varied chaotically. The one Francis Scott Key saw when he was inspired to write what later became the National Anthem was spangled with fifteen stars and fifteen stripes. In 1818 the Congress flew one with eighteen stripes while the New York Navy Yard had nine. And the pattern of stars varied, too—some flags had them in rows while others arranged them in the shape of a star, an anchor, or a diamond. President William Howard Taft finally standardized the design by executive order in 1912.[38]

As for the anthem, its story is similarly fraught with competing candidates, partisan bickering, and political accident, and it does not end with the official designation of "The Star-Spangled Banner" by Congress in 1931. Today there are still occasional complaints about the militarism and torturous grammar of the lyric, not to mention its tendency to be butchered at the ballpark. Many Americans would prefer "America the Beautiful," and with good reason.

Notwithstanding the difficulties with which Americans sought to canonize events, people, and objects as foundations of their national heritage, these symbols did emerge. Today Americans who don't share a religious or ethnic commonality readily acknowledge their common links to these myths and symbols, however muddy their origins. Even as Americans disagree about the meaning of the symbols—whether the flag represents liberty and justice or conquest and exploitation, for example—they still agree on their ability to represent the individual's connection to the nation and to other Americans. These symbols represent the civic basis of American nationalism, the connection of citizens to a set of abstract principles of self-governance and civil rights. Today it remains true that despite vigorous disagreement on the extent to which the United States fulfills its promise, few Americans dispute the values embodied in the promise itself. The integrity of the vote, the rights of the individual, the wisdom of the democratic process, and most of all, the dependence of the state upon the authority granted by its citizens remain nearly universally held axioms of American life.

The Weakness of Civic Nationalism

Civic nationalism is a pleasant myth, and not an entirely false one. The symbols and legends of American life, made familiar and shared through public education and national celebrations, really do constitute a sort of currency of national identity. Generations of immigrants have followed Crèvecoeur's advice to shed the trappings of the old country, making themselves—or failing that, their children or grandchildren—the new men of the American amalgam.

But the new man was not melted into a new race of men. He was incorporated into an old one, a preexisting culture, and even that incorporation was not a sure thing. This unacknowledged American culture was so ubiquitous and predominant as to be invisible, as water is to the fish. It did not even seem like a culture or ethnicity in the old European sense; rather, it seemed more like a foundation on which a new culture might be erected. But it could not be denied that the biographies, the mythical figures, the legends, and all the rest embraced three critical elements of what the American was assumed to be: white, Protestant, and English speaking.

Civic nationalism was taken for granted as the predominant American ideal throughout the nineteenth century, but as the tide of immigration threatened to swamp the dominant English culture toward the century's end, Crèvecoeur's ideal became less attractive. This concern became a basis for the foreign and domestic policies of Theodore Roosevelt's administration. Facing repeated waves of European and Asian immigrants, Roosevelt worried that the civic basis of American life would be threatened by a babel of foreign enclaves and traditions. He favored the new man ideal, by which the huddled masses would be Americanized not so much by adding layers of American culture but by discarding layers of European culture. Roosevelt also genuinely believed that discarding European culture was the immigrants' best hope of enjoying the fruits of their new country: "democracy and prosperity lay within the grasp of any man who shook off—or was liberated from—superstition, irrationality, and blind obedience to monarchs, clerics, and demagogues, and became a free and self-governing individual."[39]

But there were limits to what could be melted and reformed. European culture and ethnicity could usually be alloyed with the English stock; the colonists, and later the immigrants, could shed their old culture for the shared American civic values. But race seemed a different matter altogether. Those Asians, African, and Natives could not be combined with whites because racial differences could not be cast off. While one could learn a new language or new set of values, one could not change one's color. This problem was manifest, of course, right at the beginning: conflicts with Indians and the importation of African slaves were intrinsic to the American nation's origins.

The distinction between the Indian and the European, for example, is ratified in the Declaration of Independence itself. Once one gets past the lofty sentiments of the document's opening paragraphs (the part learned in elementary school), the bill of particulars that follows lays out a litany of the Americans' grievances against the king. Among these is the complaint that "he has excited domestic insurrections amongst us, and has endeavoured to bring on the inhabitants of our frontiers, the merciless Indian Savages, whose known rule of warfare, is an undistinguished destruction of all ages, sexes and conditions." It is unclear by this wording whether the savage character of the Indians is viewed as a cultural or racial trait, though it seems plain that the authors did not anticipate an easy accommodation with them. Indian conflicts, displacements, and massacres constituted part of the fabric of American history right through to the end of the nineteenth century.

As for Africans, slavery's fundamental relevance to both the economic life of the new country and its ethnic identity cannot be exaggerated. It was present in the American colonies of the English, Spanish, and Dutch, and its persistence solidified a belief in the inherent biological differences between whites and blacks. These too were codified in the nation's founding documents: the Constitution gave the black populations of states only a fraction of the weight of whites in reckoning congressional representation. And while the Constitution contained no explicit exclusion of blacks from political or social rights, later amendments made its implicit exclusions clear.

The real power of the idea of race, though, was that it could be handily applied to any non-Europeans, and later even non-western Europeans, who simply seemed too culturally different. In this way, the new man myth could be preserved even as the country excluded any number of ethnic groups from assimilation. With the help of evolutionary theory and its stepchild, the eugenics movement, those of non-Western cultures were simply declared to be of a different race. By the twentieth century, race offered a powerful logic for limiting immigration of any number of less desirable— by then called degenerate—racial groups. There was, apparently, no end to the genetic predispositions a people might have. Poles and Slavs, Turks and Hungarians, Russians, Greeks, and Croats were thought likely to carry any number of physical, psychological, and social diseases—often considered genetic in nature—or were considered to be inherently in- capable of taking part in democratic life. Their languages, religions, and customs posed a greater difficulty than had those of earlier immigrant groups. Many were Catholic and represented a significant threat to the American landscape's Protestant character. Their presumed obedience to the pope made it difficult to imagine they could shed their ethnic baggage for the new civic national persona. Others were Eastern Orthodox, which was deemed even more exotic. And many were Jews, considered a problem even to the Europeans themselves and thought unlikely to attach themselves to any nation at all.

The American response to these groups and their perceived deficien- cies was a series of legislative actions at the state and national levels. Asians, brought to the West Coast to construct transcontinental railroads, were later kept out by a series of exclusionary acts and marginalized by various state laws. The Espionage and Sedition acts of 1917 and 1918 featured a series of deportation and internal espionage policies against foreign-born radicals. Even Prohibition was aimed at least partly at the Irish and other Catholic immigrant groups.[40]

The American assimilationist ethos lay in a quandary for it appeared that some people (including most, but not all, Europeans) would be welcomed by the still-expanding nation while others would not. Through careful measurement of biological characteristics, aided by the central processing of immigrants at disembarkation centers like Ellis Island, the scientific community could be enlisted to provide rationale for the exclusion of some groups and the inclusion of others into the American fabric. The logic that was eventually adopted was clear and simple: some groups were inherently incapable of becoming American, owing to a predilection for excessive obedience, laziness, clannishness, or simple feeblemindedness.

The ideals of civic nationalism were maintained by a simple sleight of hand. Those groups deemed capable of attaching themselves to the American civic ideals were welcome to take part in it while those not so capable were excluded either by restrictions on immigration or by ghettoization and marginalization.

Perhaps Americans shared a common ethnic bond after all. Samuel Huntington and others have considered this Anglo-Protestant culture to have been the core of American identity. Upon it was built the structure of civic nationalism and the central values of American life: individualism, the work ethic, and moralism. In its name, exotic groups were assimilated, excluded, or ethnically cleansed for more than three centuries. And as seen in the next chapter, "whiteness" became the standard by which groups might be permitted to assimilate, even though whiteness was variously construed and attributed over the years according to social conditions and circumstances.[41]

Still, aside from the dominance of the English language, it does not seem quite accurate to say that Americans felt a bond to a shared culture. Race, language, and religion were useful tools of exclusion, but except in certain enclaves they were not consciously felt as sources of deep connection to others or to the country. White racism was felt more as contempt or fear of others than as a love of white identity itself. Few English-language societies or fraternal orders were organized around the celebration of English literature or arts. And while religious identity did provide deep bonds among many Americans, the pluralist ideal always held sway where faith was concerned. Though even today many would like to see the state officially endorse Christianity, few have ever suggested a ban on other faiths.[42]

In any case, whether an American cultural tradition has ever existed, most agree that its time has passed. According to Huntington, the forces of large-scale immigration of Spanish speakers, the discreditation of race as a source of identity since the Holocaust, the worldwide rise of subnational groups, the decline of the Cold War, and the motives of liberal academics and bureaucrats have all hastened the decline of American identity. Others have noted this decline, too, though less mournfully, and there is much evidence to support the claim.[43]

Today it would be difficult to define even one widely shared American cultural trait. Most Americans would be hard pressed to identify any, and many would take pride in that. In the arts, for example, few styles or genres are considered essentially American or, more pointedly, most Americans regard few, if any, styles as their artistic heritage. A few painters and composers have approached an American style or vernacular: Thomas Hart Benton comes to mind in painting, Aaron Copeland in music. Popular music offers a better example, as jazz, blues, country, rap, and rock are recognized, at least by the rest of the world, as uniquely American contributions. Of these, only country and rock would be embraced by most Americans as their music, and in few cases would the same people like both.

The same is true for other areas of taste. Frank Lloyd Wright's Prairie School formed a distinctly American style in architecture, as did the earlier Carpenter Gothic residential vernacular and the skyscraper in commercial architecture. Likewise, in literature, dance, clothing, and industrial and commercial design there are no doubt recognizably American styles. But none of these art forms, from painting to music to architecture to clothing, are really embraced by the majority of Americans, or even by the elite arbiters of American taste, as emblematic of their commonly shared culture. The fact is, there simply is no desire to identify or develop such an emblematic cultural product or any impetus to recognize a common and shared cultural heritage.[44] What's American about American culture is its very diversity and not just in the trite sense. American culture is a pastiche of artistic styles from Fredric Remington to Jackson Pollock, from Samuel Barber to Aretha Franklin, from Herman Melville to Stephen King. The arts are viewed as a smorgasbord of products from which the consumer can pick and choose. The individual is king, and personal taste is what matters.[45]

Even the English language has been less than completely effective in forging a common heritage. Through centuries of immigration and despite the ebb and flow of xenophobic and exclusionary policy, English has never received an official mandate as the national language. This is largely a matter of simple pragmatism, for as immigrant groups have formed sizable pockets within larger communities, commercial interests and public institutions have found it expedient to reach out linguistically to customers and clients. It is not uncommon, and never has been, for hospitals, merchants, and government agencies in Chicago, New York, or even Minneapolis to post their signs in half a dozen languages, sometimes excluding English. Today every major city converses in a few of the tongues of its major immigrant groups.

As for cultural values and ideals, it might be possible to identify a set of core American principles, but any such list would be almost completely self-contradictory. Americans value both equality and competitive achievement, religion and science, conformity and individualism, and on and on.[46] William Bennett tried to resolve it all in his *The Book of Virtues*, but he succeeded only in highlighting the perennial dispute over which values are most important.[47] Similarly, in the early 1990s Sheldon Hackney, chairman of the National Endowment for the Humanities, set as the endowment's mission the conduct of "a national conversation about what constitutes the shared heritage of American culture."[48] While scholars were only too happy to couch their grant proposals in terms that embraced that mandate, not much of a conversation emerged. In fact, there was a good deal of criticism from many scholars who viewed the initiative as an attempt to squelch diversity and to promote Eurocentric values.

It's fair to say that a shared artistic, literary, or historical heritage simply is not a part of most Americans' thinking. While Americans might relate to cultural or ethnic traditions, to the extent that an individual might identify with a collective sense of aesthetic taste or even moral priorities or historical understandings, those ideas are often the ideas of a subgroup within American culture—that is, one's religious, ethnic, racial, or even demographic group. Today one might say that age and income identification are the strongest determinants of aesthetic tastes, as the target markets for pop music, films, and television shows are defined very narrowly in these terms. Americans have formed distinct communities around all of these demographic categories, as well as around identification with ethnicity and sexuality. But they haven't formed strong identification with an American culture as a whole.

Other Forms of Nationalism
The legacy of the Jacksonian era still provides Americans with a strong sense of economic nationalism. Thanks to the recession of the early twenty-first century, we are more keenly aware than ever that we are part of an integrated economic and financial system that the federal government controls to a fairly large extent by regulating banks, securities markets, industrial safety, corporate labor practices, and the like. Theodore Roosevelt busted the trusts to promote competition in America's most important industries, and later Franklin Roosevelt used the government's buying and regulatory power to end the Great Depression. Today the government remains a major force in the American economy, consuming about 20

percent of the gross domestic product. More than five million Americans draw a paycheck from the federal government, and more than fifty million people receive an entitlement check from it, either through Social Security or any number of other programs. These figures will only increase over the next few years. Whether Americans like the government's economic policies or not, they recognize they are enmeshed in them and in the economic business of the nation as a whole.

Identification with the national economy extends beyond one's connection with government policy. Americans have also become more closely bound to the fortunes of corporate America, through widespread investment and their own consumption, and this association too is more acutely felt today. Since the New York Stock Exchange opened in 1817, ordinary citizens have had access to the profits and policies of most of the firms that control their lives. To be sure, for more than a century this access was manipulated by the robber barons who controlled the companies, but that didn't stop ordinary people from gradually gaining a place in the corporate economy. Today Americans are among the most invested people in the world. Through their own portfolios, mutual funds, and retirement plans offered by their employers, fully 50 percent of American households have a personal stake, for good or ill, in the American corporation.[49] And these investors pay attention: financial news, opinion, and advice are prominent features in the popular media, and they are consumed by a broad range of the American demographic. Whole cable networks are devoted to finance, and stock quotes appear on the screen during HLN's news broadcasts. The most reliably predictable news story in December is the relative success of the Christmas shopping season, where the ups and downs of the retail sector are analyzed. Even the gross ticket sales of popular movies are reported in the daily news, demonstrating as much interest in their revenues as in their entertainment value.

In addition, Americans enthusiastically play their role as consumers and recognize its importance to the economy. Shopping has become as much a pastime as a way to furnish one's needs and wants, as evidenced by the development of shopping destinations, such as the Mall of America. For a large proportion of the public, a day at the mall or in a downtown commercial district is a celebration of one's freedom of choice and economic power. In a telling phrase, Americans "vote with their dollars" to express their aesthetic tastes, class aspirations, and even ethical values. The importance of consumption to the American economy was dramatically underlined by President George W. Bush after the September 11 attacks, as he exhorted everyone, almost as a patriotic duty, to continue consuming so as not to stall the economy. His concerns were at least partly vindicated when the real-estate collapse a few years later was deepened into a recession by a slowdown in retail spending.

Finally, Americans continue to display a high degree of militarism, though it is of a different form than the militarist tradition of the Germans. It's true that the country has been more or less constantly engaged in military activities, including large-scale warfare every twenty-five years or so, but until the twentieth century the military had but little presence in the rest of American life. The United States had no officer corps tradition whereby the sons of aristocrats took their place in society, no large standing army, and no constant border disputes. Each American war, all the way through World War I, was followed by a general demobilization of the citizen-soldiers who had mostly fought it.

It was not until the end of World War II that military activities and values permeated the American experience in a large way. The United States, at the war's end, had become a preeminent global power, having developed an enormous military and at the same time having gained control of bases and outposts around the world. Moreover, the Soviet Union had emerged from the war in much the same condition. This uncomfortable parity in military power and the West's long-gestating mistrust of the Soviets brought the United States immediately into what came to be called the Cold War. Since then Americans have supported an enormous military. As of 2009 there are 1.5 million men and women on active duty, and the military budget consumes about 40 percent of the federal tax dollar when indirect expenses are counted. This budget does not even include the costs of the current wars in Iraq and Afghanistan, funded by supplementary appropriations to the tune of $188 billion in 2007.[50] As the only remaining superpower, the United States finds itself extended around the world in a variety of military ventures.

The tax burden alone of these activities demands a great deal of public support for military institutions and values. This sort of public sacrifice can be maintained only if the society's people and institutions are conditioned to a military footing, and thus America has become a much more militaristic society since World War II. The fear of nuclear attack encouraged Americans to view themselves both as targets and soldiers in the Cold War while round-the-clock patrols by nuclear bombers persuaded them that peace was possible only through strength. In short, the Cold War provided the foundation of modern American militarism.[51] Its end, however, has not resulted in demobilization. Rather, the United States has found new threats, and its response to these threats has kept the game alive.

American Sonderweg

In many ways, American nationalism is different from the nationalism that brought Germany and much of Europe to ruin in the last century. The strongest and deepest strain of German nationalism was the ethnic type, by which people viewed themselves as part of a great and timeless river of German humanity and as a people who struggled through the millennia to improve themselves, to achieve harmony with their surroundings, and to purify their race. The Germans had yearned to unite their culture under a single nation and finally achieved that aim late in the nineteenth century. They had spent more than a century exploring the essential meaning of Germanness through the arts, literature, philosophy, and most other aspects of intellectual and ordinary life. They viewed nationhood as coterminous with the volk, the ethnic and racial group naturally and profoundly rooted to the German land.

Americans are nationalistic, too, but in different ways. We have become a militaristic people and a people united by a common sense of economic interdependence. But what Americans do not value is a shared cultural heritage, a belief in a common ethnic identity. If we ever did feel such a kinship—of whiteness or a Protestant worldview or a language community—that has largely eroded. Nonetheless, there is one important way that American nationalism does closely resemble German nationalism. Since shortly after the republic's founding, Americans have nurtured a very strong belief that the United States is a special nation, destined not only to take its place among nations but also to be the exemplar of what nationhood should be. This special path of a rationally planned nation based on a set of principles of human nature and natural law is rooted in the nation's constitutional foundation. Nothing like it had been seen before. The founders believed that "the laws which governed politics were ultimately the same as those which governed Nature herself."[52] This rational basis made it possible for Americans to claim that the nation was "more principled, more civilized, than those tribally defined societies" of old Europe.[53] And because the country's founding was grounded in the

Enlightenment, Americans took it for granted that these principles—that all men are created equal and endowed by their creator with certain rights, for example—were universal ones. America's values were the world's values.

The exceptionalist view of America was reflected in the deification of George Washington. On his death he was lionized as no man had been in anyone's memory, save for Christ himself. One notable painting depicted him as a kind of saint in resurrection, surrounded by lesser beings basking in his aura. His death actually posed a problem for some mythmakers, who had difficulty depicting him as mortal at all. Indeed, many descriptions of his deathbed scene found it necessary to claim that he died "without any infirmity or decay."[54]

The end of the War of 1812 saw a new explosion of exceptionalist fervor. The stunningly unexpected victory was widely seen as evidence that the hand of God must have intervened to guarantee the survival of his chosen people. Newspapers and broadsides went wild with hyperbole in describing the war, using such phrases as "holy war," "God of Battles," and "the rod of God's anger." Americans were likened to Israelites, saved by Andrew Jackson from the depredations of the Philistines.[55]

Exceptionalism carried the nation westward on the wheels of Manifest Destiny. The very idea of "destiny," a sense that America had a preordained future that could not be denied by mortal caution or moral restraint, was, of course, romantic at its heart. Moreover, this destiny was manifest, made visible to all who had the insight and courage to see it. Those who could not recognize it were, by definition, lacking in vision or brashness or patriotism and could easily be dismissed.

The American sonderweg persisted even as the deepest rift in American history grew. The abolition movement, in addition to its antislavery focus, had become symbolic of a fundamental division in the American identity that had existed since the signing of the declaration itself: the struggle between the goal of egalitarianism and human rights on the one hand and the desire for moral purity and national greatness on the other. These two positions—essentially reflecting civic nationalism and ethnic nationalism—amounted to "competing understandings of what the nation should be."[56] It was similar to the strain seen later in Weimar Germany, as newly unleashed forces of freedom and egalitarianism clashed with desires for ethnic purity and traditional morality. In Germany, the strain was reconciled by a Nazi ideology that deflected the conflict to various non-

German elements, whose purge could save both the purity and the equality of true Germans. In the United States, however, it erupted into civil war.

While the war ultimately brought political reconciliation, it did not solve the question of America's national identity. Throughout the second half of the nineteenth century the ideological poles competed by establishing various fraternal organizations and by staging national displays of patriotism. For example, two competing associations of Civil War veterans struggled over whose traditions and memorials would dominate the national memory. While the Northern veterans' Grand Army of the Republic (GAR) had dominated in the years immediately following the war, the United Confederate Veterans worked to represent and shape Southern appeals for reconciliation. It came in 1897, when the GAR's national reunion adopted the principle of reconciliation under the slogan One Country, One Flag, One People, One Destiny.[57] The Nazi regime's later adoption of a similar slogan (One Volk, One Reich, One Führer) was almost certainly a coincidence, but it expressed the same ideal and attempted to manufacture a romantic sense of oneness around a symbol.

But under which ideals were Americans to reconcile? The solution for the veterans' associations was to exclude blacks from membership, thereby appeasing Southern interests. In the larger society, this ban threatened an abandonment of the egalitarian side of American identity altogether. The contradiction was reconciled by of a new sort of nationalism, wholly abstract in form and unencumbered by any principles that might interfere with the national consensus. In the 1890s the flag became a symbol of that abstraction, worshipped as a sacred totem and symbol of whatever the viewer imagined America to be. Along with the flag cult, there were other patriotic cults, including a drill craze in which the bonds of school, temperance society, fraternal, and even church groups were translated into national loyalty through practicing military drills complete with uniforms and guns.[58]

With the Spanish-American War, the strain between the egalitarian ideal and the ideal of national greatness was at last resolved. The military victory gave the final blow to the egalitarian interpretation of American identity; it would forever be consigned to second place, easily dismissed at the first sign of threat from within or without. All that was left was exceptionalism itself, an abiding faith that Americans were a chosen people and that the United States had a destiny to lead the world on a righteous path. This belief has never changed as the ideology of American exceptionalism has been a cornerstone of national sentiment for nearly two centuries. Its most recent manifestation, the Bush Doctrine, is the belief in America's obligation to bring democracy to the rest of the world while banishing Islamic fundamentalism. When the threat of Saddam Hussein's weapons of mass destruction evaporated, this sacred mission served handily to justify the war in Iraq.

This American patriotism has come to mean an ideologically empty love of country, a turgid and unreflective belief in American exceptionalism. George Lipsitz has called this new form of patriotism "defensive and insecure," and John Higham called it a "truculent and gasconading patriotism" created and maintained by "unifying abstractions" like the flag, George Washington, and a host of rituals and parades.[59] While these descriptions might be unfair representations of the genuine love of country felt by many, it does seem true that when a threat to national security arises, the truculent unifying abstraction is what emerges, often as a cudgel.

Remarkably, the word "exceptionalism" became a part of the stump speeches of John McCain and Sarah Palin in the 2008 campaign, as they attempted to keep the ideal of spread-eagle patriotism attached to their party. But what had worked for Ronald Reagan (America as the shining city on a hill) and for George W. Bush (America's mission to spread democracy) was drowned out by more pragmatic issues closer to home. The dissatisfaction with the wars in Iraq and Afghanistan and the economic collapse caused a majority of Americans to focus on how to salvage what reputation the country still had and to repair the political and economic damage done over the past couple of decades.

THE THREAT OF NATIONALISM

Nationalism was a central factor in Germany's adoption of the National Socialist philosophy and doctrine. The Nazis were first and always a nationalist party. Although they offered other ideological appeals beyond plain nationalism as a way to attract votes, their appeal to national identity—to Germanness, to fear of enemies, to anti-Semitism—could usually be counted on to bring an unresponsive crowd to its feet. Often all were included in the same sentence, as when Jews were cast as an international conspiracy dedicated to de-Germanizing Germany, through pernicious cultural and economic infiltration.

Nationalism then, as now, was thought to transcend partisan interests, party platforms, and policy aims. The various parties that called themselves nationalist parties in the 1920s asserted they were nonpolitical and above the bickering and byplay of party interests. In this way, of course, they were also antidemocratic, since the bickering they so disdained was nothing other than the normal activity of the democratic process as it hammered out compromises among competing interests. The nationalist parties, and thus the National Socialist party that overtook most of them, were able to rise above the partisan fray and at the same time paint the opposition as less loyal, less patriotic, and less German.

Americans are nationalists, too, and this trait is a worry. The simple escape would be to say that Americans are bound by civic ties, grounded in the belief that the rule of law engages us all in a shared social contract. Americans nourish and celebrate the myth that ethnicity is irrelevant (despite glaring exceptions for race) and that our diversity itself has created a new kind of citizen. "The genius of America," wrote Schlesinger, "lies in its capacity to forge a single nation from peoples of remarkably diverse racial, religious, and ethnic origins."[60] Americans neither believe in nor have much desire for a common heritage or shared culture, and this attitude, at least, is one advantage in avoiding fascism.

But there is a problem. While Americans observe the symbols of civic nationalism—perhaps sometimes obsessively so—they tend to be quick to abandon the principles those symbols represent. If the Constitution is the most sacred and fundamental document that cements the nation together, it receives surprisingly little respect when it is needed most. In fact, it seems the most patriotic Americans—those who display Old Glory on their sleeves and car bumpers, who sing loudest when the anthem is played, who are quickest to demonize the country's critics and enemies—are so often the very people who place security above law, who grant the government extraordinary powers to control citizens, who criminalize dissent, and who despise Congress and the judiciary. They often have only the vaguest understanding of what the Constitution and Declaration of Independence even mean. In many ways, it seems Americans' love of country is similar to youthful romance: based on an idealized image of the object of affection and thus prone to frustration.

And here is the problem for Americans: nationalism poses an inevitable paradox in democratic societies. Democracies are faced with the dual tasks of defending individual liberties while at the same time demanding a certain amount of individual sacrifice and submission, and this contradiction is exacerbated in times of crisis. At such times, nationalism is inherently antidemocratic because it always transcends democratic discourse. Appeals to this transcendent but empty love of country always squelch the democratic process because opposition and dispute are easily cast as unpatriotic and un-American.

In the face of such attacks, appeals to civic nationalism—that pride in democratic principles, legal rights, and social obligations that ought to bind Americans most deeply—seem hollow and weak. Civic nationalism is a luxury to be enjoyed in carefree times. The problem is that those times are all too rare, and crises can be inflated or manufactured almost at will by the skillful use of the media. When they are, the pernicious forms of nationalism, fed on fear or revenge, actually erode civic nationalism. Those very rights and principles that are the bedrock of civic nationalism are challenged as aliens, political opponents, immigrants, activists, and other generally suspicious characters are investigated, harassed, or imprisoned. Citizens are offered the depressing choice of signing on to a turgid jingoism or retreating into an opposition that actually does become vaguely anti-American. This is the box into which the American citizen has been squeezed over the last decade or so.

The clear failure of the Bush Doctrine's brand of nationalism was expressed at the polls in 2008. A majority of voters rejected the focus on winning the war in Iraq and heeded a more thoughtful, if less concrete, approach to finding a solution. They concluded that America's mission for the near future should focus on domestic harmony by restoring some balance to the spiraling consumption and debt of middle-class Americans. They retracted their aspirations for permanent American supremacy in the world. At least, a majority did.

But the competition between jingoist exceptionalism and civic nationalism constitutes an ongoing strain in the American identity that won't be eliminated by the current retrenchment. This strain is similar to that faced by the Germans in the Weimar era, and it can be resolved in either of two ways. First, the Right might permanently take possession of the symbols of American identity. Efforts in this direction have been the bedrock of the post-Reagan Republican domination of the national discourse, as the party's base of Christian fundamentalists, antiabortion groups, and pro-family and antigay forces has aligned to advance the purity and dominance definition of American identity. Oddly, for all these forces' influence in selecting Republican candidates and electing them, they have not succeeded in advancing any of these issues politically or legally and probably have not really tried.[61]

The other way in which the strain in American identity might be reconciled is by uniting the values of civic nationalism with the desire for moral purity. Achieving this combination was the true National Socialist triumph: ethnic and militarist nationalism was called on to serve the goal of civic nationalism—that is, to protect the freedoms and rights of true Germans from the insults that had been visited on them by international Jewry, international communism, and other enemies. Such was the crusade in postwar America for a Cold War against communism and, more recently, the Bush administration's call for a war on terrorism. In both cases, appeals to militarism and national purity were united with appeals to civic nationalism into an exceptionalist holy mission to use our mighty force to spread and preserve democracy worldwide. This uniting of heretofore opposing ideals—of joining the Left and the Right, conservative and liberal—into adventurous policy is the way in which fascist ideology is advanced.

___6___

RACISM

IN MODERN HISTORY, THERE have been only three overtly racist regimes, governments that have explicitly and legally recognized race as a basis for conferring differential rights and rewards. The most notorious was the Third Reich, which made Jewishness itself a crime and which set for itself the task of eliminating European Jewry through deportation and murder. The most recent was the apartheid regime of South Africa, a nation formed in 1948 but officially split into two castes—a ruling white minority and a subordinate black majority—in 1968.

But the world's first overtly racist regime was the Jim Crow South of the United States.[1] This regime, which took root at the end of Reconstruction and lasted until the 1960s, served as a model for the other two to follow. It perfected methods of social and political disenfranchisement, economic subjugation, stigmatization, and separation that were thorough and effective. It elevated the concept of race to the level of both scientific fact and an article of faith, and it did so even under a national Constitution that guaranteed the rights of all Americans under the law. It was a remarkable achievement of political duplicity, if only for its endurance.

Racial disparity was not restricted to the South. Many of the beliefs and structures that formed the underpinnings of the Jim Crow era were readily adopted throughout the rest of the country after blacks migrated there in large numbers early in the twentieth century. Examples include official or de facto segregation of residential neighborhoods, schools, amateur and professional sports, and the military; formal as well as informal barriers to membership in professional and social associations; overt discrimination in higher education and employment; strong barriers against social or sexual contact between the races; and perhaps most insidious of all, the taken-for-granted assumption that the United States was a white nation.

African Americans were not a uniquely disparaged caste. The country hadrid itself of most of the native population and confined the rest to reservations in the West, and the government had imposed a ban on Chinese immigration as well as racially based quotas for other groups. All this occurred despite the fact that America comprised more cultural and racial groups than anywhere else. Most Americans were immigrants themselves or recently descended from them and had felt the sting of at least informal discrimination. But upon integrating themselves into the American fabric—by becoming exemplars of the new man envisioned by the nineteenth-century nationalists—these Irish, Poles, Swedes, and the rest had been raised from the bottom of the social and economic pile. They were white, it mattered, and they were glad of it.

Thus at the beginning of the twentieth century, the United States was clearly a far more racist country than was any nation in Europe. But Germany, not the United States, a few decades later would make racial extermination the hallmark of its political and social system, ultimately discrediting race forever as a basis for social order. The anti-Semitism that had long been a staple of religious and then nationalist thought became in the 1930s a central focus of National Socialist policy.

What role, exactly, did anti-Semitism play in the rise of the National Socialists? The question might seem absurd for everyone knows the Nazis played on anti-Semitic hatreds that had smoldered within Germany since Martin Luther's day and before. Hitler railed against world Jewry in *Mein Kampf,* clearly foreshadowing his intention to resolve the Jewish "question" once and for all. On the way to power, the Nazis nourished stereotypes and fears of *der Jude* in their political campaigns, and on achieving it they wasted no time in enacting all sorts of laws curtailing Jews' political and social rights, ultimately resulting in the Jews' near-annihilation. And the proof of it all lies in the ashy muck of Auschwitz and Majdanek and Treblinka and the rest, and in the identification tattoos of the dwindling community of survivors.

Indeed, seen in hindsight the entire National Socialist era appears to have been the single-minded development of a vast apparatus whose sole purpose was to exterminate the Jewish people. But the problem with hindsight is, it makes historical events appear to have been planned, such that the results were foreseen from the beginning and destined to turn out the way that they did. It is the equivalent of intelligent design in evolutionary thinking, and just as wrong. The fact is, it would have been very difficult for an observer in fin de siècle Germany—or even as late as the Nazis' accession to power in 1933—to imagine that the government would actually undertake the eradication of Jewish life in Europe.

It is certainly true that the German culture contained a considerable streak of anti-Semitism, and in fact, race and ethnicity seem still to be relevant and widely used distinctions among many Germans. Obviously the National Socialists were also avowedly anti-Semitic, but it is not at all clear that anti-Semitism was their primary appeal. In fact, they used it strategically early on, when it could capture votes (particularly in Bavaria), and toned it down when it could not (particularly in Prussia). The more they broadened their political base, the less shrill the Jew-baiting speeches were.[2] This modulation of tone is significant: anti-Semitism was a central philosophical tenet of the party and an evident leitmotif of Hitler's worldview, yet the Nazis had to control the tenor of their appeals because the broad base of the German electorate simply did not respond to that sort of thing. The question then is, what was the nature of German anti-Semitism in the early part of the century? It is not a simple question of degree or of how racist the Germans were but rather a more difficult and subtle question of what race meant to Germans.

THE MEANING OF RACE IN 1900

It is impossible to gauge the racism of German society without some understanding of the meaning of race in the Western world at the time. Seen from our century, the world of a hundred years ago was barbarically racist. It was the peak of the Age of Empire, when any nation worth its mettle exploited the black and brown peoples of the world with hardly a blink of compunction. The sun constantly shone on the British Empire, from India to the Middle East, to central and south Africa, across the Caribbean and Central America, and clear to Asia. Throughout, native peoples served an imperial engine of economic and military power. But the British were not alone. Spain, Belgium, France, Portugal, Denmark, the Netherlands, and finally Germany—all grasped at the riches of the earth, bringing civilization and enslavement, more or less, to those without the blessings of European heritage and white skin.

America would not be left behind. Having conquered what was thought to be its rightful share of the North American continent, the United States

126 | FASCISM: WHY NOT HERE?

thirsted to be a player in the world system. The Spanish-American War was the perfect opportunity to seize a broad holding all at once. At its conclusion, American protectorates included Puerto Rico and other holdings in the Caribbean, Guam and other central Pacific islands, and the Philippine archipelago. This latter was the most difficult to possess, as the locals had hoped in their liberation from Spain to achieve self-rule. William McKinley's administration saw things differently, deeming it inhumane to leave such a childlike race to their own devices. The soldiers sent to quell the uprising took a more simple view. Some of their letters home reveled in such joys as "killing niggers," which "beats shooting rabbits all to hell."[3]

Being the most distant of the new holdings, the Philippines also most captured the public's imagination. The St. Louis World's Fair of 1904 featured an authentic village inhabited by actual Filipinos, for example. Curious fairgoers could see for themselves how these exotic primitives lived and could thus appreciate the virtues bestowed upon the white race. When the fair ended, some of the Filipinos took up residence in a neighborhood that is today still called Dogtown, a reference to their alien diet, or so the locals say.

The United States had eradicated slavery only a few decades prior to the turn of the century, but now Jim Crow laws ruled the South while the bulk of the great black migration North was yet to occur. And the Indian "wars" were still fresh in the minds of most Americans, having concluded ignominiously with the Wounded Knee massacre of 1890. Meanwhile, Asians had migrated to the western states in large numbers, with more to come, and Europeans were flooding the eastern ports. All of these movements would usher in decades of fear of racial mongrelizing.

Back in Europe, anti-Semitism was hardly a uniquely German development. The Dreyfus affair, in which a French army officer was sent to the Devil's Island penal colony on fabricated evidence of "Jewish treason," brought to a head the deep undercurrents of anti-Jewish sentiment in France and, indeed, through much of Europe. In czarist Russia, Jews had been subject to repeated pogroms, which only hastened their westward migration—largely to Germany, where they were better treated.

Race was simply a more concrete and more meaningful reality a hundred years ago than it is today. In a world where there had not yet been much assimilation or mixing of any kind among the races, it seemed clear to everyone that the peoples of the world were inherently different. These differences were thought unchangeable, just as the pigmentation of skin and the shape of the eye were unalterable. And in an imperial world of rapid industrial and economic growth, ever cheaper transport, and increasingly solid control by a few monarchies, the idea of race was an absolute cultural necessity. The notion that the world was composed of peoples of varying worth and talents made sense of imperial splendor, military pomp, and Christian righteousness, not to mention the plunder of colonial empires. With the help of convenient interpretations of scripture and, later, of Darwin's theory, race came to be a concrete reality that made sense of the world as the ruling elites of the West saw it and lived it. The idea that people of different races merited equal regard was widely viewed as silly or even dangerous; the modern taboo against the use of racial epithets would have seemed quite puzzling. Depending on the context, the speaker, and the subject, the other peoples of the world were conventionally referred to as brutes, heathens, savages, throwbacks, or simply darkies and wogs. It was in this world that German anti-Semitism glowed, smoldered, and finally burst into flame.

EVOLUTION OF GERMAN ANTI-SEMITISM
There is no question that anti-Semitism was a fixture of German culture and had been for a millennium and more. Rooted in a hodgepodge of theological and social teachings since the beginning of the Holy Roman Empire, Christian anti-Semitism was based on the beliefs that Judaism was outdated, having failed to recognize the messiah; or that Jews threatened the promise of salvation through Christ; or that Jews had killed the savior and bore the guilt of murder for all time; or a combination of all three.[4] Jews were thus a threat to the very basis of social organization throughout the Middle Ages, insofar as the Christian church offered the only refuge for Europeans from abject chaos. The Jews occupied a place in the social and cultural taxonomy not too different from Muslims and the heathen peoples of Africa, Asia, and uncivilized parts of Europe.

How were such people regarded by the Christian world? The Muslims had been the subject of an obsessive and unsuccessful extermination campaign, as we know; the brutality of the Crusades attests to the degree of hatred felt toward this alien group. But at the same time some Christians, by virtue of their unorthodox interpretation of seemingly small details of scripture, were also subject to trial, torture, and burning at the stake. These heretics—whose beliefs ranged from the notion that Jesus became divine later in life instead of being born that way to disputes about whether

the Holy Trinity was one being or three—fared little better than foreign
infidels. Moreover, they were nearby. The treatment of Jews throughout
this period can be likened to that of any of these other unorthodox
groups. Believed to pose a threat to the principal social order of the day,
just as Muslims, pagans, and heretics did, they were consigned to the same
depredations when the threat was acute.

Christian anti-Semitism took a distinctly German turn with the
Protestant Reformation. Some have suggested that a direct line can be
drawn from the thinking of Luther to that of Adolf Hitler, but if so, that
line is not straight.[5] In his pamphlet "On the Jews and Their Lies," Luther
did indeed refer to Jews as an "arrogant, vengeful, foreign presence" and
called for the burning of synagogues and for the forced labor and removal
of Jews. But here, too, Jews were little worse in the Lutheran mind than
Anabaptists, Zwinglians, and a host of other unorthodox movements within
the Protestant house itself.[6] What was new in Luther's formulation was the
repugnance of the Jews' foreign presence among the German people. He
viewed Jews as one of many foreign predators who had humbled Germans
over the centuries.[7]

To Christian anti-Semitism, Luther had thus begun to add a strain of
German nationalist anti-Semitism, and it would grow more important as
German national sentiment, and its frustration, grew over the next several
hundred years. Through the Thirty Years' War, through the Revolution of
1848, and through the nineteenth century, anti-Semitism waxed and waned
as the intensity of feeling for Germanness also waxed and waned. At the
end of the eighteenth century, for example, it diminished as the German
flirtation with the Enlightenment included at least some acceptance of the
universal inherent rights of humankind. Prussia consequently granted
citizenship and political rights to Jews in 1812.

But at the same time there was a backlash against the emancipation of
Jews. In Germany, the Enlightenment was, as everywhere else, more popular
among the aristocracy than among the lower classes since it justified rule
by the educated elite. It was a universalist worldview as well, which also
appealed to the aristocrats, who often felt a stronger identification with their
class than with their country. At a time of emerging German nationalism
and populism, the nobles' universalism created an intolerable strain. The
liberalization of 1812 fueled sporadic riots and pogroms in scattered towns
and cities in various parts Germany, becoming somewhat institutionalized
in the "Hep! Hep!" Movement of 1819. So called because of its battle cry—

"Hep! Hep! Hep! Death and destruction to all the Jews!"—this vicious outburst was among the first to couch anti-Semitism in nationalistic terms, identifying Jews specifically as an enemy of Germanness and not just of Christianity.[8]

The essence of all forms of nationalism is the definition of a people not only in terms of their own virtues but also in terms of what they are not: aliens, foreigners, the other. Often the other is an enemy nation or people; in these cases geographical boundaries easily serve as the frontier between us and them, civilization and the barbarians, the free world and the enslaved. But sometimes the boundaries are not geographical but cultural, and in these cases the logic of enmity is both more convoluted and more cruel. One's nation can't be protected from such internal enemies simply by a boundary line or defensive wall. The Great Wall defined the Qin dynasty, Hadrian's Wall the extent of Roman Britain, and the iron curtain the division of Eastern and Western Europe, but no physical wall could define "true" Germans from Jews—that is, not until the Nazis' establishment of the ghettos and camps. In the early nineteenth century, however, Jews were excluded by cultural walls, or ideas that promoted German solidarity and identity at the expense of Jewish humanity.

Thus nationalist anti-Semitism could be even more virulent than Christian anti-Semitism, because by the beginning of the nineteenth century, nationhood was a more important social bond than religion was. Heresy wasn't the crime it used to be; treason had taken its place. And because Jews were mixed among the German population, the simple enmity of the foreigner, dealt with by the relatively benign means of distance and separation, would not do for them. Jews amounted to civic heretics, or people who stood outside the German community and yet existed within it for all to see as living examples of apartness within the group. This distinction made them a greater threat than any foreign enemy for whereas foreign enemies strengthen the solidarity of a nation, internal enemies threaten it.

How could this strain between the Germans' national aspirations and the other's presence in their midst be resolved? Could Jews be incorporated into the German nation? This matter actually caused considerable thought and debate among German thinkers and ordinary people over the next century. The *Judenfrage*—the "Jewish question"—became the subject of an extensive literature that lasted for a hundred years, beginning in the 1830s and extending right up to the Third Reich.[9]

The Jewish question might have resolved itself over time. Gradual accommodation and assimilation might have continued through the end of the century, and the distinctions between Jews and true Germans might have diminished to the vanishing point. But there were barriers to such an orderly and incremental process. For one, the Germans had not yet achieved nationhood as the rest of Europe had. Still divided late in the nineteenth century among a bagful of kingdoms and lesser principalities, they took seriously the question of who was a German. Meanwhile, they were undergoing the other wrenching cultural changes of the modern world—industrialization and the new institutions and values that accompanied it. The new economy challenged traditional cultural values as finance and speculation came to be more lucrative than frugality and patience, and Jews were thought to have benefited the most from this change. The new forms of employment in industrial factories and bureaucratic offices changed the character and meaning of work as well as the family structures and routines of many Germans. Jews were thought responsible. And the densely interdependent economy tended toward instability, with booms followed by busts punctuated by the occasional dire crisis. Jews were thought to be at the bottom of them all.

The Germans were not wrong in associating Jews with the oncoming modern age and its values. German Jews, a people who had come to the German lands during the Enlightenment to escape pogroms in the east, embraced the Enlightenment's values and taught them to later arrivals. They tended to be middle class, nonorthodox, and educated. Their birthrates were low, and they had a high rate of marriage outside the faith. Quite a few converted to Christianity.[10] The problem was, even as the German aristocracy led the nation's economy into the modern age, average Germans were, as we have seen, deeply suspicious. Through their interests, their habits, their aspirations, and even their religion, Jews came to stand for everything that was modern, and a good many Germans held most of that in contempt.

Thus even while the various German states accorded Jews greater social and political status, the deeper cultural animosities toward them became more virulent. It seemed as if each gain in social equity was offset by a backlash of popular anti-Semitism. The Revolution of 1848, for example, gave way to a confederation of the various German states that bestowed unprecedented political rights to Jews, only to be followed within a year by more brutal reaction. As the aristocrats became increasingly liberal, the public's growing populist and nationalist sentiments made them angrier toward the upper class. This postrevolutionary bitterness toward the elites spilled over to the Jews, the beneficiaries of the elites' liberal policies. New thinkers like Paul de Lagarde railed against Jews as the "vermin" who had victimized the "poor, exploited Germans" for so many long centuries.[11]

But again something new was happening in the way Germans thought of Jews. When the French aristocrat Arthur de Gobineau, among others, began to describe Jews in the allegedly scientific terms of race, they became regarded not only as religiously or culturally different from Germans but also now as inherently so because of their inborn physical characteristics. Thus the perceived threat to Germanness was greater than ever: the mixing of Jewish and German blood through assimilation and marriage would dissipate the German race by pollution and degeneration.

Jews in the Second Reich
The cycle of liberalism and reaction revolved again in 1869 with the passage of the "Law Concerning the Equality of All Religions with Respect to Civil Rights and Citizenship" and in 1871 with the formation of the unified German state to enforce it. It was another in the long series of attempts to assimilate Jews, but as with the other attempts, it created a backlash. In so strongly inviting Jews to assimilate fully, it placed an onus on the Jews themselves to abandon their traditions and effectively acquiesce in their elimination as a people. Not going along was seen as stubborn resistance and as spurning the German people's generous and inclusive nature.[12] In fact, Jews had already been assimilating to a fairly large extent throughout the nineteenth century, but it just never was enough to convince the Germans that Jews could be like them. Daniel Goldhagen has called this and other extensions of rights to Jews a sort of probation by which rights were granted politically, with the implied proviso that Jews would either assimilate over time or at least act more German. The idea that Jews were different from Germans and alien to them was not challenged by any of the new laws.[13]

In 1873 the new nation suffered its first economic crisis, and in response the government turned to the political Right. The liberal agenda Bismarck had at first pursued was thrown overboard, and anti-Semitism became a handy cudgel for flogging political opponents. Avowedly anti-Semitic candidates began to increase in strength, and by 1893 sixteen of them had been elected to the Reichstag. As anti-Semitism gained legitimacy in politics, it did in other institutions as well. For example, the Jews' access to civil service jobs gained in the 1870s evaporated in the 1880s. Access to university professorships declined, too, though it helped if one had been baptized. The diplomatic service all but closed to Jews, and the army in 1879 barred Jews from appointments even as reserve officers. The navy had not a single Jewish officer.[14]

To Christian anti-Semitism and nationalist anti-Semitism, the Bismarck era had added political anti-Semitism. Election to public office had made Jews fair game in open political discourse, for they could now be blamed for whatever went wrong in German politics. And even at that, Jewish representation in politics was declining. This reduced participation was the result not only of increased anti-Semitism among voters but also of demographics. Jews had become so concentrated in a few urban areas that they were an insignificant presence in most districts. More than a quarter of all Germany's Jews lived in Berlin while most others were concentrated in a few other large cities. Consequently, it became nearly impossible for a Jew to get elected anywhere else. Thus by 1893 all Jewish members of the Reichstag were from large cities.[15]

By the start of World War I in 1914, the brief golden age for German Jews was over. In the previous century they had benefited from the liberal tendencies in German political and social thought, but German folkish cultural values had always exacted a cost. For each gain in rights and access Jews had had to forfeit some of their cultural identity. Germans did not acknowledge this sacrifice; in fact, the harder Jews worked toward assimilation, the more their attempts at assimilation were seen as duplicitous and sly. Further, the Germans felt it provided proof that the Jews had no culture of their own; rather, they were opportunistic parasites who were able and willing to attach themselves to any host culture in order to prosper. And in doing so they became increasingly identified with the avant-garde, the political Left, and the decline of decent German culture.

By now it was widely understood that the Jews were different and that they were fundamentally un-German. In Goldhagen's usage, anti-Semitism had become "common sense."[16] In a time when multiculturalism was as yet unknown and when celebrating diversity would have been a puzzling and alien idea, being different was dangerous. Homogeneity was viewed as the only basis on which to found a strong national community, and difference was always a threat to that desired outcome. It wasn't that Jews particularly wanted to stand out; they didn't seek to maintain a separate language or other visible signs of their uniqueness. Instead, they sought most of all to assimilate in a pluralist and secular state, keeping their customs to themselves in a society where everyone else did the same.[17] But the Germans would not have it that way. Their idea of nationhood was based on the volk, and no amount of assimilation could make a Jew fully German. By 1914, as the guns of August roared, the Jewish question had still not been satisfactorily resolved.

Weimar and the Third Reich

During the political turmoil of the Weimar era, Jews became increasingly pushed to the Left. Centrist parties were increasingly unwelcoming, and the Social Democrats were the only party to embrace them fully. Thus over time the Jews became increasingly identified with socialism. This association did not discomfit most of them much, as the socialist way of thinking was a better fit to their changing role in the economy as well as their increasing role as wage earners rather than small businessmen. As they moved to the left, they also became associated with opposition to World War I, even though they served in the war in large numbers in a last hope for full assimilation. In fact, as increasing numbers of politicians later found success in claiming that the Jews had been shirkers during the war, the military actually commissioned a "Jew count" to provide evidence. The report was suppressed when it found the opposite was true: Jewish participation in the war turned out to be disproportionately high.[18]

The Weimar Republic represented a hard swing to the Left, and on paper it seemed to promise the final liberation of German Jews. But the republic had been born of defeat, and while its liberating influence led the moderns, the urbanites, the internationalists, and the avant-garde to new heights, a deep sense of resentment and disillusionment simmered among enough others to cause persistent trouble. Jews had achieved high positions in the government, but as always, this progress was met with the opposite and more than equal backlash. Walther Rathenau, a Jewish industrialist's son, was foreign minister. He paid with his life for the privilege, assassinated by two right-wing army officers in 1922, but not before becoming the butt of a popular ditty:

> Knallt ab den Walther Rathenau
> Die gottverdammte Judensau!
> (Pick off that Walther Rathenau,
> The Goddamned Jewish sow!)[19]

The Weimar Republic offered fertile ground for populist, nationalist, and anti-Semitic political parties, including the National Socialists. The latter were not by any means an immediate success. After the aborted putsch of 1923, they had risen to only 2.6 percent of the vote in the 1928 elections, but in this election the center of German politics collapsed. Moderate parties either faded out of existence or were taken over by radical wings, left or right. A tipping point seemed to have been reached, at which it simply was futile to be a centrist. Whether one was a supporter of the Left or the Right, there was a sense that the other side had become so extreme that one had to do the same, similar to the way one might move farther out on a seesaw to keep it in balance. If one's opponents were shrill, one had to be just as shrill; if the opposition made outrageous claims, they could not be disarmed with modest ones.

Each extreme propelled the other further from reason, and the Germans bemoaned the unraveling of their nation and of the unity they had strived for so hard. It looked as though the dream of a united German people, so long in coming, was about to fall apart altogether. But now Adolf Hitler offered a way to unite all Germans under the same banner. The Far Left and Far Right could become one under National Socialism, with himself as the embodiment of the whole German volk. The party's only prerequisite was that the anti-German forces among them—principally, the Communists, various misfits and criminals, and Jews—would have to be crushed. This promise of unity was compelling, and with it the Nazis grew. In 1930 they received almost a million votes; in another election later that year 6.5 million; and in 1932, 14 million, or roughly a third of the votes cast. And as threats to the promise of unity were exaggerated, Germany became "a world intoxicated with hate, driven by paranoia, enemies everywhere, the Jew lurking behind each one."[20]

Upon accession to power in January 1933, the Nazis wasted little time in making good their promises. They began to cultivate anti-Jewish hysteria among the populace through a series of political displays and propaganda campaigns, kicked off by a national boycott of Jewish businesses in April of that year. It is not clear whether the boycott was widely approved by ordinary people, but it didn't matter. The boycott served to cement the Jews' status as outsiders, officially despised by the government. After that, all their social and political gains of the previous century were gradually retracted through a march of laws requiring compulsory retirement of Jews from the Civil Service, disbarment of lawyers, exclusion of physicians from medical associations, and prohibitions from public baths, the armed forces, intermarriage with Aryans, and eventually citizenship itself. Jews were encouraged to emigrate, and many did. Germany lost 200,000 academics, artists, scientists, and others, including twenty Nobel laureates. There were proposals to resettle those who remained in a new homeland of their own, with Madagascar considered as one possible site.

After a few years of this campaign, the public was convinced: "People who earlier would not have known what a Jew was, now blamed them for every misfortune."[21] But all the new laws, the harassment, and the sheer uncertainty about the status of Jews in Germany led to consideration of a "Final Solution" of the Jewish question. For most Germans, this phrase did not inspire the dread that it does today; rather, most people sought some sort of legal compromise or accommodation that would once and for all put an end to the street violence, the constant harangue, and the vulgar displays of anti-Semitism.[22]

The turning point came in 1938. With the annexation of Austria in March, Germany suddenly acquired 195,000 new Jews, just as it had been trying to export them. This development resulted in an anti-Semitic orgy that even many Nazi Party regulars worried was getting "out of hand."[23] It was brought to a head in November when a minor party official was murdered in Paris. The suspect was a Jew, thus presenting an opportunity for a hastily organized response against the entire German Jewish community. *Kristallnacht* (The Night of Broken Glass), the nationwide vandalism of Jewish shops, synagogues, and homes, thus marked the kickoff of a new and more vicious wave of anti-Semitic hysteria. Whether one was horrified or gratified by the display, one could no longer doubt that the Jews were the reich's enemies and could be dealt with as harshly as one liked. It was clear, too, that there was no turning back the anti-Semitic tide.

With the start of the war in 1939, Germany acquired an even larger population of Jews, and these were not the urbane Westerners the Germans were accustomed to but the bearded and shawled Polish Jews of the east. If the Nazis were to find their lebensraum for the German people in Poland and beyond, then these aliens would have to be dealt with, too. It wasn't long before the German people finally had their Final Solution to the Jewish question. In 1940 Auschwitz was chosen as the site of the first of a series of extermination camps.

AMERICAN RACISM

If German anti-Semitism was complex and changeable, American racism was more so. Since the first Europeans set foot in the New World, various

conceptions of race—color, ethnicity, religion, and others—have determined one's position in society, one's political rights, one's economic
circumstances, one's humanity. But the precise effects and meaning of
race have varied greatly, with the very rules for classifying individuals by
race changing with time. Moreover, Americans have contacted, imported,
subjugated, and incorporated an entire world of human types and groups.
Unlike the Germans, who were able to focus their issues of nationality
largely on the Jewish question, Americans have grappled with an Indian
question, an African question, an Asian question, a Hispanic question,
their own Jewish question, and a catchall immigrant question. The way
these questions have been posed and addressed constitutes one of the
central skeins of American history. That history can be divided into three
eras: the pre-racial, during which differences among people were viewed
as arising from religion, culture, or other sources; the racial, in which
biological definitions of difference were invented and imposed; and the
post-racial, which began as race became discredited as a legitimate concept
in the mid-twentieth century.

The Pre-Racial Era: 1600—1830

America's racial history begins with the first colonists. The first Africans
were imported to the Jamestown colony in 1619 to address a crisis of
starvation and a shortage of labor. The colonists themselves, according
to Howard Zinn, were generally unsuited to farming, being for the most
part either skilled craftsmen or "men of leisure" who were unaccustomed
to hard labor. Though their English heritage did not suit them to slaveholding either, they borrowed the idea from Portuguese colonists in South
America.[24] At the same time, the settlers were already in conflict with the
local Indians, at first over small thefts and insults, but often escalating
beyond reason out of fear and suspicion of each other. Revenge attacks and
counterraids became war when the local Indians decided in 1622 that the
growing settlement of exotics had to be gotten rid of once and for all, and
they massacred 347 settlers.[25] The country was thus born of ethnic contact,
competition, and conflict. A similar chronology characterized the relations
between the English Pilgrims and the Wampanoag in Massachusetts: first
cooperation, later encroachment, mistrust, raids, and finally open warfare.

But at that time neither Africans nor Indians were yet viewed as a race.
For that matter, the concept had little meaning and little utility at the time.
The colonists, like other Europeans, were accustomed to regarding various

groups and types of people as different and unequal; thus there was little need for elaborate justification. There had always been distinctions based on religion, for example; Europeans had always considered non-Christians worthy of subjugation and sometimes extermination. As for other ethnic types, the Europeans regarded Arabs, Moors, Mongols, and other exotic peoples as aliens in the deepest sense of the word and automatically saw them as potential enemies. But Europeans also considered the simple accident of birthright to be sufficient cause for relegating people to one caste or another. One was either highborn or lowborn; it was simply one's identity and could not be changed. And one's birthright was significant because the position of one's ancestors determined his legal, economic, and even moral position in the hierarchy that was European society. Whether people were inherently unequal—that is, whether their circumstances were established by biology or culture, nature or nurture—was immaterial. It was just the natural order of things. If the aristocracy itself was not imported to the New World, its ideas of inherent difference and relative worth certainly were.

Throughout the 1600s, slavery became a fixture throughout the colonies, though in relatively low concentrations. The slave population was varied and included, in addition to kidnapped Africans, a mix of opportunists, outcasts, adventurers, zealots, debtors, and laborers pressed into service by one form of coercion or another. Most slaves were indentured and not all were black. Furthermore, not all blacks were enslaved. One-third was free and had access to the legal system, and some owned property. Moreover, in none of the colonies did slavery permeate the social fabric; it was simply an economic expedient.[26]

Late in the century things began to change. Economic conditions made indenture less attractive while at the same time the price of imported Africans declined. The following hundred years saw an explosion in the black slave population. In Virginia, for example, the number of slaves increased from 3,000 to 187,000, or from 7 percent to 42 percent of the entire population.[27] A practice this widespread could no longer be viewed as a temporary or makeshift expedient; the sheer numbers of slaves required that an overall system was needed to justify and regulate the practice. In short, slavery was becoming institutionalized.

As early as 1664, a Maryland law had decreed that all slaves imported to the colony from then on would serve *durante vita* (for life). By 1700 other laws proliferated among the colonies to govern titles to slaves, their inheritance by the owners' heirs, their purchase and sale, their proper treatment, and penalties for their insubordination or escape. A dense network of customs and social expectations guided owners on the most effective use of slaves, how to judge a slave's value, and most of all, the rules of separation between slaves and their masters. Slaves had become a caste and were now mostly black.

The ubiquity of slavery as a social institution—and not just as an economic accommodation—was illustrated by the "Great Negro Plot" of 1741 in New York. Slaves constituted a full quarter of the city's population at the time, and the colonists had become increasingly edgy about their numbers. A series of suspicious fires that erupted around Manhattan only served to heighten tensions, until a handful of blacks and Catholic whites were seen leaving the scene of one of them. More than a hundred suspects were ultimately brought to trial, most of whom were banished from the colony. But what was remarkable was the barbarity of the punishments meted out to the chief suspects: roasting alive, breaking on the wheel, and hanging in the gibbet. So brutal an outburst suggests that slavery and race were such important underpinnings of social order that symbolic punishments had to be imposed for those who upset it. Their crimes were not simply regarded as arson or even murder. Indeed, because they were thought to be perpetrated by slaves, they were considered violations of the very social fabric upon which the colonists depended for their survival. The punishments were meant to terrorize blacks and reassure whites, just as the punishments for heretics had done in an earlier age.[28]

By the time of the revolution, America had been transformed into a "genuine slaveholding society."[29] Blacks had become an alien caste, different from Englishmen and other Europeans, and thought suspect or deficient in many areas. But these distinctions were still not considered biologically inherent. Race was thus far an unnecessary concept, simply being non-English or a heathen was sufficient to place a person outside the circle of humanity. But that system was about to change. By the end of the century, economic exigencies had made the South far more dependent on slaves than the North was. The 1790 census counted 757,000 blacks in the new nation, 90 percent of whom were slaves, 99 percent in the South. With the invention of the cotton gin, the demand for cotton and thus for labor exploded in the South; consequently, 100,000 more slaves were imported by 1808.[30] Slavery became the pillar upon which all of southern society was based and shaped every aspect of daily life: economics, politics, family, and religion.

Thus began of the racialization of the African American. Particularly since the new republic had been born of the lofty rhetoric of the Declaration of Independence and the Constitution, the strain between the liberal values of the Enlightenment and the vulgar reality of chattel slavery became untenable. In a triumph of legal misdirection, the strain was actually expressed in Congress and the courts as the conflict between individual freedom and the sanctity of private property. Americans of the South needed a way to rationalize the hypocrisy of slavery in a republic of God-given rights and equality before the law. The result was the gradual development and acceptance of an explicitly racist conception of the Negro as a lower species of human and not just as a culturally different alien like one of Shakespeare's Moors.

The African's racialization was accomplished in much the same way that an ideology or doctrine is developed and sold today. Some philosophers, naturalists, essayists, and ordinary cranks had doubtless been peddling racist ideas for centuries. Some probably had a modest following, perhaps within a religious or political community, but in the tenor of earlier times had not been widely accepted. Publishers, editors, professors, and other gatekeepers thought them outside the mainstream and unlikely to draw an audience. But times were different now that blackness and slavery had become synonymous. People began purchasing the racialists' pamphlets and attended their lectures. They were buying into racism because it helped them understand something they had had no need to question in the past. They wanted to hear how the experts made sense of an uncomfortably nonsensical situation.

They got what they needed. Religious thinkers, for example, used scripture to rationalize the differential position of whites and blacks. The doctrine of polygenesis—the idea that Adam and Eve were not the only original humans—was tried, but it carried the scent of heresy. A safer approach was to reckon blacks' descent from the cursed Old Testament tribe of Ham. Some simply asserted that Genesis was an account only of the white race. Where religion was too hazardous or unconvincing, phrenology was sometimes effective. One practitioner identified racial differences in thirty-five capabilities according to head contours and regions of the brain, concluding from his observations that blacks were inherently unfit for freedom.[31] All sorts of thinkers attributed all sorts of characteristics to race. Anthropologists and naturalists found a ready audience for their views both in America and abroad; even though they often reported highly specific traits that any observer might easily have refuted. A paper presented at the London Anthropological Society noted that the gray matter of the Negro brain is "of a smoky tint" with brown spots, that "the Negro frequently uses his toe as a thumb," and that he "rarely stands upright." An 1866 paper titled "The Six Species of Man" placed the Negro at the bottom of the human hierarchy, reiterating the observation that blacks were incapable of erect posture. By the 1830s scholars generally agreed that blacks were "at least a permanently inferior variety, if not a completely separate species," of human being.[32] The racial era had begun.

The Racial Era: 1830–1950

With the Civil War came not only abolition and emancipation but also a backlash. As happened later with the German Jews, emancipation came with a price, especially vicious in this case since it had been gained all at once. Legal rights ran far ahead of cultural sentiment and practice, and whites in the South sought to control the black population by violence, both legal and extralegal. As racialization became more entrenched and more severe, blacks became an untouchable caste as whites institutionalized the idea of ritual pollution. The extent of separation between the races became over time an all-encompassing mania. By the twentieth century, swimming pools, phone booths, restrooms, drinking fountains, eating establishments, shops, and transportation had become completely segregated. In Macon County, Georgia, it was actually proposed that two separate road systems be built.[33] Most important of all, segregated schools made racial inequality an unstated part of what every child learned. But these examples were only the obvious means. In Florida and North Carolina, for example, it was illegal to give white schoolkids books that had been used by black students (unlikely anyway, since whites would have had first call for them). Separation was clearly intended to symbolize inequality, but when it failed, violence filled the bill. Between 1889 and 1916 there were from 50 to 161 lynchings per year. The 1930s saw between 10 and 24 per year, and they trailed off to a handful each year thereafter until 1960.[34] These killings were usually public rituals, attended by crowds of onlookers, and the perpetrators often had their photographs taken with their trophies.

Both the segregation and the violence were aimed at maintaining a total barrier between the blood of whites and blacks through avoidance of sexual contact. Lynchings were most often motivated when the rape of a white woman was suspected, though actual rape was hardly necessary to merit the rope. As late as 1955, fourteen-year-old Emmett Till was brutally beaten to death in Mississippi just for whistling at a white woman. The suspects' hasty acquittal attests that race was the fundamental basis of southern society and was as energetically protected as religion had been during the Middle Ages. Back then, anyone who questioned its legitimacy or violated its requirements, even through mere symbolic acts, were subject to such communal rituals as burning or dismemberment. Just as the punishments of the worst deviants and criminals, these rituals reaffirmed the social order and the solidarity of the community.[35]

From all the theories that emerged about race, three themes arose that helped rationalize the unequal position of blacks. First, blacks were unqualified to participate in democratic society in any meaningful way. Because of their inherent inadequacies they could not vote judiciously or otherwise exercise a relevant political voice. Thus they could not carry out the moral, economic, or cultural obligations of citizenship. Second, whiteness was the default race, or the lack of race, of the true American. Since there was even from the beginning no cultural or geographic common identity of Americans, the common trait of whiteness was drafted as a substitute. Finally, the mixing of races weakened them both. "Race defilement" had been thought sinful on a personal level since the early colonial era, but now it was given gravity by its putative public health consequences. A weakened, mongrelized, or "creolized" race might lose the vigor needed to rule the lesser races. It would also be at the mercy of stronger peoples who might outproduce, out-navigate, or otherwise overtake the emerging white nation. A racially weak America might even be subjugated by a foreign power.

Blacks were not the only group undergoing racialization. Indians in the colonial era had been regarded with the sort of curiosity that any exotic, previously unheard-of people might engender. Sometimes an enemy, sometimes an ally, the native was considered a cultural throwback, a people who had not developed the virtues of civilization. Yet the whites uniformly regarded the Indians as people and overwhelmingly admired their physical characteristics. The Indians were considered "biologically admirable but socially abhorrent; nature had blessed them but nurture had cursed them." Color was not typically used to describe them for they were thought to be born white and colored by the sun over time. They were not yet called red men, except in reference to the markings painted on their skin.[36]

Because their shortcomings were not inherent in their nature, the common wisdom was that the Indians would sooner or later be assimilated, or culturally exterminated by Christianization, civilization, and habit. For all their perceived odious traits, among them "cannibalism, barbarism, idolatry, devil worship, brutality, lechery, indolence, and slovenliness," the Indians were thought capable of acquiring civilization with time, as any alien people might.[37] Indeed, some did seek to civilize, by taking up farming and land ownership as the principal means of their existence. For example, the Choctaws of Mississippi became successful at raising crops and livestock. Some of the New England peoples had developed elaborate governance and treaty structures.

But after a couple of centuries of uneven accommodation, conflict, and open warfare, white America gave up on Anglicizing the Indian. As the nineteenth century began, whites were frustrated and puzzled at the Indians' reluctance, overall, to give up the hunter's free life for the farmer's stolid existence. Indians also remained hostile—unaccountably, to many whites—to encroachments on their land. Further, when they did not in large numbers accept the plain and simple truth of holy scripture, it appeared that maybe they were incapable of reasonable thought in the European manner after all. Consequently, racial theories about the native cultures began to catch on. One sign was that they came to be described in terms of their skin color, most often described as "tawny" or "copper-colored."[38]

The realization that native cultures could not be eliminated by assimilation came when the United States was finding its national identity after the War of 1812. When Andrew Jackson, hero of the Battle of New Orleans, became president, he did more than centralize control over economic and monetary policy. The new doctrine of Manifest Destiny meant that the American culture and people would inexorably cut a broad swath across the continent. The judgment that the Indians were unlikely to be a part of that American culture led to the beginning of their removal. It began in the East, where pressure on land was greatest. The Choctaws were relieved of both their sovereignty and 10.5 million acres of their land. The Cherokees fared even worse: the Trail of Tears was the deadly culmination of a series of laws designed to remove them from the Southeast. In the end, they were simply snatched from their homelands and forcibly marched a thousand miles to Indian Territory in the West. The history of the other Indian peoples is much the same—a sorry litany of encroachments, conflict, short-lived treaties, removal to reservations, and often new encroachments.

The Melting Pot

Race thus became a basic ingredient of American nationalism. It was the basis for a set of tacit principles that guided the nation's political and cultural history for more than a century. These principles included the belief that the races were hierarchically arranged, that America was a white nation, and that its ruling white caste must be preserved intact and pure. These three tenets would require a good deal of effort to maintain in the face of the waves of immigration that were about to arrive, for as the United States both industrialized and opened vast expanses of farmland and resources, it invited the world's huddled masses to provide the labor.

There had always been sizable numbers of immigrants arriving in waves from one country and then another, depending on where some disaster—war or civil unrest or crop failure or religious persecution—had most lately erupted. The early arrivals had been Germans, often those sectarian Protestants who had carried Luther's reforms too far, or not far enough, or in the wrong direction. They tended to focus on cult personalities like Menno Simons or Jacob Hutter or Ulrich Zwingli, or on specific practices like infant baptism or foot washing. Rejected and harassed by both the Roman church and the Reformation, many had looked unsuccessfully for respite elsewhere in Europe but finally gave it up for a new start in the New World. Many had come during the colonial era, and most had integrated into the American fabric or else found refuge in farming communities off the beaten track.

By the middle of the nineteenth century, things were changing. The Irish famine of the 1840s, coupled with England's abysmal handling of it, drained the island of a substantial portion of its population. Many died in place, but many others migrated to Canada, the United States, or Australia. More than 1.5 million people arrived in the United States between 1841 and 1860.[39] These were not small groups of wayward European Protestants; instead, it was an invasion of Catholics, practitioners of an alien faith and obliged, it was thought, to do the bidding of a Roman potentate. Having had the poor timing to arrive in America just as Darwin was becoming popular, they were also roundly characterized as evolutionary throwbacks, possessing all the vices and inadequacies attributed to blacks: sloth, intemperance, uncleanliness, violence, and all the rest. The same

Anthropological Society of London that heard treatises on the Negro's incapacity for upright posture also heard papers on the Irishman's apelike features. The English had long cultivated these ideas, and some even referred to the Irish as "their Indians."[40]

But the Irish were not the end of the immigrants. Successive waves of Europeans—no longer northern, Protestant, and Anglo-Saxon—arrived in their turn. Italians, Poles, Serbo-Croatians, Slovaks, and Greeks were pushed from the old country or pulled to America's economic dynamo at the end of the nineteenth century. During roughly the same period, Asian peoples were arriving on the western shore. At first, a trickle of Chinese were lured away from civil strife to the land they called Gold Mountain during the same 1849 gold rush that drew so many New Englanders, Pennsylvanians, and Kentuckians. The trickle became a flood in 1865 as Charles Crocker contracted for laborers to speed up the Central Pacific Railroad's construction. By 1870 "Crocker's pets" had become 90 percent of the railroad's labor force and had swelled the Chinese population to 63,000 people. Though most had intended to return to their homeland when they had made their fortunes and when the Opium Wars and other conflicts died down, about half stayed in the United States permanently.[41]

The Chinese fared pretty well with the railroad, but when it was completed they became a glut on the California labor market. Many were able to move into tenant farming and have been credited with establishing California's agricultural industry, converting it from wheat to fruit. The rest were thrust into the bottom caste of the labor market, as threatened whites raised widespread public concern about America's growing Chinese problem. The usual negative traits—"heathen morality," savagery, lust-fulness—were attributed to them just as they had been to blacks and Indians, and political and legal initiatives played their usual part. The Chinese became officially nonwhite in a California Supreme Court case that involved the prohibition against nonwhites testifying against whites. The murderer of a Chinese man went free because his accusers were Chinese, whom the court had formally declared to be equivalent to Indians and blacks and thus without legal standing in the courts. An 1880 California law also prohibited marriage between whites and "Mongolians" as well as blacks. Newspaper editorials expressed the general opinion that California should resist being overrun by the "Chinese invasion," as President Rutherford Hayes put it.[42] The state legislature deliberated over a slew of exclusionary bills, from protections for white laborers to complete removal of "all Mongolians in the state."[43]

By 1882 the anti-Chinese drumbeat was being heard in Washington, and Congress passed the Chinese Exclusion Act, which shut off Chinese immigration for twenty years, with exceptions for certain categories of workers. President Chester Arthur vetoed it, not out of moral principle, but because it violated an earlier treaty made with the Chinese government. He requested and got a modified bill he could sign. Later the Geary Act required registration of all Chinese already residing in the country and restricted the legal rights of Chinese in the courts. Further bills narrowed the range of workers eligible for immigration. By 1898 virtually all Chinese were barred from American shores.

Toward the Post-Racial Era
Thus was the state of race and ethnicity when the twentieth century began. Since the first English colonists had arrived nearly four centuries earlier, the identification, definition, division, and relegation of peoples to statuses according to their identity had been a constant concern. The Indians had been, by turns, considered curious and exotic savages, ruthless enemies, objects of redemption and assimilation, and a broken and isolated people. Africans had been a ready source of labor, fearful heathens, articles of private property, emancipated freemen, and an oppressed caste. The Chinese had been seekers of fortune, valued laborers, inscrutable celestials, and an invading horde. The various other European, Latin American, and Asian peoples who had come to America filled much the same roles in their turn.

In 1891 the Census Bureau announced the end of the frontier, for white America had settled the West densely enough that the country now consisted of a contiguous span from sea to sea. Non-Americans—that is, nonwhite people—were mixed in either sparsely or in isolated, dense clusters, or they had become white by assimilation. The Irish, for example, were no longer the degenerate Catholic menace of half a century ago; instead, they had advanced to an annoying clan of cops, politicians, and other minor undesirables.

It was in this environment that Theodore Roosevelt sought to forge a new, modern nationalism. As seen in chapter 5, the goal of Roosevelt and other progressive and liberal thinkers of the time was to melt ethnicity and difference from the immigrant, leaving a sort of tabula rasa on which to drape the flag. The new American was supposed to be bound to his country by civic, not ethnic or clan or tribal, bonds. The rights obtaining to Americans thus came with duties as immigrants were expected to rid themselves of their ethnic identities and fully adapt to the American way of life. Any group that failed to show sufficient progress could be characterized as incapable of doing so. Moreover, the level and rate of progress thought sufficient could easily vary from one group to another, depending on the need for immigrant labor at the time of arrival, the relative similarity to the dominant English culture, U.S. foreign policy involving the home country, the group's politics, or the inclination of the group to change. The latter was especially damning, as any group could easily be labeled unwilling to become American owing to its clannish ways.

Any and all of these factors were used to marginalize one group or another as the need arose, but the rise of the eugenics movement in the 1920s introduced a new racialization of all sorts of cultural differences. By new purportedly scientific methods, the eugenics movement gained the attention and respect of Congress as it pondered an ongoing policy of restricting immigration. These policymakers came to view the world as a collection of a great many racial groups, all differentially endowed with the capacity for citizenship and thus of varying value. The concept of the degenerate race—one that had gone backward on the evolutionary path or failed to match the northern Europeans' progress—combined with fears of mongrelization gave rise to the Immigration Act of 1924. This law effectively stemmed the tide of immigration and, moreover, controlled the kinds of people who were allowed to immigrate. The act's racial quotas remained in place, with various adjustments, until the 1960s.

———

Though America harbored the first overtly racist regime, it was not the United States that fell into fascism in the twentieth century. Jim Crow did live on until the 1960s more or less intact, and successive waves of immigration provided fodder for the eugenicists and other racists. The great black migration brought sizable numbers of African Americans to the northern cities during and after World War I and with them came the explosive industrialization and urbanization of the United States, along with its concomitant social and cultural changes. Whites thought the blacks were the harbingers of those changes—which were mostly undesirable— just as the Jews were thought to be the carriers of the modern age to Germany.

By mid-century the cities of the North were already becoming black enclaves as the automobile, high-speed highways, and the postwar housing boom made the suburban life available to middle-class whites. The cities themselves declined as families and businesses found new homes in the outlying areas. Those whites left behind noted the correlation between the blacks' arrival and the erosion of the city core and concluded that the blacks were the source of the blight. Northern America settled into a kind of tacit apartheid, enforced by custom and income.

But in the South, apartheid was still the de jure variety, and it was open to challenge on the most fundamental legal and moral grounds. With the end of World War II and the horrors of the Holocaust, race had become discredited as a basis for making legal distinctions, if not social ones. In this climate, civil rights activists made visible the inconsistencies between the Constitution and local laws and customs, challenging voting barriers, segregation in public facilities, and blocked access to the courts. In the era of strong national government, the southern states found it increasingly difficult to invoke the old Federalist notions of sovereign states. The American nation had just won a world war. It was holding back the tide of Communist aggression and protecting the entire free world. It rebuilt Europe and saw a great economic boom at home. America was about to put a man into space and then on the moon. It was not the time for small rural states to claim sovereignty.

The post-racial era had begun. While racial inequality persisted in both personal attitudes and in social structures, the task for policymakers became one of reducing it or at least downplaying it, rather than justifying it as scientifically warranted. With the passage of the Civil Rights acts of 1957, 1964, and 1968, America entered a period of reforms in housing, employment, education, and nearly every other aspect of public life. Earlier African Americans had entered major league professional sports, but their token numbers now rose to equitable levels. Blacks and other people of color were seen increasingly in the public media, in positions of authority and power, and in formerly white enclaves. By the end of the century, a growing middle and affluent class of African Americans had begun to diminish residential segregation, one of the linchpins of the American caste system.[44] Interracial dating and marriage became far more common than a generation ago; 12 percent of blacks today marry outside the race. And most whites today believe the impact of the civil rights era to be positive.[45]

These changes, however, are structural. The cultural changes have followed, slowly and haltingly, often after the old law, policy, or habit was forgotten. The schools' desegregation by various means began to pay off as kids of different ethnicities felt a reduced sense of their differences. Black film stars increasingly played leading roles as detective and doctors, not as black detectives and black doctors. Over time, the Census Bureau found it increasingly difficult to reckon the race of its subjects because the American consensus on race had eroded. Black people gradually became "normal" to white America, and the same might be said of Asian Americans, Indians, and Latinos. Finally, the election of Barack Obama brought these gradual changes into sharp focus. In the face of alarming economic and foreign policy crises, most white Americans seemed simply to have forgotten about his race.

The election of an African American president did not lead to a general decline in the cultural awareness of race; rather, it was a consequence of it. My students, while mostly excited about the election's outcome, were not astonished by it. Indeed, the Obama presidency could not have happened if it were astonishing. Regarding other positions of political power, a great deal had happened even in just a few years. For instance, while President Clinton had made a great show of appointing a cabinet that "looked like America," neither President Obama nor his successors will bother to mention it. To its credit, the Bush administration continued what Clinton had trumpeted, and if there was tokenism involved, it still had the same effect.

RACISM TO FASCISM

The question remains whether racism is a necessary prerequisite to the rise of the fascist state. It is clear that anti-Semitism was a pillar of National Socialist thought and action, as discussed early in the chapter. If anti-Semitism wasn't absolutely essential to the Nazis' rise to power, it certainly was an asset. More important, anti-Semitism was deeply incorporated into all of the tenets of National Socialism. It was not simply an add-on that could get votes or that could continue to energize the base of Nazi support, as we might say today. Rather, it was completely consistent with and intertwined with the folkish nationalism of the Nazi philosophy. Jews were not part of the German volk; thus, they could not be a part of the folkish reich. They were people of the Enlightenment, wedded to the values of reason, order, and universalism, and for these reasons could neither identify with nor take part in the romantic flights of imagination and heroism upon which the German nation was to embark. The Jews were a distinctly modernist people, only too eager to abandon the past and embrace the new and the modern, which many Germans considered crass. They would inherit and thrive in a world many thought was without meaning and without values, grasping for advantage and power without direction. Finally, the Jews were of the urban, educated, and merchant classes and did not identify with the German farmer or villager. In short, they could be used to illustrate a point for any of the basic planks of the Nazi platform. Anti-Semitism served as a consistent thread that could be woven through Nazi propaganda, and it seems unlikely that they could have succeeded without it.

But while Jew-baiting and scapegoating were useful and perhaps even essential to the Nazis, it doesn't follow that racism is an inherent component of fascist regimes. Mussolini's fascist party was not anti-Semitic, having formally rejected anti-Semitism in 1931. And though a hundred thousand Italian Jews were rounded up in 1943, this action appears to have been ordered by the German occupiers, who by then controlled much of Italy. In any event, 85 percent of Italy's Jews survived the war.[46] There were also many other fascist parties and movements around Europe early in the century, but they were not uniformly founded on anti-Semitic or other racist principles.

While fascism doesn't require a racist medium in which to grow, it does require a revolutionary spirit of struggle against perceived injustices perpetrated by insidious and potent enemies. For the Germans, the Jews fitted the bill perfectly: they were generally middle class, so they could be portrayed as powerful enough to threaten the German way of life. They could be labeled "foreign" or "alien" even if they had been in the country for several generations, and they were associated with the vanguard of unwanted social change. They had been characterized as both capitalist overlords and Communist anarchists; therefore, they were beneficiaries of the two modern cultural forces that kept Germans awake at night. It was no small feat to be cast on both sides of what was viewed as the social and cultural struggle of the century, but it's not unusual for racist ideologies to contain mutually inconsistent stereotypes. Finally, at a mere 1 percent of the population, the Jews were small enough in number that most Germans didn't know any personally. They could fit whatever stereotype was needed at the moment, they could play the role of the distant other for almost all Germans, and they could ultimately be made to disappear without being missed.

What group could serve Americans in the same way? What group could be identified as the pernicious enemy that threatens to ruin all that is good about American life? In some ways, African Americans could provide such a scapegoat. They continue to be thought of as somewhat alien and resistant to assimilation by white America, never mind that this perception is almost entirely the result of white America's own exclusionary structures and practices. African Americans have been at the forefront of, and are seen as beneficiaries of, social change that is thought by many to be of dubious benefit. School desegregation, affirmative action, and a hundred other laws and structures aimed at guaranteeing civil rights or reducing the effects of discrimination—all of these are viewed with a wary eye by a sizable portion of the white community. As for culture, it's easy for whites to blame blacks for decrepitude in the arts—first jazz and blues, then rock, soul, and now rap, for example—or for the vulgar overcommercialization and brutalization of sports. The image of the African as a brute is readily projected onto millionaire athletes and hip-hop stars; at the same time they are stereotypically thought incapable of handling their fame, stardom, wealth, and other blessings of American life.

But even assuming African Americans are targets of simmering white animosity, they are simply too numerous to serve as America's scapegoat in a crisis. While Jews amounted to only 1 percent of the Nazi era's German population, blacks constitute 13 percent of Americans. And even though blacks continue to endure discrimination in most areas of life, it appears that we may be seeing the beginning of the end of America's apartheid. Some have attributed this decline in caste to the globalization of the economy and, by extension, of the culture. Today's popular culture—particularly youth culture—as expressed in fashion, music, cinema, and television, is largely multiethnic. American culture has "obliterated walls" between whites and others, and whiteness itself is evaporating as a form of identity.[47]

No, African Americans won't emerge as enemies of the American people, for they are neither alien enough nor rare enough. The same is true of Latinos, who constitute majorities or large minorities in parts of the Southwest as well as many eastern and northern urban centers. If Americans are to be persuaded to target an internal enemy, it will have to be a smaller group, one that is visible yet rare enough so that most Americans will not have had a great deal of interaction with its members. It should also be a group with some economic position; not so downtrodden that they pose no threat to the majority of Americans or to American values. It should be a group that exists in sizable numbers outside the United States, such that they can be accused of loyalty to an external government or movement.

And it should be a group that can be viewed as both alien to and a threat to core American values.

The most obvious choice is Muslim Americans. There is considerable dispute regarding their numbers in the United States, since questions on religion are by law not asked in the U.S. Census. The most systematic attempt to measure their numbers is the American Religious Identification Survey, which estimated the Muslim population in 2001 at just 1.1 million people. Although less than 0.5 percent of the American population, this number was double the measure taken just a decade previously.[48] Islam can also be easily linked not only with terrorist attacks on American targets but also with a worldwide movement against the globalization of Western culture. This connection amounts to a conspiracy that opposes the very core of American values—progress, individualism, modernism, and enterprise—that the fundamentalist wing of the Muslim world consider sinful. On the one hand, this group will not be poor enough to gather sympathy from the general public; on the other hand, for the foreseeable future there will be sufficient new immigrants to be perceived as benefiting from what remains of the American welfare system. In all, Muslims possess an essential characteristic of all scapegoated people: they can be made to appear strong even as they are weak. Equating Islam with terrorism makes every Muslim a larger-than-life potential threat even while the Muslim community's economic and political power is fairly small.

The continuing wars against Muslims—if not against Islam itself—adds to other suspicions the potential for the sort of irrational stigma that was applied to Japanese Americans during World War II. And as long as the Muslim world's most recognized spokesmen are Osama bin Laden and Mahmoud Ahmadinejad, it will be difficult for Americans to decouple Islam from terrorism. This would be especially so if an aggressive American administration finds it useful to fan the flames, or if another terrorist attack strikes the United States.

Americans have generally been quite tolerant of religious difference per se. But when combined with foreignness, as in the case of the Catholic mobs that arrived from Ireland and later from southern and eastern Europe, religion can become a potent symbol of difference and a rationalization for discrimination. In fact, religion itself could be irrelevant, giving way to ethnic identity symbolized by wearing the chador and other traditional garb, by adhering to prayer and other rituals in public, and by generally resisting assimilation or even encouraging a resurgence of traditional ways.

In this case, Muslims will be subject to the same probationary tolerance that was shown the German Jews—that is, a legal and social acceptance coupled with the demand for complete Americanization. Some will comply, some will fall short, and some will resist. Those who fail could readily become potential targets of private, and possibly public, wrath.

Despite the extent of structured inequality among races in America, and despite the subsurface resentment whites harbor toward African Americans as well as immigrants and other people of color, it seems unlikely that race per se would be invoked intensively by a fascist regime. Race just isn't the useful construct that it used to be. Hitler and the Nazis did humankind one service anyway, in forever making it a disreputable notion. Americans will instead draw on different "others" when crisis demands an accounting of who is to blame. These people will consist of one or more of the usual suspects—a religious minority, the avant-garde, or one of a growing host of foreign enemies—who will help create the "us against the world" mentality on which fascism feeds.

__7__

AUTHORITARIANISM

IN 1961 A YALE PSYCHOLOGIST NAMED Stanley Milgram set out to see whether a German penchant for obedience could explain the rise of the National Socialists and the ensuing fall into totalitarianism, war, genocide, and ruin. His intent was to compare Germans with people of other cultures in terms of their willingness to follow orders, even when those orders were morally odious.

He established a baseline using American subjects. He contrived an experiment by which subjects would be cast in the role of "teachers" who monitored "learners" as they tried to memorize pairs of words. Each time a learner failed to remember a word pair, the teacher was required to administer an electric shock as a negative reinforcement. The shock was to be increased with each error and could go up to what seemed to be a lethal level. The teachers were unaware that the learner was always the researcher's confederate, a professional actor making errors according to plan, and that no actual shocks were delivered.

Expecting that most teachers would refuse to administer the punishment as soon as it became apparent that the learner was suffering, Milgram was stunned to find that fully half the subjects continued to administer shocks all the way up the scale to the maximum voltage. The confederate learner by that time had screamed, begged to be released, and finally ceased responding altogether. It appeared that for many teachers, simply nothing could prick their consciences enough to stop tormenting their fellow humans. Milgram never got around to studying the Germans. He had already learned that many people, Americans included, had the capacity for following the dictates of a morally questionable authority.

Milgram was just one of many scholars who reacted to the Third Reich with research seeking to explain how and why people could be made to support such a criminal regime and to participate in its crimes themselves. Even before World War II ended, scholars had taken up the question of how National Socialism and other forms of totalitarianism could have taken root in the technologically and socially advanced twentieth century. Erich Fromm had raised the question in 1941, observing that the modern age and its freedoms had removed many of the comforting constraints of the past; instead, in times of crisis and uncertainty, people sought an "escape from freedom" in authoritarian political regimes.[1] In 1950 Theodor Adorno and his colleagues had explored with several associates the possibility that there might be an authoritarian personality type that could account for the rise of fascism in Germany. Using psychometric techniques that were advanced for the time, they found that certain kinds of beliefs and values seemed to occur together in individuals, creating a syndrome of personality traits. This authoritarian type tended to show overly rigid respect for convention and authority, of course, but at the same time exhibited a tendency to believe in mysterious forces or secret conspiracies that control things. They admired toughness and rigidity and detested tenderness or imaginative thinking. They tended also to have an exaggerated concern with controlling sexuality and other pleasures.[2]

Such a personality type's predominance in a society would seem to go a long way toward explaining why Germans might respond to crisis by seeking an authoritarian leader or accepting an authoritarian regime. It's not hard to see that this personality type would be more accepting of the National Socialist view of the world and that the founding members of the party itself would be disproportionately composed of such types. After all, the Nazis promised strict enforcement of convention and harsh punishment for violators. They also promoted aggression in the pursuit of German ideals and inculcated militaristic toughness in German youth through the schools and youth associations, especially the Hitler Youth. And of course, the shadowy international Jewish conspiracy was their bread and butter.

But there were two problems with this psychological approach to understanding the rise of authoritarian regimes. The first was that if differences were found between Germans and other peoples, this discovery would only raise a further question: how had these differences been created? Why might Germans be more psychologically predisposed to obedience than, say, Americans? In fact, many researchers looked for answers to this

question, hypothesizing that rigid gender roles, patriarchal family structure, strict discipline of children, or some other characteristic of German
life might account for such a difference. It turned out that research
findings did not bear any of these hypotheses out.[3] This approach was
essentially a dead end anyway, because even if these characteristics were
instrumental in producing authoritarian people, it would only point away
from the personality type and toward the culture in which the personality
was formed. Put another way, the authoritarian personality was just the
product of an authoritarian culture, and it might be just as well to forget
about the idea of a German personality type entirely and instead examine
German cultural values and norms as the source of German obedience.

The second problem was that authoritarian types were not much
more common in Germany than in America, as Milgram's work and later
research showed.[4] So why had Germany succumbed to the appeals of
National Socialism while countries like France, England, and the United
States had not? Why had the Germans acquiesced to genocide of their
fellow citizens? What was different about them?

OBEDIENCE AND AUTHORITY

Though the psychological approach was unhelpful in distinguishing
between the Germans' and Americans' behavior, Milgram's social-psycho-
logical orientation made a genuine breakthrough by asking how the
personality could be overridden by social situations and cultural values.
His obedience studies are now part of the common cultural knowledge
of Americans, and they offer profound insights into why human beings
succumb to authority. But these insights are available only if one goes
beyond superficial interpretations of the results. On learning about
the study most people conclude that it demonstrates how people fail to
engage their moral conscience in obeying authority. This conclusion is
understandable, especially since it gives people a reason to claim that they
would not behave in the same way, living as they do in a better-educated,
more sophisticated age. Daniel Goldhagen gave Milgram's work just a few
sentences in his 631-page opus, concluding that the study failed to show
that people obey blindly.[5] But the "blind obedience" interpretation misses
the point. Milgram's own documentary film of the experiment makes it
clear that the teachers—the ones administering the electric shocks—are
anything but blind or unthinking. They protest, they beg the experimenter
to let them stop, and they develop strategies for minimizing their guilt

(pressing the buttons for the shortest possible duration, coaching the learner, and the like). Many of them repeatedly refuse to continue, but when told the experiment will be ruined, they reluctantly go on.

So what makes them continue? The experimental environment gives a few clues. It is conducted in an isolated set of rooms, removed from the familiar world of most people. The experimenter is dressed in a white lab coat and speaks with academic precision and coldness. The subject has already been paid for his or her participation and told that "no matter what happens, the money is yours." The role of teacher or learner is determined by an apparently fair draw of lots. Finally, when subjects object to going further with administering shocks, the experimenter accepts full responsibility for the learner's welfare and safety.

Thus the subject is placed not in a situation of simple obedience to authority but in a complex and ambiguous moral quandary. First, he has accepted payment for a task and feels obligated to perform. Many subjects actually try to give the money back as a means of escaping, but the experimenter refuses to take it. Second, he has been given responsibility for correctly performing a task that will allegedly advance the cause of science and human knowledge, and it is strongly implied that reneging will set that cause back in a substantial way. Third, the subject is aware that he himself could have been receiving the shocks, and he would like to think he could endure them if that were his lot. In short, the experiment presents a situation in which doing the wrong thing feels very much like doing the right thing.[6]

In the 1980s Bob Altemeyer went a step further in connecting the authoritarian personality to the community in which it is produced. In defining what he came to call "right-wing authoritarianism," he condensed the relevant findings of his own and previous work into a few critical elements. The right-wing authoritarian is characterized, as he put it, by

- submission to authority that is perceived as legitimate
- authoritarian aggression, believed to be sanctioned
- high adherence to social conventions endorsed by authorities[7]

This description is notable not only for its informative definition of personality traits but also for its inclusion of distinctly social and cultural elements. The authoritarian type, according to this definition, submits to authority that he or she perceives as legitimate. He or she takes out aggression under the assumption that it is sanctioned. He or she rigidly conforms to conventions that are endorsed by authorities. On close examination, it appears that authoritarianism is not a matter of personality but of social structure. That is, in societies where aggression is sanctioned, authority is legitimated, and the regime takes efforts to endorse conventions, one might expect to find a great deal of obedience. In societies whose institutions don't reinforce these assumptions, obedience to authority is less rigid.

In fact, Milgram's work itself had shown that these social structural factors—legitimacy of authority, social sanctioning of aggression, endorsement of convention—are the most important elements in creating obedience in subjects and, by extension, in citizens. He made this conclusion all the more clear by replicating the experiment under a variety of conditions: changing the physical settings, varying the closeness of the contact between teacher and learner, and scripting different instructions from the experimenter himself. These variations had at least as much effect upon the outcomes as did the personality variations of the subjects, strongly suggesting that the social context has as strong an influence over moral choices as do the individual's personal traits. But this finding can't be surprising for it is demonstrated time and again by police officers, by prison guards, and especially, by soldiers. It takes only a few months' training to transform the average nineteen-year-old into a combat-ready soldier and only a few encounters with the enemy to render the act of killing commonplace.

The subjects in Milgram's study obeyed not because they were personally disposed to follow orders but because they perceived those orders as legitimate. More important, the authority of the researcher lay not in a crude power to coerce or in some magical charisma but in the subject's faith in the organizational and institutional system in which he operated. Surely the experimenter would not let a man die from these shocks just for an experiment. Surely Yale would not have such a madman on its faculty. Surely everyone must know what they are doing. In short, the subjects went along not out of obedience to authority but out of trust in the social system that legitimates it.[8]

This observation is the key to understanding Milgram's findings, as well as to understanding human obedience to authority in real-world contexts. People commit evil, or acquiesce as others do it in their name, when it is sanctioned and legitimated by the community in which they belong. They endorse war on enemies and punishment of criminals if the enemies seem real and the criminals are found guilty by some process perceived as legitimate. And under the right circumstances they will follow their government over a cliff, as the Germans did during the Third Reich.

GERMAN OBEDIENCE

The question of German obedience thus becomes a question about how the National Socialists could exploit an authoritarian German culture to gain votes during its rise to political power and, later, to marginalize and silence opposing voices. Though the tradition of research on the authoritarian personality finds little difference between Germans and Americans, those familiar with the two cultures consistently report clear and apparent distinctions in their values and norms, often noted by ethnographic or anecdotal methods. Moreover, casual travelers to Germany are often struck by myriad small culture shocks that seem to add up to Germans' greater tendency to follow rules and, very possibly, to their greater acceptance of authoritarian government. And though tourists are prone to stereotyping the peoples they encounter based on scant experience and observation, they do tend to have a heightened sense of awareness of cultural expectations brought on by newfound difficulties in catching a bus or ordering lunch. If Germans are neither inherently more authoritarian as measured by psychological scales nor more inclined to inflict pain on victims as implied by Milgram's experiments, there seems to be a fair amount of agreement that German cultural values emphasize certain forms of obedience and conformity even in the present day.

Ordnung Muss Sein

The most pronounced—but also possibly the easiest to overemphasize in one's everyday encounters with German society—is the German insistence that "there must be order" (*Ordnung muss sein*). Stability, organization, regularity, and clarity of expectations seem highly prized in both personal and public life. The trains really do run on time, remarkably so given the density of traffic and the complexity of the system. Bike lanes are verboten to pedestrians, and escalator etiquette (stand to right, pass on left) is observed punctiliously. Housing codes require that new homes be built in a style harmonious with the neighborhood. Workers in many trades are required to register with the authorities in order to practice their occupation. Changes of address are similarly registered; thus, the police always know where you can be found. Even baby names are subject to approval by local authorities so as to conform to acceptable standards. It does not take long for the American observer to conclude that in Germany, the individual is expected to conform to the state's restrictions. By extension, the Germans seem particularly suited to submission to the state.[9]

But this conclusion is based on at least a partial misinterpretation of the facts. German obedience to rules is as much a ritual of solidarity with one another—with their Germanness—as it is conformity to externally imposed rules. Each act of compliance is a gesture to one's fellow citizens and a sign of respect for one's community. It follows that noncompliance is a sign of disrespect for all, and so Germans are only too happy to enforce the rules themselves when they see a violation of some norm or convention. One anecdote depicts a German car needing a wash. Instead of writing in the dust the simple American "Wash me," someone had traced on its rear window "Der Zustand des Autos läßt auf den Zustand Ihres Geistes schließen" [The condition of your car says a lot about the condition of your mind].[10] On a recent visit to Germany, one of my students was scolded in the middle of a Nuremberg street by a German man for her poor use of the *English* language: "You have just used the word 'like' five times in one sentence!"

When dealing with neighbors or other familiars, Germans seem quick to call on the authorities to enforce the rules. This propensity might be a way of avoiding confrontation with those one has to live among, though an American might call it passive-aggressiveness. Thus a neighbor mowing his lawn on Sunday or making too much noise in the evening might be reported to the police rather than confronted directly. Even trivial disputes in public (arguments over a parking space, for example) can result in a call to the *polizei*. And where necessary, Germans readily bring their grievances to court. One annoyed citizen sued the tennis club next door over some encroachment on his quietude, even though he was himself a member.

Many have noted with puzzlement one apparently glaring exception to the ordnung ideal—the mad sprint of the autobahn—but even this may not be as contrary to good German order as it seems. The absence of speed limits is a shock to American drivers, especially in a country that so venerates rules and their enforcement. But they misinterpret the German view. The autobahn's high speeds are possible only *because* drivers are expected to rigidly obey the more fundamental rules of the road—that is, keeping strictly to the right except to pass, maintaining a minimum speed so as not to create bottlenecks, zero-tolerance enforcement of speed limits where posted, and so on. The penalties for infractions are severe; for example, driving under the influence can result in revocation of one's license on the first offense. German cars shun the cup holders and other accoutrements of home for their drivers do not engage in multitasking. Moreover, qualifying for a driver's license is a more rigorous process in Germany than in the United States, requiring many hours of professional training and high fees.

Finally, both the autobahn and the vehicles that use it are maintained at a high level. Roadworthiness inspections for cars and trucks are meticulous; even rust spots can disqualify a vehicle. The roadway itself is built to a very high standard—double the thickness of an American interstate, for example—and groomed such that a driver can have confidence that a pothole or frost heave won't endanger his 120 mile-per-hour reverie. In short, the German motorist is able to trust the social institutions that govern road safety in a way that Americans cannot, and a high-speed *fahrt* on the autobahn is more a celebration of good German order than an escape from it.

The ordnung ideal is a central component of German culture, but it is not a simple pattern of blind obedience to authority. Far more than Americans, Germans view the community—local and national—as a source of, rather than a barrier to, self-actualization. Holding one another to seemingly trivial rules of comportment is an ongoing ritual of solidarity and of the individual's respect for the community. Sublimating one's individual prerogatives to community standards and state approval is a way of acknowledging mutual interdependence while ensuring relative peace and stability—something the Germans may reasonably claim to have had too little of over the years.

The primacy of the community over the individual and of the individual's obligation to that community has deep roots in German history and culture. Germany was the first nation to have a national health care system, which Bismarck devised not long after unification. And after World War II, the West German Parliament passed the Equalization of Burdens Law, which required those who had escaped major financial losses from the war to give up half the value of their postwar assets, payable in thirty-year installments, to assist refugees.[11] Individualism of the sort Americans revere is not a major theme in German culture. Aside from the rare hero, there is little in German myth of the individual rejecting convention and making his own way. Germans never had a wild frontier, no Manifest Destiny (until, of course, the abortive quest for lebensraum in Poland and Russia), no history of people striking out on their own in a land boom or gold rush. There's little immigration and assimilation of other cultures. For Germans, the main problem has been to bring Germans together in a German nation centered around German ideals and values. The sublimation of the individual to that community and to those values has thus retained a deep significance to the German mind.

Inside and Outside

Germans also make rigid distinctions between in-group members and those outside the group, and on many levels. There is, of course, the concern with Germanness and the German identity on a national scale. Even today it is very difficult for immigrants to acquire German citizenship; consequently, several generations of German-born people of Turkish descent remain *Gasterbeiters* (guest workers) and until recently were ineligible for citizenship except in a few cases. At the other extreme of social interaction—the intimate world of the home and family—Germans maintain a strong barrier to penetration by outsiders. An invitation to a German's home can be a highly significant overture to a deeper social relationship, and it tends to be a fairly formal occasion. Neighbors and work associates seldom socialize in this way.

At the intermediate levels, between the nation and the home, the Germans devise myriad ways to belong to associations, clubs, and other communities. The rise of musical groups discussed in chapter 5 is but one example among many others: shooting clubs, *Landschutzen* (amateur local defense societies), hiking societies, philosophical groups, and the array of similar hobby and interest societies. On a more informal level, one will find in many bars and restaurants a *stammtisch*, a table reserved for groups of regular customers. What's significant about the stammtisch is that the stammtisch sign on it invokes a whole set of social norms and judgments involving whether one's party is "regular" enough to claim it. The process of making these judgments, even among those who conclude they are not stammtisch worthy, reinforces feelings of belonging and consensus among those who are able to make the correct decision.

It is the association, the stammtisch, the hobby club, or the singing society that fills the German's need to belong and to connect with others on a personal but non-intimate basis in German society. If neighbors and coworkers are held at arm's length, then these associations are the loose bonds that offer Germans an ongoing personal connection with the larger community. It is no mere coincidence that a German sociologist, Ferdinand Tönnies, described the distinction between *Gemeinschaft* and *Gesellschaft*, or the personal involvement in the community and the more distant connection of the individual and society, respectively.

Ordnung, Obedience, and National Socialism

As discussed in previous chapters, Hitler and the Nazis gained power on a combination of appeals to German values: romanticism, nationalism, populism, racism. But in many ways, all of those themes are manifestations of the overarching concern for the unification of the German people into one community. The racist appeal defined Germans and created a boundary against those who threatened Germanness while the populist appeal equalized all German people and pitted them against those who would divide them into social or economic classes. The nationalist appeal tapped the deep yearning for a unified volk and promised to deliver it against all enemy forces. Finally, the romantic appeal set the stage for all the others by preparing the German mind to think "outside the box," to accept the mystical, to imagine the impossible, and to act boldly to realize them.

These themes were wrapped into a coherent package when Hitler promised to restore German order—the sort of order enjoyed before the Weimar era's cultural exuberance and uncertainty—by crushing the Communists, removing Jewish influence in German society, and controlling artistic expression. The Nazis also constantly overemphasized the "crime wave" that had beset Germany and boasted of their harsh methods for dealing with it. Their "lock 'em up and throw away the key" approach was well received.[12] At the same time, they complained that too many people had been pioneering new lifestyles, "Americanism" was invading culture as well as commerce, economic life was uncertain, and the nation that had taken so long to forge was in danger of dissolution. Never mind that the Nazis themselves had played a large part in exacerbating the Weimar Republic's political instability by agitating and harassing opponents or by routinely and systematically disrupting parliamentary debates. Hitler promised that if his party could achieve legitimate power, it would restore the good German order that the good German people deserved.

They did so through a variety of mechanisms and principles. Even before taking the chancellorship, the Nazis had instituted the *Winterhilfe* (Winter Aid program), which cemented the principle of a shared German community as a part of Nazi ideology. It also helped the party establish credibility as an orderly and organized institution capable of governing, and not just a mob of goons. Upon accession to power, the regime consolidated Germany's various unions into a single, national German Labor Front. Uniting all workers, of both hand and mind, into a single group further symbolized the end of partisanship and division in a zero-sum game. All Germans would henceforth prosper together or wither together.

The Nazis endeavored at all times to legitimate their power so as to reinforce the idea that they were restoring order rather than dismantling it. The Enabling Act was a brilliant example: the duly constituted legislative authority of the Reichstag enacted, in a legal and orderly way, the policy of dictatorial rule by one man. Autocracy was legitimated by democratic process. When Hitler combined the presidency with the chancellorship into the single role of führer after Hindenburg's death, he subjected the act to popular vote just to give it a legal imprimatur.

What, then, was the nature of German obedience during the reich? It was rooted in a sense of threat to the community, whose members were ready to take radical action to protect that community. They would give up their personal freedom and security, and even more readily give up the freedom and security of others, to protect it. Just as citizens were willing to call the police to report a neighbor working on the Sabbath, they would also readily report neighbors they suspected of being Communists, of speaking against the state, or of harboring Jews. They would burn books and accept the censorship of un-German films or insist that it wasn't really censorship at all. They would acquiesce in the state's control of the arts. They would stand by and pretend not to notice the disappearance of Jews and other undesirables from their cities. In a period of intense crisis, which the regime itself sustained by going to war, they were willing to sacrifice all for the perpetuation of the German state. They were willing, in short, to oppress themselves.

ARE AMERICANS OBEDIENT?

The German penchants for order and a sense of community might help explain why Germany, rather than other nations undergoing great crises early in the twentieth century, succumbed to the appeals of Hitler and the Nazis. But can the same be said of Americans? If these cultural traits led Germans over the cliff in the first half of the twentieth century, do Americans have similar traits that might, when conditions are right, cause them to do the same?

The evidence is not simply mixed; it is fundamentally ambivalent. On the one hand, Americans have a history since the nation's beginning of fierce individualism and of resistance to authority. The national mythology is replete with challenges to every social institution—state, family, church, school—and Americans tell and retell the stories of dissidents and rebels.[13] One of the abiding national myths is the revolution against the English mother country—the most powerful empire of its day—which gave birth to the nation itself. And viewed from this perspective, we have been a nation of rebels ever since, from the Shays and Whiskey rebellions, to slave revolts and the Underground Railroad, to the abolition movement and John Brown's insurrection, and to the Civil War itself. More recent social and cultural movements have also challenged popular convention if not the authority of the state: a variety of populist and labor movements; women's suffrage; Prohibition; religious and utopian revolutions like those of the Quakers, Shakers, Amish, Latter-day Saints, and a slew of communal experiments in the sixties; the counterculture movement of the Vietnam era; gay pride; and dozens of other departures from what was considered normal at the time.

But though these challenges to authority are often taken as cherished examples of American independence of thought, our memories are selective. The episodes of defiance that we remember tend to be either movements that succeeded or ones that occurred in the distant past. It's easy to forget how strenuously the majority of Americans resisted most of them, both through acquiescence in state suppression and through public marginalization. Popular and official reactions to abolitionists, Mormons, suffragists and their granddaughters in the modern women's movement, early labor agitators, civil rights activists, gay activists, and antiwar protestors have ranged from disdainful to murderous. As for those movements that failed, schoolkids don't celebrate Eugene Debs's birthday or observe the National Organization for the Reform of Marijuana Laws (NORML) week.

It is true that Americans have not hesitated to defy authority when they found it necessary, but they also have been astonishingly conformist and willing to acquiesce in their own oppression when faced with uncertainty and threats. Even the most revered acts of resistance to authority—women's suffrage, civil rights, and many other movements—usually brought negative reactions from fellow citizens who viewed the causes as un-American, immoral, sinful, or just weird. Clearly, the question of whether Americans are conformists or rebels is a complex and ambiguous one. How can we be both?

The Obedient-Rebellious Americans

One possible explanation for Americans' ambivalence is that the right to rebel and pursue one's agenda is an integral part of the individualist ideal while the right to defend one's own opposing agenda is similarly valued. While passions have often run high in many of these conflicts over cultural values and social policy, citizens have generally been willing to air the dispute in the streets, in the courts, in Congress and the legislatures, or in the rhetoric of a political campaign and to see who wins the day. In a sense, Americans seem genuinely to believe in the right to dissent, though they also show little hesitation to crush the dissenters with all available means.

Unlike the Germans, then, Americans view the world of values and ideals as a kind of free-for-all in which everyone has a right to advance his or her interests rather than as a forum in which the common interest is hammered out. Americans expect cultural change, even if it is not welcomed. While old-timers or other cultural conservatives might yearn for the past— whether it is a racially comfortable past, or a sexually unambiguous one, or a male-dominated one, or something else—they recognize and accept that change is inevitable. "That's progress," they say, and they might either yield to change or plot the next counterattack in the culture wars to be launched when political or social circumstances allow.

American obedience-rebelliousness is also a frank pursuit of self-interest or, put in more noble terms, the pursuit of happiness. That sentiment, so deeply institutionalized in the American value system, clearly implies an inherently pluralist society that is structured in such a way that everyone can define for themselves what is most valued and pursue it with little regard for the sensibilities of others. To call this tolerance of dissent would be misleading; a better characterization would be a contest among interests. It is the ultimate democracy of ideas, but this description also implies acceptance of tyranny of the majority or of those with the cultural clout to make their values stick.

In a sense, then, Americans find a sort of consensus on the core value of dissension, the raw conflict of ideas in an open market. If all points of view are not equal, they have an equal opportunity to be heard. If they are bad, immoral, or un-American ideas, they are fair game to be dispatched by any rhetorical or political means necessary. In this way, Americans can tolerate expression even as they crush unorthodox thought by the most defamatory and even violent methods.

A second explanation for Americans' tendency toward both authoritarianism and dissent is that their level of authoritarianism varies in several ways. A sizable body of research shows that authoritarian views vary not only by social class but also by gender, age, and a host of idiosyncratic factors, including one's profession and major area of study in college.[14] But more important, their endorsement of authoritarian values has varied greatly over time, principally according to the level of threat to the society or even to levels of personal stress. In times of economic stability and quiescent international relations, the overall level of authoritarianism declines; conversely, in times of rapid cultural change, recession, or especially, war, it increases.[15] Overall, the findings confirm Fromm's original claim that people respond to uncertainty by seeking authoritarian solutions to problems in an escape from freedom. Such threat effects can be surprisingly immediate. For example, according to national survey data, the September 11 attacks created a spike in authoritarian feeling among Americans, but another study based on an examination of letters to the editor showed a more complex effect—that is, an increase in both authoritarian and antiauthoritarian views.[16]

Whatever the level of authoritarianism at a given time, it does influence people's behavior. For one thing, during threatening times, Americans tend to elect presidential candidates who are perceived as strong or powerful leaders, and this tendency has been true since the early nineteenth century.[17] Thus President Bush's 2004 reelection campaign rested almost entirely on cultivating his image as a strong leader, even if that meant promoting policies that were inconsistent with party ideology or, for that matter, the Constitution.

A third explanation for the dual obedient-rebellious character of Americans is that there has been a long-term change in the very way Americans view the individual's relationship to society. Irene Taviss Thomson examined the contents of magazines, self-help books, and social science literature and observed a shift in the way this relationship is viewed. It has gone from one of conflict—the individual versus society—to one of embedment in which the individual depends on society. From the early twentieth century to the 1960s, the individual was most often seen as struggling against social control either as a self-indulgent egoist in need of moral restraint or as an innocent free spirit subjugated by convention and conformity. This individual-versus-society view began to change in the 1970s as a more complex view emerged. Conformity came to be viewed as something helpful and empowering for the individual. The individual was still viewed as most important, but the self could only be completely fulfilled by a commitment to the larger community. Alienation became the principal problem, and narcissism was its personal manifestation. Pitting the individual against society was a "false dichotomy," and the "rugged individualist" gave way to the "relational self."[18]

This view sounds similar to the German model of the individual in which one's essential humanity can only be fully realized within the context and the constraints of a larger community. Rampant individualism is alienating and narcissistic; being part of something larger is the way to fulfillment. And the emergence of the new embedded self has corresponded to the growth in various intermediate-level communities and subcultures to which the individual could belong: newfound ethnic identities, support groups for sufferers of various diseases, recovery groups, new religious communities. This search for gemeinschaft was not so different from the musical society and stammtisch of German life.

SYNTHESIS: CULTURE, PERSONALITY, AND HISTORY

The question of whether Americans are as authoritarian as Germans may be impossible to determine. Americans are both obedient and rebellious, both authoritarian and tolerant, individualists who long for community. American culture may simply be more complex than others are, given its history of immigration and cultural mixing, both voluntary and involuntary, which has characterized the nation's history. The distinct pluralism of American society, divided by any number of ethnic, socioeconomic, gender, generational, and regional identities, suggests that there is likely to be a good deal of difference on fundamental values and on how they are interpreted. Every American may agree that personal freedom is a bedrock of the American creed, but there are distinct differences in how that freedom is construed between the rich and the poor, men and women, blacks and whites, Christians and Muslims, and so on.

Such pluralism makes it easier for Americans to live with contradictory values. We embrace both personal freedom and strong community spirit. We are generous, yet we hate taxes. We are patriotic yet suspicious of government. We revere the Bill of Rights but often complain when it is invoked. We believe in equality but strive mightily to acquire symbols of status. Of course, none of the exceptions noted here are true of all Americans—not everyone hates taxes or chases after status—but that is the point: American values are fluid and dependent on historical circumstance and one's social position and identity.

We know Americans score about as high on psychological measures of authoritarianism as Germans do, but these scores vary by social class, age, and numerous other social categories. More important, they vary from time to time, depending on the level of threat people feel not only to the nation but also to their own personal well-being. This fluctuation suggests the possibility that authoritarianism as a psychological construct, or even as a relatively stable cultural one, may be a useless idea. If it can vary so widely among people within a culture and be influenced so quickly by historical events, does it explain anything at all?

It does, but only if we accept that the level of authoritarianism is neither constant across time nor uniform across the society. The level of authoritarianism in a society depends on a relationship among several forces: the society's culture, the personalities of the people socialized within and by that culture, and the historical forces that impinge on it. This relationship is complex because each of the three forces is both cause and effect of the other two. A culture in which respecting authority is a source of social cohesion will produce people who respect authority. And when such a people finds itself in national crisis, they will seek out leaders who can best make the case that sublimating one's own liberties is the solution.

Though the personalities of Americans are no less authoritarian than Germans' personalities are, it does seem true that American culture does not accord the same degree of authority to social and political institutions that German culture does. But Americans' hesitation to follow leaders may be a matter of historical circumstance—the degree to which Americans feel a threat to the social order and to their material interests. As will be seen in chapter 8, Americans in times of war are as rabid a bunch of conformists as anyone, all too willing to censor their own doubts or have them censored, and to turn their backs on fellow humans and even fellow citizens in the name of a rigid orthodoxy, which is usually whatever orthodoxy the political administration has endorsed. But it is not necessary that such threats rise to the level of all-out war to instigate public obedience and self-repression. Americans have gone along with all sorts of compromises of and outright assaults on the Constitution in suppressing labor unions, religious cults, civil rights activists, and aliens.

Gradualism and the Evolution of Consent
The sort of obedience the Germans in the Third Reich displayed was made possible by a perfect conjunction of history and culture. A deep sense of crisis and malaise, the inherent weakness of the Weimar government, a people who were culturally predisposed to seek order and to legitimate whatever regime could restore it, and an opportunistic leadership—all of these combined to create an atmosphere of desperate obedience among enough Germans to submerge the worriers and silence the dissenters.

But though the descent into fascism happened quickly, it did not happen all at once. It took the Nazis longer than a decade to seize the reins of the German state, and a good deal of trial-and-error was involved. Hitler miscalculated early with the Munich putsch; it drove the party underground and earned him a prison term. But as with so many of Hitler's miscalculations, the putsch also brought long-term benefits. His trial gave him a national platform for his undisputed oratory skill, and it also brought a certain legitimacy to the right-wing leanings of the judiciary. The token sentence it meted out gave legal sanction to the Nazis' platform and was widely approved by the public. And Hitler's imprisonment resembled a sabbatical leave: he got the chance to sit down in peace and quiet with a few colleagues, sort things out, do a little writing. *Mein Kampf* was the result, and with Hitler's release nine months later (although the crime nominally carried a life sentence), the party was off to a fresh start.

Hitler had learned that despite the instability of the Weimar government, a revolutionary takeover was not the way to go. Instead, he told the party faithful that they would have to "hold their noses" and seek power through the electoral process. The ensuing decade saw the Nazis feverishly organizing, fund-raising, campaigning, and reorganizing. They became a national party and ran candidates for Reichstag seats in most districts of the country. Their success came in fits and starts. A particular issue or theme might reap rewards in Franconia in one election; a few years later a seat might be gained in Saxony on some other appeal. There were sudden surges of popularity and disappointing reversals, too.[19]

Even after their accession to power, the Nazis had to be careful. Hitler had become chancellor, but he was an inexperienced outsider who was only nominally in charge of a fragile coalition that he had not forged. Moreover, the country was in turmoil, and previous governments, even though they were led by experienced and sober politicians, had not remedied the situation. His best hope was to try to unite the country politically as best he could by silencing opposition while developing a strong base of support.

Hitler and the Nazis moved quickly under an atmosphere of crisis, partly real and partly fabricated. Less than a month after taking the chancellorship, Hitler swore in forty thousand SA and SS men as auxiliary police in an extravagant display of his intent to restore "good German order." A few days later the Reichstag burned and offered the Nazis an opportunity to heighten the sense of crisis and fear. The Communists were blamed for the fire, and the following day the Nazi government pressured President Hindenburg to use emergency powers granted him by the still-active constitution to suspend legal process and make it easier to imprison them. Only a month later Dachau was built for the task, and before long it also contained hostile journalists, gypsies, gays, dissident religious groups, and other troublemakers. Himmler was careful to remind people that "good citizens had nothing to worry about."[20]

These actions and more had all taken place in less than two months. One might think that the German citizenry, accustomed to more than sixty years of democracy, would have recoiled in shock and rebellion at the sheer pace of the clampdown. Few did. Facing the prospect that the German state might collapse entirely and given the reassurance that the new regime was taking bold action to save the day, it was all too easy for most people to stand by and hope for the best. Once the situation was brought under control, one might hope the Nazis would restore normalcy by retracting the Reichstag Fire Decree, by returning policing duties to the experienced and institutionalized civil police forces, and by gradually reeducating and emancipating the Communists and other internees or trying them for legitimate crimes. As for those who did resist, it was easy for the rest of German society to believe that it was not the time to stand up for naysayers and troublemakers. The new government had to be given a chance to do what it promised to do.

But something else was happening. Under the surface of popular worry about the regime and its policies, a steady trickle of acquiescence was building in the public discourse. Each repressive measure tended to be self-reinforcing, and each undermined the average citizen's resistance to high-handed government. Once the Communists were imprisoned, they appeared all the more criminal. Once the legions of SA police were on the streets, it seemed as if there must be an awful lot of criminal activity around, and it was just a good thing so many extra police were available to control it. Once dissidents were rounded up, it was easy to see that there was less divisiveness, less demagoguery, and fewer disorderly mobs. Say what one might about the Nazis, it seemed to many that they had been right about some things.

Not all Germans felt this way, of course, perhaps not even a majority did. Most probably had grave doubts, at least at this early phase of National Socialist rule. But how could one resist effectively when the Nazis enjoyed the support of such a determined and ruthless political base? It seemed too easy for doubters to be cast as villains, anti-German even, for the slightest departure from orthodoxy. Politicians were shouted down in the Reichstag for talk of moderation, and editors were harassed for criticizing party policies. Since the most vocal critics were already jailed, there remained no voices to lend credibility or legitimacy to dissent. All dissenters looked like cranks or worse, because they always appeared to be small minorities at the fringe of society.

In short, each act of repression that went unchallenged legitimated the next act of repression. On April 1, 1933—barely two months after the accession—the party organized a boycott of Jewish shops and other businesses. Most Germans probably did not rigidly obey it, but the sheer spectacle of it made an impression. It must have felt at least a little uncomfortable to walk into a Jewish bakery, haberdashery, or barbershop with one's fellow citizens watching. And the legitimacy lent to the boycott by the government's endorsement sent a clear message that Jews were becoming officially marginalized. They were different, not fully German. On the eleventh of the same month, an official decree defined exactly who was and was not an Aryan. Since there had been no widespread outcry over the boycotts, the decree only seemed to reduce the ambiguity about who was who.

On May 10 the government organized a mass burning of non-German books in various cities and towns around Germany. Looking at photos of this event, it appears that many who participated did so enthusiastically while many others watched, possibly with concern and even puzzlement. Many others, of course, stayed home. The burning of books wasn't really meant to keep ideas away from Germans; rather, the goal was to invite

Germans to make the leap and commit themselves to the Nazis and the
Third Reich by participating—or at least acquiescing—in this odious affair.
Once you've thrown a book into the fire, it becomes difficult to believe you
stand outside the Nazi circle. Even acquiescence is a way of being pulled
in, for just watching others without expressing protest is an unconscious
step toward acceptance. The mounting of such spectacles, with no visible
demonstration of dissent, went a long way toward making resistance seem
pointless and perhaps even wrongheaded.

Autumn of the same year saw further escalation of the march toward
total control with the establishment of the Reich Chamber of Culture.
This move enabled the Nazis to control the arts and the media and thus
to exclude Jews from participation in either. Next were various other
prohibitions against Jews from newspaper editorships, land ownership, the
practice of law, and membership in the official national labor union, the
German Labor Front. By now the steady march of anti-Semitic decrees had
become routine, expected, numbing.

The drumbeat of political agitation—by the government itself—
continued through 1934 and 1935. It seemed as if Germany was locked in
a permanent political campaign, in which everything—the arts, the news,
entertainment, sport, science, even religion—had deep political consequence. The difference was that this campaign only involved one party;
there was no one to voice an opposing point of view. Instead, Germans
were constantly forced to take sides, either for or against the regime, and it
was always much easier and safer to side with it than against it. This process
had an ongoing ratcheting effect on the German political, social, and moral
consciousness, and each bit of acquiescence made it all the more difficult
to justify resistance to the next depredation against democracy. How could
one speak against the establishment of the Chamber of Culture, when one
hadn't denounced the book burnings? How could one resist the arrests of
Jews if one had not opposed the boycott? It was less stressful to convince
oneself that such acts were just. And why say anything at all when so many
of one's friends and neighbors seemed satisfied with the way things were?
The Germans gave themselves up to the Nazis gradually in a steady process,
and each step was politically and legally justified by the previous one in
what Karl Bracher called a "legal revolution."[21]

The Authoritarian Threat

We know how things ended for the Germans, but they did not foresee their
calamity at the time any more than we Americans will foresee ours if and

when it comes to us. How would a fascist takeover of American society happen? Would there be a sudden crisis, a shocking repudiation of the Constitution, or a putsch in Washington? Would the public be cowed by a show of brute force, such as tanks in the streets, the seizure of the media, or public executions of resisters?

The German experience, as well as our own history, suggests not. The Nazis were nourished by the Weimar era's economic, political, and moral upheavals and by the deep bitterness of the German people over their nation's decline. They indulged that bitterness, deepened it, and gave it increasingly shrill expression until they had enough political support to gain the chancellorship. By then they had come to be viewed not as agitators and destroyers of good German order but as saviors who would restore it through radical departures from business as usual.

It's worth noting, too, that the Nazis did not enjoy the support of the majority of Germans when they gained the chancellorship. A relatively small but powerful political base was able, by manipulating values through pageantry, propaganda, and violence against non-Germans of various stripes, to silence the majority who neither loved nor despised the Nazis. Even after achieving the chancellorship, the Nazi regime was not the irresistible and disciplined monolith most people imagine it was.[22] The Nazis ruled by promoting fear of enemies both within and without, through brutal repression of marginalized groups, and through constant display of revolutionary fervor. They ruled with the consent, either explicit or tacit, of a critical mass of Germans, and they cultivated that consent carefully through propaganda, rallies, favors, and flattery of the German volk. And they were careful to grasp power a little at a time rather than all at once, taking two steps forward and one back when necessary. How much was done with the consent of the Germans and how much through coercion? It is impossible to say because, as Robert Gellately put it, the two were "intertwined."[23] Like Milgram's subjects, the German people's sense of good and evil, as well as their sense of responsibility, had become fatally confused.

The deep lesson of the National Socialist revolution is that the loss of freedoms, the decline of law, and the slide into barbarity often occur in steps and not in a sudden convulsion. No reading of German history can tell us the precise time when most Germans understood that their society had taken a disastrous turn. Even those who lived through it would be hard pressed to say with clarity when the turning point came. Some never acknowledged it at all.

Are Americans as prone to falling into step as the Germans were? It seems that American cultural predispositions are different from those of the Germans. In ordinary times and under ordinary circumstances, Americans take pleasure and pride in a certain disrespect for institutions and traditions of all types. This attitude offers some hope for those Americans who worry about the possibility of a fascist era in America's future. American pluralism, individualism, and factionalism may indeed retard the rise of nationalist and totalitarian sentiment, even when the worst crises loom.

But haven't Americans succumbed to the same appeals to fear and uncertainty from time to time? Where was American individualism and love of liberty when German Americans were hounded from the streets during World War I? Where was the Bill of Rights when Japanese Americans were sent to concentration camps during World War II? And how many have dared object to the increased surveillance of and suspension of civil liberties of suspected terrorists, or to the indefinite imprisonment, "rendition," and torture of "enemy combatants" who do not have the protection of the law or of the Geneva Convention? Who dares even to question whether everything has indeed changed since 9/11?

It seems a small sacrifice of freedoms to remove our shoes and endure inspection at the airport. We say it's all to the good as long as it makes us safe. Widespread phone tapping and the interception of e-mails are not big issues for most of us, so long as the authorities are only listening to the terrorists' conversations. So what if the phone companies have collaborated in our own surveillance? Good Americans have nothing to worry about. And if a member of the White House staff suggests during this time of war that those who object to administration policies "should be careful what they say," isn't that just politics?

It appears we have escaped further descent into authoritarianism this time, but the end of the Bush era has not brought an end to the problems it created. In fact, as the world economic crisis deepens, it could well threaten the reforms promised by the new administration. How will Americans react when great masses of Americans are unemployed and losing their homes? Will we continue to find hope in "change we can believe in"? Will we still value our individualism and love of liberty? Or will we find a leader with a bold plan that requires new conquests, new enemies, or a new world order? Will Americans reject the cool rationalism of the Obama presidency and rush to a bold outsider with a simple explanation and audacious plans?

A skilled and opportunistic regime might under such conditions be able to ratchet public sentiment against a scapegoat responsible for our miseries. It would not matter who the scapegoat is—Iran, Saudi Arabia, Russia, the banks, immigrants, terrorists—for any would do. More executive power would be required to take the extreme measures required, whether military, domestic security, or financial. Through careful manipulation of the media and creation of a series of crises, a desperate public could be lulled into a graduated series of minor compromises to authority. If that time comes, each brutalization of a suspected terrorist will justify another; each compromise of the rule of law will make the next one that much easier to accept. Each war will make peace seem like cowardice. Each difference will threaten American solidarity. Like the Germans, we will participate in our own seduction until we believe all elections are rigged and all politicians are bought, all knowledge is ideology, and all dissent is treason. By the time we recognize the beast we have created, it will be too late.

__8__

CAN IT HAPPEN HERE?

AMERICANS ENJOY A SENSE OF POLITICAL SECURITY that many around the world have reason to envy. The Constitution, ratified more than two centuries ago, rules over an active and partisan government whose leadership and philosophy change with the shifting fortunes of various interest groups, demographic categories, and innovative movements. The Constitution balances the powers of the three branches of government so exquisitely that only a few amendments have been needed to keep its principles aligned with the tremendous social and technological changes that have taken place since its adoption. Americans take for granted the provisions of the Bill of Rights, and for most people, most of the time, they can have confidence those rights will be protected.

Americans are so assured of the stability of their government and the solidity of the rule of law that many overlook, or forget, or never learned of the lapses that have occurred. In fact, the Constitution has not stood inviolate and constant over the full course of American history. Even setting aside its fundamental, initial shortcomings regarding the status of women and blacks—resolved only after more than a century and only in legal terms—there have been quite a number of occurrences in which the provisions of the Bill of Rights have been significantly trampled. Moreover, most of these cases have had the acquiescence and even enthusiastic approval of the bulk of the citizenry. Thus examination of the question, can it happen here? must begin with the recognition that Americans have already had occasional flirtations with authoritarian and populist repression.

AMERICAN SELF-REPRESSION

The first major attack on the Bill of Rights came in 1798 in the form of the Alien and Sedition acts. Facing the threat of war with France, President John Adams saw an opportunity to use the citizenry's patriotic fervor to advance the aims of his Federalist Party by silencing its Republican critics. The Federalist-dominated Congress passed the measures, which, in addition to providing for the arrest of foreigners who were subjects of enemy powers, criminalized criticism of the administration. The Sedition Act's centerpiece was the threat of fine and imprisonment for publishing or uttering "any false, scandalous, and malicious writings against the government of the United States . . . or the President of the United States, with the intent to defame [them] or bring [them] into disrepute." Whatever the political or ideological intent of the measure, in practice it accomplished little but the prosecution of several Republican newspaper editors and politicians.

But though passage of the Alien and Sedition acts is among the most egregious compromises to constitutional principle, it doesn't serve as a good cautionary example of American tendencies toward fascism. In those times, the Constitution was just being tested, and American political parties were just taking shape. It is significant, too, that there was widespread protest over the measures, both in Congress from the Republicans and among the citizens and the media of the time. Most newspaper editors ignored the law, assuming correctly that the government couldn't put them all in jail. The outcry probably cost Adams the following election, which brought the Republican Thomas Jefferson to the presidency. Thus the Alien and Sedition acts might well be viewed as an early test of the strength of the Bill of Rights, enacted only a few years earlier, rather than as a failure to uphold its principles. Further, it is impossible to think of this episode as an early move toward fascism, which was not invented until the twentieth century and, in fact, could not have emerged until the modern age. Still, the political maneuverings surrounding the acts displayed some of the key methods by which citizens might be persuaded by opportunistic politicians and other elites to surrender some of their most basic freedoms: the invoking of an external threat as a cause for radical action, the scapegoating of foreigners to increase nationalistic fervor, and the labeling of opponents as traitorous in times of foreign threat.[1]

There were no further significant attacks on the Bill of Rights until the Civil War. Local or state authorities harassed abolitionists now and then, but Americans and their leaders apparently had been shaken by the struggle over the Alien and Sedition acts or had come to a reasonable consensus on what the Bill of Rights meant. But as the nation was split and the war sapped the strength and morale of what was left of it, President Lincoln faced mounting pressure to put a lid on the increasing sense of chaos and dissent in the Northern states. Though he refused on principle to squelch criticism of himself or the administration, it began to seem that dissent regarding the war might ultimately bring down the Union more readily than Robert E. Lee's armies could. These differences became a particular problem in border states, such as Maryland, Kentucky, and Missouri, where substantial Confederate constituencies agitated for secession. In the end, Lincoln suspended the right of habeas corpus, thereby making possible the arrest of suspected agitators and traitors without due process.

Though Lincoln had intended the measure to be strictly a matter of maintaining security, others were more zealous. Gen. Ambrose Burnside, for example, had the featured speaker at an antiwar rally in Ohio arrested, tried by military tribunal for "treasonable utterances," and sentenced to two years' imprisonment. The problem was, the speaker was not an insurgent advocating the end of the Union, but a former congressman advocating an end to the war on moral and practical grounds.[2]

Lincoln had to publicly support Burnside's actions but not without careful analysis of its implications. He based his decision on the constitutional provision that habeas corpus could be suspended "when in time of Rebellion or Invasion the public Safety may require it." He noted that the speech was not a simple criticism of the war's aims or its conduct but an attempt to discourage enlistment, to encourage desertions from the army, and generally to interfere with the war effort. And he made clear that the arrest could not be legal if the speaker was simply criticizing policy. This example, then, is of another abridgement of rights, but again, it need not be taken as an example of self-repression parallel to the beginning of the Third Reich. This suspension of habeas corpus was undertaken during a time of genuine and total war, it was temporary, and it was limited.

Hun Scare, Red Scare
A better example arose during World War I. President Wilson, reluctant to involve the United States in a foreign war, found he had to do so when Germany began to challenge American security through unrestricted U-boat warfare and the threat of a Mexican invasion of the Southwest. But though reluctant, Wilson was astute enough to recognize that this was

a new kind of war, which required a total mobilization of society. It would require extraordinary efforts to bring the public along and make the human and material sacrifices that would be needed. That meant control of information and of assembly, which meant censorship, surveillance, and harassment.

These controls would need to be strenuous, as there was plenty of opposition to the United States entering the war, even after the Germans sank the *Lusitania* off the coast of Ireland. Antiwar activists ranged from pacifists like urban social reformer Jane Addams to Socialists like Eugene Debs, who wanted to take over the government, and to anarchists like Emma Goldman, who wanted to abolish it altogether. In 1917, only a few weeks after the declaration of war, Congress passed the Espionage Act, which criminalized acts or speech intended to interfere with military success or to promote the success of America's enemies. It was not a blanket suppression of freedom of speech, but in practice it encouraged such suppression. Since it was always difficult to know where the line might be drawn, one was well advised not to speak up too loudly.

Wilson had also established the Committee on Public Information (CPI), a propaganda campaign that exceeded anything the nation had seen up to then. Established to arouse support for the war, the committee used the most advanced advertising methods and media of its day: short films of German atrocities, enlistment of academics and prominent essayists to lend authority to administration claims, the flooding of newspapers with press releases, and the training of seventy-five thousand Four-Minute Men to give brief pro-war speeches in their town halls, schools, and workplaces.[3] It also encouraged the formation of citizen groups to monitor fellow citizens for signs of disloyalty. George Creel, head of the CPI, summed up its purpose in a memoir a few years later:

> What we had to have was no mere surface unity, but a passionate belief in the justice of America's cause that should weld the people into one white-hot mass of instinct with fraternity, devotion, courage and deathless determination. . . . Every task was a common task for a single purpose.[4]

The description could have applied almost verbatim to the techniques of Adolf Hitler or Joseph Goebbels a generation later.

In any event, the campaign was effective. Much of the nation fell in line behind the war and against anything German, Austrian, or pacifistic.

The Department of Justice was flooded with thousands of reports daily from those citizen groups concerned about suspicious activities. One of them, the American Protective League, grew to more than two hundred thousand members. By the time the CPI had gone into full swing, all opponents of the war were tarred with the same brush. Jane Addams and similar pacifists were considered as disloyal as the anarchists; consequently, they were anathematized by various patriotic groups and shunned by much of the press. Even mentioning Addams's name in a speech could get a speaker booed off the stage.[5]

By 1918 the Espionage Act was not enough to quell all opposition. Responding to court decisions that had gone in favor of to the war's vocal opponents, the administration introduced to Congress the Sedition Act of 1918. This law made it illegal to publish "any disloyal, profane, scurrilous, or abusive language about the form of government of the United States," or about the flag, or about the military. It also forbade the publishing of such language that would bring any of these institutions into "contempt, scorn, contumely or disrepute" or to in any way "oppose the cause of the United States." Throughout the debate in Congress, every member found it necessary, for fear of being accused of treason, to proclaim his loyalty even though he might only quibble over a word or two.[6]

Freedom of speech was not the only casualty of World War I. There were numerous cases of vigilantism, some by local law enforcement authorities. People were harassed and beaten for failing to salute the flag or for a passing remark about the president, the generals, or the war. A man named Robert Paul Praeger was lynched in Illinois for making anti-American remarks and preaching the virtues of socialism to miners. In Montana, seventy-eight men and a woman were convicted of sedition for various criticisms of the administration and the war, usually made in saloons when tongues were loosened. One had called it a "rich man's war," while another had poked fun at food rationing.[7] And four thousand German and Austrian aliens were arrested, removed from such strategically important areas as seacoasts, and imprisoned for the duration of the war.[8]

The Espionage and Sedition acts and the other legal and administrative measures taken during World War I are good object lessons regarding the American capacity for endorsing fascism. These laws were not simply an opportunistic grasp at power or an effort by one sector of society to advance an ideological position while another sector pushed back. Instead, they were largely successful attempts to galvanize the entire society behind a national crusade, and not only in terms of its economic production or military effort. The Wilson programs galvanized thought itself in a way that made dissent or even reasoned debate impossible. Dissent was squelched not only by law but also by the pressure of fellow citizens and the threat of denunciation, job loss, or the humiliation of being called a traitor. If one had a German surname, which was not at all uncommon since the great waves of European immigration, so much the worse.

An additional danger arose in this period of American history. As the war came to a close, new threats made Americans nervous. One was the Bolshevik Revolution in Russia, which introduced communism to the world as a genuine political force that could topple regimes. The fear of communism, stoked in large part by American business interests that felt most threatened, came at about the same time as the American labor movement was gaining momentum. Some elements of the movement were sympathetic to the Communists and some were Socialists, but most were simply workers trying to use political power to wrest a little more control over the fruits of their labors. But all were thought vulnerable to Communist infiltration and indoctrination.

The Communist threat might have been taken in stride if there were not also significant dislocations that accompanied the end of the war. It had been the first truly industrial war and the first that mobilized whole societies on a grand scale, including the harnessing of labor, industrial capacity, finance and capital, communication, transportation, and, as seen above, public opinion and discourse itself. The rapid industrialization had changed the character of much of American life, turning the nation's population from one of mostly farmers to one of mostly urban factory workers. Its insatiable need for labor had brought great numbers of blacks from the South to the industrial centers of the North and Mexicans to the fields of the West and Southwest. Nine million workers had been employed in defense production, and four million others had served in the armed forces. The institution of the family was changed, too, as the nation's lifestyle and work habits changed, not to mention the family separations and dissolutions that resulted from the war itself. The war had also brought inflation, which made it difficult for those on low incomes to manage. Between 1914 and the war's end food prices had risen 84 percent and clothing 114 percent, but salaries only increased 10 percent. Not surprisingly the American Federation of Labor grew eightfold between 1914 and 1919, in which year some thirty-six hundred strikes were staged.

Industrialists resisted, sometimes using violence, and as they got stronger, labor became more militant. Though these changes in American life were under way before the war began, they were markedly accelerated by the conflict. The deaths and often hideous wounds of thousands who had gone to fight on another continent had their effect too.[9]

The country had been united by the war, but it was an artificial unity based on enmity and propaganda, much of which was overblown or simply false. Thus it was understandable that there would be a sense of let-down and deflation even in victory. At the same time, there were political and economic elites who were only too ready to capitalize on the national malaise. For one, the administration was worried about the impending collapse of nationalist feeling and what it could do to the Democrats' hold on power. The administration sought a way to rekindle a sense of unity and carry the party forward into the new century. The industrialists worried about organized labor's growing strength and militancy and were especially alarmed by Communist and Socialist gains not only in Russia but also by smaller increments elsewhere in Europe. Bavaria actually became a Soviet Republic, if only for a few weeks.

Finally, a third force emerged that was neither government nor commercial; it was cultural and moral. Those citizens groups the Committee for Public Information had encouraged were still around but now without a meaningful purpose since the "Hun scare" had ended. They included established elite groups like the Daughters of the American Revolution, the recently formed American Protective League, and the brand-new American Legion, formed in 1919 by the veterans of World War I. When the war ended, these groups exhibited a classic case of "goal succession": having lost their original purpose, they cast about for another. They became what Murray Levin called "superpatriotic societies" and were dedicated to nativism, antiradicalism, and what came to be called "one hundred percent Americanism," which was essentially a blank slate on which the American brand of content-free nationalism could be projected. With large and devoted memberships, the superpatriotic societies had no difficulty refocusing their mission. The American Protective League's goal of finding and reporting suspicious foreigners and war resisters could work just as well in turning up radicals, Socialists, and "parlor pinks." An examination of the American Legion's weekly publication during 1919–20 shows the transition in focus from pro-war patriotism to the dangers posed by radicals and leftists.[10]

The superpatriotic societies would not have lasted long on their own. The malaise of the postwar dislocations gradually eased, and life settled in to what had become normal. Chasing radicals and other evildoers would have become less and less satisfying, especially if there was no one to whom they could report them. But as it happened, the superpatriots were just what the administration needed to continue to maintain nationalistic feeling and public support. They were also useful to the industrial interests in stemming the tide of organized labor. These three institutions—government, industry, and the superpatriots—combined with the press to create what became the most serious episode of political repression in American history and a good cautionary lesson for understanding the possibility of American fascism.

It came to be called the great Red Scare of 1919–20, and while it was a temporary outbreak of political hysteria, it demonstrates how Americans can be led to abandon their constitutional principles out of fear of almost nothing at all. It began with a few individual superpatriots in the government and elsewhere in the public eye who caught people's attention by connecting the unease they felt to scapegoats they could understand. One example was Seattle mayor Ole Hanson, who responded to a shipyard strike in his city by requesting federal troops and denouncing the strikers as people who "want to take possession of our American government to duplicate the anarchy in Russia." The Seattle *Star* saw an opportunity to use Hansen's hyperbole to sell papers. When the strike failed, the paper stirred the pot by declaring "FULL STEAM AHEAD . . . today this Bolshevik nightmare is at an end."[11]

When the public rewarded people like Hansen with greater attention, other institutions saw opportunity as well. The superpatriotic societies joined the fight against anarchists and radicals. Corporate officials saw a chance to characterize labor as infested with Communists. Finally, as the antiradical sentiment caught on, government officials of both parties were forced into line. Who could sit idly in Congress or in the White House when the press so eagerly reported a growing tide of fear and concern over the country's future? Before long, everyone was talking about the threat that the Reds and anarchists posed, so the press had no choice but to redouble its coverage. The Red threat became the only important story, and, of course, this emphasis made it seem all the more real. In the end, each of these institutions reinforced the others, creating a vortex of fear that drowned out debate and reason. The citizenry became convinced that there was a worldwide conspiracy to destroy America, and desperate measures would be required to root it out and defeat it. Before long, the Red Scare had become a nationwide hysteria:

In 1920 a salesman in Waterbury, Connecticut, was sentenced to six months in jail for having remarked to a customer that Lenin was "the brainiest" or "one of the brainiest" political leaders in the world. In 1919 a citizen of Indiana, in a fit of rage, shot and killed an alien who yelled, "to hell with the United States." The jury deliberated for two minutes before acquitting the killer. In Weirton, West Virginia, during the great steel strike of 1919, a mob of enraged citizens forced 118 aliens, who were on strike, to kiss the American flag. In western Pennsylvania, steel workers were tried and fined in cases where the charge was "smiling at the State Police." In New York City a riot ensued in the Waldorf-Astoria when a man shouted, "to hell with the flag." The American Legion, in that year, demanded that "enemy aliens" buried in Arlington National Cemetery "be removed . . . and given proper burial elsewhere." In the state of Washington, school teachers were forbidden to answer student questions concerning Bolshevism "or any other heresies." Twenty-eight states passed laws banning the display of Red flags. . . . In Centralia, Washington, after radicals shot and killed three members of the American Legion, local citizens removed a member of the IWW [Industrial Workers of the World] from jail, castrated him, lynched him by throwing him off a bridge with a rope around his neck, and then riddled his body with bullets. Senator McKellor of Tennessee argued that native-born American citizens who were radicals should be sent to a penal colony in Guam. In 1920 the legislature of the state of New York expelled five duly elected members of the Socialist party.[12]

It was true that radicals had engaged in some incidents of disruption: assassination attempts, shootings, bombings. But in this sort of super-charged environment, incidents that were highly scattered and might normally have been reported only as local news became national headlines. When a shooting in Chicago or a speech in Seattle was carried in papers around the country, a fairly normal rate of crime and unrest became a "reign of terror." And when disparate events were linked together in the public mind, it was all too easy to believe that they were linked in fact and part of a centrally contrived conspiracy to destroy America.

186 | FASCISM: WHY NOT HERE?

Between the superpatriots, the politicians, the corporations, and the press, "bits and pieces of reality" were "woven together" into a coherent myth: a shadowy cabal of Bolsheviks, foreign labor, and anarchist Jews, whose intersecting interests created an almost superhuman foe, was bent on destroying America. Like the international Jewish conspiracy imagined by the Nazis, these conspirators were considered to have an unstoppable will and to be capable of any sacrifice or deprivation in pursuit of their mission. They also possessed the most extraordinary patience and might lie dormant for years before striking America in its most vulnerable moment. These and other demonic characteristics made them appear to "transcend the normal limits of humanness."[13] They sound also very much like the Islamic terrorists of today.

Over time the Red Scare ran its course, weakened, and collapsed. It did not plunge the United States into a fascist dictatorship. Instead, America turned to Warren Harding and the Republican Party after the Wilson era ended and elected him on a promise of a return to normalcy: "America's present need is not heroics, but healing; not nostrums, but normalcy; not revolution, but restoration; not agitation, but adjustment; not surgery, but serenity; not the dramatic, but the dispassionate."[14] Harding's rhetoric was a nearly exact mirror image of Hitler's, who could easily have given the same speech in Germany but with each of the key word pairs reversed.

The American public turned in the opposite direction from the Germans' course, owing to a number of factors. The most important was that for the Americans, World War I had ended in a noble victory and not an ignominious defeat. It brought the country the respect of the world's nations, rather than the shame of surrender and reparations. The 1920s became an era of American economic expansion, and as the labor movement continued to prosper, an increasingly well-off working class felt less and less like blaming the unions for any problems. Communism and anarchism were still concerns, but they came to be viewed as social and political ills that could be dealt with by normal means. It's likely, too, that the American political structure helped keep things from spinning out of control: the opposition party's initial disadvantage when defeated for the presidency diminishes over time as their rivals take responsibility for governing the nation. By the time Wilson was finished, the Republicans had built a political and electoral advantage.

Still, a historical precedent had been established, and the techniques for galvanizing the nation around a common cause had been proven.

Political and moral opportunists would not forget the lessons learned: given the right kind of enemy threat and the increasing social dislocations of the modern age, it was possible to manufacture a crisis out of thin air to advance an agenda. Although it could not be done on command whenever a political leadership or other opinion-dependent elite needed a boost, a careful observer might be able to see when the political and cultural forces were aligning in an opportune way. They were aligning again in 1945.

Red Scare Redux

When the German reich collapsed in a heap of smoking ruins in 1945, the United States had again emerged from a world war with both a victory and greater international standing than before the war had begun. Moreover, the country was economically stronger than ever, as the war had helped upgrade industrial facilities, and the bounty of commercial goods ushered in a new American consumer age. But the structural and cultural dislocations caused by the war were even greater than those brought on by the first one. The economy had been entirely converted to war production and had to be retooled for civilian needs, the war had created a massive national debt, and families had been strained and often broken by geographic relocation, by abrupt change in women's roles, and by men's military service, disability, and death.

The war had also produced the same jingoist hangover as the first war. The turgid anti-Nazi enmity and the more visceral hatred of the Japanese were not easy to relinquish after years of wartime propaganda and the often true accounts of atrocities. Worse, the postwar rebuilding effort had created jarring inconsistencies in the way Americans had to think about their enemies. Under the Marshall Plan, the Germans received enormous amounts of aid at largely American expense, even though they had resisted until nearly the last bullet, pointlessly and lethally for many American troops. Who had won the war, anyway? As for the Japanese, Americans had to reconcile their contempt for the "Jap" with the reality that thousands of innocent Japanese American families had been held by executive order in concentration camps for the war's duration. Their return to ordinary society created an awkward historical moment.

As Americans tried to learn to embrace their enemies, they also had to acknowledge that the victory depended largely on their most powerful ally, the Soviet Union. The same Reds who had threatened the American way of life a generation ago and whose leader, Joseph Stalin, was little

188 | FASCISM: WHY NOT HERE?

improvement over Hitler himself had made inroads into Western Europe.
The Soviets held the eastern part of Germany and made the allied sector
of Berlin a lonely outpost in a desert under Moscow's control. Though the
United States had made a convincing claim to world military leadership
with its detonation of two nuclear weapons, it seemed certain that it would
be short lived as the Soviets would do anything they could to get the bomb,
too. Toward the end of the war, some felt that Germany's defeat merely
realigned world power, the Soviets pitted against the West. A few even
whispered that the United States may have chosen the wrong side.

Meanwhile, by 1945 the Democratic Party had occupied the White
House for thirteen years and would do so for at least three more. Throughout this period the Republicans had had to swallow a decade of New Deal
reforms that expanded the government's role in every phase of life, as well
as emergency wartime centralization that brought even more of the same.
In addition, labor had made gains during the war, at gunpoint in the eyes
of many, and on top of it all, blacks had leveraged their labor power to
force equity concessions from the railroads and other industries. On the
latter, even elements of the Democratic Party gagged.

By the 1946 midterm elections, a few Republican congressional candidates were trying out a Red-baiting approach to getting votes. Who had
created this new imperial presidency? Who had issued an executive order
conceding to the demands of the Brotherhood of Sleeping Car Porters
when they shook down the country in wartime? Who had decided to
reward our enemies after they had started the war? And who had sat down
with Stalin and allowed him to enslave East Germany and much of Eastern
Europe? Richard Nixon, Joseph McCarthy, and many other Republican
candidates accused their Democratic opponents of being allied with the
Communists. Senator Hugh Butler of Nebraska linked communism to
the New Deal: "[I]f the New Deal is still in control of Congress after the
election, it will owe that control to the Communist party." The chairman
of the Republican National Committee flatly stated that Democratic policy
"bears a made-in-Moscow label."[15]

This campaign was tremendously effective, as the Republicans gained
fifty-four House seats and eleven in the Senate. Moreover, it became
increasingly difficult to voice opposition to the anti-Red rhetoric. As had
been the case in 1919–20, Red-baiting was becoming a hysteria. Everyone's
loyalty became suspect, and every politician again was forced to find ways
to demonstrate his by introducing Red-baiting legislation or by opposing

anything that might be made to appear sympathetic to Communists. Before long, even the Truman administration found it necessary to prove its loyalty; various cabinet members called for the outlawing of communism or imposing a loyalty test for voting. The president himself had to state flatly, "I want to get this straight now. I hate Communism."[16] To further appease critics, Truman also instituted a stringent program by which federal employees would be investigated for disloyalty and be required to take a loyalty oath. This effort only lent legitimacy to the growing atmosphere of fear and mistrust.

Red-baiting continued through several election cycles. In 1947 Congress passed the Taft-Hartley Act and then in 1950 the McCarran Internal Security Act, both over Truman's veto. The former required labor leaders to swear they were not Communists; the latter required the registration of all Communists, which in practical terms meant that the simple fact of not being registered as a Communist could instigate an investigation of whether you were one. In 1952 the anticommunist line worked better than ever. Presidential candidate Dwight Eisenhower and his running mate, Richard Nixon, both fanned the fears of communism, with Nixon actually referring to the Democrats as the "party of communism" and calling Truman and Stevenson "traitors."[17] In 1954 the Communist Control Act was overwhelmingly passed (with only one dissenting vote in the Senate). It outlawed the Communist Party and barred its members from serving in various government capacities. It was this sort of legislation that gave the House Un-American Activities Committee (HUAC) so much latitude in investigating the political views of Americans.

As in 1919–20, the key ingredients were again aligning to kindle anticommunist hysteria. As the Republicans were making political headway with Red-baiting, others joined in. Represented by the Chamber of Commerce, corporate interests published a report that claimed various government agencies had been infiltrated by Communists. It was all Senator McCarthy needed to fuel a formal investigation of every government agency in which the Democratic administration had a hand, and that was of course all of them. Even the U.S. Army was targeted. The superpatriotic organizations participated, as did the press, which now included radio and television. Religious organizations signed on as well, as Cardinal Francis Spellman, Archbishop Fulton Sheen, and the Knights of Columbus all declared war on the godless Communists.

In the end, the hysteria collapsed in much the same way as that of 1919–20 had. McCarthy and the HUAC overreached, casting the net of disloyalty beyond the government to the academic profession, novelists, Hollywood actors and writers, and even diplomats. McCarthy used the HUAC to create a new kind of populism, which cast these literati and glitterati as the new elite, replacing the old corporate and moneyed interests. As journalists and his colleagues in Congress began to suggest that he tone down the rhetoric, McCarthy became increasingly arrogant and shrill, pointing a finger at "egg-sucking liberals" and "queers." His attacks on the army infuriated Eisenhower, and even Richard Nixon turned against him. As others saw the tide turning, they were emboldened to speak up. When Joseph Welch, an attorney representing the army, delivered his "Have you no sense of decency?" tirade, the packed hearing room exploded in applause. It was over.[18]

And it had come to nothing. The House Un-American Activities Committee's proceedings did not lead to any prosecutions, and Truman's loyalty program, which had investigated more than 4,000,000 federal employees, led to the firing of only about 350 people. The country was not riddled with Communist conspirators; even the unveiling of the Soviets' atom bomb and the Korean War failed to result in the sort of mass hysteria seen at the end of World War I. But as with the Red Scare, again dozens of political careers had been launched and others ruined as the Republicans, this time, had taken the ascendancy. The American people had found a way to reconcile the dislocations of war, the inconsistencies of American policy, and their own duplicity by deflecting them to a shadowy conspiracy bent on America's ruin. In doing so, Americans had again gone along with the abridgement of their fellow citizens' political rights, and even the United States Senate had been cowed into acquiescence.

The War on Terrorism

The global realignment at the end of World War II became the foundation of the Cold War, which lasted until 1991, when the Soviet Union was dismantled as a world power. During that forty-six-year period, the threat of annihilation by a Communist state bent on our destruction shaped much of America's foreign and domestic policy. The bipolar world of foreign relations—the East versus the West, or the free world versus the Communist Bloc, with the two sides divided by the iron curtain—was, if frightening, at least simple. Many of the world's nations were drawn to either of these poles by opportunism, coercion, geography, or historical accident. Bristling with enough nuclear weapons to end the humans' reign on Earth, this bipolar arrangement was remarkably stable. In fact, the two poles were engaged in a constant state of warfare, usually through client states such as Korea, Vietnam, Middle Eastern countries, and other nations in what was then called the third world. More often, they agitated internal strife within developing nations by using political factions aligned with one pole or the other. There were also the constant patrols of B-52 bombers near the Soviet border and the mythic doomsday figures of young U.S. Air Force officers sitting in the bottom of missile silos, waiting for the order to begin the end of the world. But the world did not end, because both sides had everything to lose from total war.

They had much to gain, however, from maintaining the Cold War. The threat of a dangerous enemy was a powerful political tool for silencing opposition in Congress, in the Politburo, or for that matter, in the town meeting. In the United States, the Cold War revived a moribund Republican Party by giving it an issue with which to flog opponents, not only those of its foreign policy but also of its domestic policy. In the long run, it gave the political Right a lasting advantage in the voters' minds where foreign policy and defense of American interests were involved.

When the Cold War ended, the American political agenda was seriously disrupted. The Right, which claimed to have "won" the Cold War, suddenly was without one of its guiding political themes. Being strong on defense had less political value without an enemy equal to the task of destroying the American way of life. When the old binary alignment of nations collapsed, attempts to restore the old game by expanding the North Atlantic Treaty Organization (NATO) into the former Soviet sphere seemed hollow.

George H. W. Bush tried to extend American influence with peace-keeping and nation-building operations, but the U.S. military was ill designed for the task. An incursion into Somalia failed after a firefight in Mogadishu resulted in dead American troops being dragged through the streets. President Clinton pulled the plug on the operation. Meanwhile, the "no-fly zone war" over Iraq slogged through the Clinton years without resolution while American troops helped to stabilize the Balkans with some success. But all of these actions, in which American might had the overwhelming advantage, seemed like so many popgun wars. Even the Gulf War—a "dream war" fought on American terms that showcased American power splendidly—had failed to excite public fears, as the supposed supermen of the Iraqi army surrendered in droves.

But a gnawing worry had been growing for decades. Since the Munich Olympics of 1972, the specter of Islamic terrorists lurked below the surface, occasionally exploding in an embassy bombing or airliner hijacking. In 1993 a truckload of explosives detonated in the World Trade Center. The buildings survived, and the perpetrators were caught and imprisoned for their crimes. Throughout the 1990s terrorist activity grew more intensive as well as more extensive, with high-profile kidnappings, embassy bombings, airliner attacks, and a suicide attack on the USS *Cole*.

September 11, 2001, put an exclamation point on all of it: the United States was under attack. The foe was formidable, secretive, and single-mindedly dedicated to America's destruction. Al Qaeda was only loosely organized, so it would be impossible to neutralize even by killing or capturing Osama bin Laden. It was international, recruiting members from all over the world. It was financed, it was said, partly by unsuspecting dupes who contributed to Islamic religious and charitable causes, but also by powerful figures in the Middle East and western Asia—possibly by drug and oil money. And al Qaeda was patient. Sleeper cells might lie dormant for years while things cooled off, then strike out of nowhere when least expected. In short, the global Islamic terrorists fit perfectly the mold of the conspiracy to destroy America, just as the global Communist conspiracy had done twice in the past century.

The al Qaeda conspiracy was more real than the Red Scare of 1919–20 or the Red menace of the 1940s and 1950s. The horrifying spectacle of the Twin Towers' collapse, the audacity of the Pentagon attack, and the high drama of the thwarting of a further attack on the White House or the Capitol Building were not fabrication. It has been called a more devastating attack on America than Pearl Harbor was, and though a reasonable comparison is difficult, the point can be conceded.

The obvious authenticity of the September 11 attacks enhanced their value as a political tool. The spectacular nature of the attacks, combined with the electronic media making its images available immediately and pervasively, compelled a frightened American populace to seek strong leadership at once, without any need to exaggerate the threat. In a climate of fear that further attacks might be imminent, the public was willing to trade some civil liberties for security. As it happened, the George W. Bush presidency was in a situation similar to the one the Republicans faced after World War II. The party had held its ground through eight years of the Clinton administration, but it had gained the White House in 2000 by the slimmest of margins and only after a ballot fight decided by a divided Supreme Court. With a neoconservative agenda that had been formulated over a decade but virtually no mandate to execute it, the terrorist threat offered the administration an unanticipated opportunity.

This agenda included both foreign policy and domestic goals. Since the early 1990s, a variety of conservative think tanks had housed out-of-power neoconservatives as they developed, first, a Middle East doctrine whereby the United States would gain a greater physical and political presence in the Gulf to intimidate upstart states and ensure access to oil; and second, a goal of aggressive enhancement of executive power in domestic affairs. These policymakers, who included Richard Armitage, Richard Perle, and Paul Wolfowitz, had by now become key members of the administration. Richard Cheney, who had set forth much of the doctrine while working at the Project for a New American Century, was vice president.[19]

The president wasted no time. Three days after the attacks, he stood on the rubble pile of the World Trade Center. He promised retribution while calling the people to him in the same sentence: "I can hear you, the rest of the world hears you, and the people who knocked these buildings down will hear all of us soon." In his State of the Union speech the following January, he described the axis of evil, which he said consisted of Iraq, Iran, and North Korea. It seemed a startling non sequitur at the time, given that none of these nations had anything to do with the attacks. But throughout 2002 the administration worked to link 9/11 with the goals they sought to achieve. In June 2002, Vice President Cheney and his chief of staff made a series of unusual visits to the Central Intelligence Agency (CIA) to influence the analysis of intelligence that might be used to justify an invasion of Iraq. In August, the White House Iraq Group was formed to assemble the case for war.

From then on, the administration mounted an all-out campaign for war, including aggrandizing weak intelligence about Iraqi weapons of mass destruction (WMDs), maneuvering the United Nations into passing resolutions for Iraq to dismantle its WMDs, and generally saturating the airwaves with interviews comparing Saddam Hussein with Hitler. The Bush administration also drew dismal comparisons with the appeasement of the Munich Agreement of 1938 and referred to a "mushroom cloud" as the possible result if action were not taken.[20] In October 2002, Bush again used the mushroom cloud imagery in his request to Congress for authorization to go to war. He launched the invasion the following spring.

The war was not the only item on the neoconservative agenda. In the weeks after the September 11 attacks, the House Judiciary Committee drafted a bipartisan bill to expand law enforcement capabilities in order to cope with the terrorist threat. On October 3, it passed out of committee on a vote of 36-0. But as the bill was to be discussed on the floor, the administration substituted at the last minute its own bill, the Patriot Act. In violation of the House's standing rules, it was voted on with no amendments permitted. In a reprise of 1919 and 1952, Attorney General John Ashcroft warned members that anybody questioning the necessity of its provisions would be denounced as soft on terrorism. Few in Congress even read the 342-page bill for they knew what the right response had to be. The president signed it into law later that month.

Among other provisions, the Patriot Act:

- lowered legal standards for search and seizure, allowing the Federal Bureau of Investigation (FBI) to enter a premises without notification
- empowered federal authorities to obtain various personal records on individuals while forbidding those providing the records from saying so
- enabled the FBI to demand phone, e-mail, or other consumer records without court oversight while also gagging those involved from revealing it
- granted immigration authorities more discretion in detaining and deporting immigrants

These actions were only the legally sanctioned enhancements to surveillance and law enforcement. The administration also engaged in new extralegal practices, which President Bush claimed were his prerogative as commander in chief:

- closing some deportation hearings to public scrutiny
- indefinitely detaining suspects without access to courts, without charges, and without even revealing their identity to anyone
- removing terrorism cases from the judicial system by establishing military tribunals for terrorism suspects
- eavesdropping on attorney-client communications of terrorism suspects
- jailing José Padilla, an American citizen, as an enemy combatant without access to the courts
- selectively withholding public documents requested under the Freedom of Information Act

- disregarding laws against torture
- violating laws protecting whistle-blowers
- failing to report to Congress on implementation of the Patriot Act

The Patriot Act and other measures have been "fairly characterized as opportunistic and excessive," according to Geoffrey Stone, and it seemed clear that some of its provisions "had smuggled into law" several investigative practices that the Right had sought for years but were unrelated to terrorism.[21] The administration also later proposed a second version of the law, Patriot II, which would have provided for secret arrests, secret revocation of citizenship, construction of a permanent government database containing various records of citizens as well as aliens, and the empowerment of local police to infiltrate and monitor religious and political groups. When it was met with widespread criticism in the media and in Congress, the administration withdrew the bill.

The war in Iraq did not end quickly with American troops welcomed as liberators, contrary to what the vice president had predicted. Nor did the mortal threat of further massive terrorist attacks materialize. There were some foiled plots, most notably that of Richard Reid, an Englishman who can claim to have changed the footwear habits of airline passengers everywhere. There were also several very deadly attacks in Europe and Asia, but the administration was unable to either scare the public with them or claim effectiveness in keeping them off American soil. The color-coded terror threat warning system became irrelevant in a few months after it became clear that the threat level would always hover between yellow and orange since any departure outside that range would be politically hazardous. In the absence of new serious attacks, the public's demand for security through strong leadership waned.

The war on terrorism may or may not be over, but the neoconservatives' opportunity to change the direction of American policy has slipped away, owing mostly to the blunder of Iraq and associated blunders in diplomacy. America did not slip into fascism this time, and the Left and the Right did not join together in demanding recklessly bold leadership abroad and repressive policies at home. In fact, the Bush administration's excesses were relatively slight compared to those of 1798, 1919–20, or even 1945–54. No one has been prosecuted for criticizing the war, for example; no one has been lynched for failing to salute the flag; and no parties or organizations have been banned. According to Stone, a "reasonable analogy to the prosecution of Eugene Debs in World War I would have been the prosecution of Howard Dean in 2004 for his opposition to the war in Iraq."[22]

But new crises loom, perhaps bigger and more threatening than the terror threat and perhaps more immediate as well. One assumes that the Obama administration will undo many of the overreaches of the Bush era and much of the Patriot Act will be repealed, but nothing had yet been done in the first six months of the administration. President Obama did order that the Guantánamo gulag be closed, though his own party opposed him, claiming fears of housing terrorists in their home states. Domestic surveillance will likely be moderated, and there was early emphasis on a more collaborative foreign policy. But if and when the economic crisis deepens or the war on terrorism worsens, the forces of political opportunism may well assemble a new coalition of militarist patriots, anti-government populists, and authoritarian xenophobes to challenge the new regime. They will get a hearing in the public discourse.

WHY NOT HERE?

In all the cases of American political excesses described here, three factors have been critical. The first is the impetus toward unity created by historical events. War and the threat of war have been the most effective of these events. Galvanizing the populace to accept wartime sacrifices requires a sense of enmity toward the foe and an unquestioned belief in the righteousness of the nation's cause. Even the aftermath of war, as in the case of the two world wars, can create a sense of alienation and directionlessness that agitates the population. Old hatreds have to be forgotten, sacrifices have to be accounted for and reconciled, and dislocations and rapid social changes have to be adjusted to and settled.

The second factor is the opportunism of various elites. The politicians are often in the vanguard, being the most dependent on and sensitive to the public mood. In casting about for useful campaign themes, they are frequently the first to strike the nerve of public feeling when an inflammatory speech or even a phrase is applauded, picked up by the media, repeated by others, and entered into the common discourse. This process happens much faster today than in the past, as a witty or shrewd turn of phrase is repeated incessantly by the twenty-four-hour news networks and blogs and is thus made irresistible to the more sober print and major network media. The White House press corps asks the president's staff for its reaction to the remark or to the story about the remark. If it is advantageous, the president's men bring it up themselves, carrying the nonstory into another day's news cycle. As politicians and the media score points by promoting myths of enemy conspiracies, other elites—patriotic groups, religious organizations, corporate interests—follow or are coopted by them.

But neither of these factors—historical events nor the opportunism of elites—could be effective without the underlying cultural beliefs, values, aspirations, and fears that they arouse. The politician can't make headway denouncing shadowy conspiracies unless the public is willing to take romantic leaps of judgment—what Levin called "poor reality testing on a massive scale"—as a means of coping with social and cultural strains.[23] They can't get the public to toss aside the Bill of Rights in times of crisis if American nationalism is of the civic variety, rooted in the belief that what is truly American is our very tolerance of diverse opinion. It will only work if American nationalism is a content-free sort of idolatry rooted in the exceptionalist belief that the American dream is the world's dream. American populism, too, contributes to political hysteria by discrediting the voices of the intellectuals and the experienced and often by equating them with the very enemies that threaten the nation. Finally, Americans can't be drawn into begging their political leaders for protections from internal enemies without our peculiar brand of American authoritarianism—conformity wrapped in a myth of independence.

Americans' political excesses have been nourished by a similar combination of forces that encouraged those of the Germans nearly a century ago: historical stresses and strains, largely imposed by war; skilled political opportunists; and cultural themes that the opportunists could weave into their explanations for why the stresses and strains were so severe. But the German hysteria of the 1920s ultimately lapsed into a permanent state of repression—permanent, that is, until the utter destruction of German society. This type of repression did not happen in America—not in the 1920s, not in the 1940s, and not today.

Why not? Why has the United States so far been able to retreat from the brink of fascism? Several reasons can be proposed. First, the American political system may have a built-in tendency to seek equilibrium. The two-party system of the legislative branch tends to guarantee a fairly unified opposition party that will chip away at the party in power rather than fragment or enter into a coalition government in the sort of pact with the devil that was seen in Germany's Weimar era. In a sense, the two major parties use various demographic, ethnic, and interest groups as "splinter parties" which can be brought into coalition as needs and opportunities arise. In this way, the Democrats subsumed Southern segregationists during the Populist era. When the party moved toward advancing civil rights in the 1950s and 1960s, they lost that constituency and had to reassemble the party from a new combination of groups, including blacks, labor, and small farmers. In Minnesota, the Democratic Party is still officially called the Democratic-Farmer-Labor Party, which Hubert Humphrey and others built in 1944. Similarly, toward the end of the twentieth century, the Republicans captured a large segment of the Roman Catholic and Christian fundamentalist population by making abortion one of its signature issues.

By picking off such groups by embracing issues important to them, the two parties survive more or less intact and provide credible opposition to an overreaching majority. In normal times, the ship rights itself through a rebalancing of power after the majority has gone too far, but on those occasions when the opposition is silenced by a single, overriding threat to national security, its reaction can swing beyond equilibrium. Thus the Republicans lay more or less dormant through four Roosevelt administrations, only to overreach when the Roosevelt-Truman era burned itself out. So the tendency for parties to compensate and stabilize political currents cannot be counted on in every case.

A second explanation for American political stability may be the peculiarly diverse character of the populace. Americans will never feel the sort of folkish nationalism the Germans experienced and revered for so long. The nature of American nationalism is less substantial, having risen from a national origin that is both recent and well documented. It is difficult to sustain the myth of white and English dominance, let alone the more fabulous ones about national heroes and their exploits, so long as the public is reasonably well informed and educated. At the same time, American nationalism has a certain emptiness about it, and any dominant group can project its definition of nationhood onto its blank slate. As it has worked out historically, the only themes on which there has been much consensus are militarism and exceptionalism.

Similarly, racism has been more divisive than unifying. It has been a central component of American life since long before the nation's establishment. Indians, Africans, and then a parade of immigrants groups have provided both the cheap labor on which the country was built and the exotic other by which an Anglocentric national identity was constructed.

Race, however, simply isn't the powerful idea it used to be. In any case, American society includes too many ethnic and racial groups to form a credible "them" from which "we" can protect ourselves.

As for obedience, Americans are of two minds. We value—in the abstract anyway—independence and individualism to a very high degree. This mind-set is played out in myriad ways, from chafing at housing codes to preferring home schooling, to migrating to the West or choosing the suburbs, to lodging tax protests and resisting the draft. Independence and individualism are the staples of popular arts, from television to film to popular music. But this very denial of national consensus and mutual obligation creates a kind of alienation among Americans and a desire for deeper connections to community. Thus we are also a nation of joiners, of self-help groups, clubs and associations, political movements, and online communities. The yearning for national unity is genuine and is romanticized by a good many people who remember World War II, or man walking on the moon, or even the cohesion felt on September 12, 2001. It bursts forth during times of crisis or perceived crisis, but thus far the feeling has faded when the crisis has passed.

While the above elements of America's culture and political structure do seem to offer some brakes on runaway political hysteria, they have at times been ineffective, as we have seen, in correcting political excesses in the short term. Usually the stresses and dislocations that have brought about the political extremism have played themselves out or simply become irrelevant. It would seem that the single greatest explanation for our ability to regain political stability after a crisis is that we simply haven't had a big enough crisis yet. In the present case, for example, despite the shock of 9/11, most Americans have been unaffected directly by the terrorist threat. Troop commitments in Iraq and Afghanistan are relatively small, owing to the extensive use of hired contractors in roles never seen before in a combat area. The volunteer military has allowed American youth to engage the war or to "pursue other interests," in Vice President Cheney's inapt phrase. It is difficult to imagine where the war on terrorism would have taken us had there been several more devastating attacks, as had been feared, or if the Iraq War had been a much worse mess than it has been.

The underlying cultural elements that render Americans prone to fascism remain, however, and will shape our reaction to the next such threat. The romantic exceptionalists and utopians, the populist religious Right and radical Left, the superpatriotic nationalists, and the anti-immigration racists will simmer below the surface until a new and bigger crisis emerges. That crisis may be a new series of terror attacks, a deepening and long-lasting economic collapse, a global energy shortage, a serious epidemic, a larger and more disastrous war, or perhaps a simple realization that the twenty-first century will be China's, or India's, or Russia's century and not ours. Most likely it will be a combination of several of these elements, as one tends to bring about others.

The attacks of September 11 were deadly and shocking to Americans, so shocking that they sparked armed assaults on two countries as well as several years of political hysteria. But they were not society-changing events. Compared to the German experience of the 1920s—or, for that matter, the upheavals roiling any number of societies today—the war on terror is the sort of crisis that can be managed by responsible government and weathered even when less-responsible government is at the helm. The political and social opportunists did not have enough to work with this time.

The Bush Doctrine of American intervention abroad, exceptionalist nationalism, antiliberal populism, and increased executive power seems to have been repudiated by the 2008 election. The dissenters—of which there were many, although they were voiceless in the face of such strong nationalist sentiments—found a leader and a platform through which to articulate a new political and social direction. That is, a new majority was able to couch its dissent in terms of the contrasting American values of equality, reason, and internationalism. But this turnaround was made possible largely by the failures of the Bush era: a misdirected war and a collapsed economy, brought on by promiscuous consumption and widespread chicanery at the top. There is reason to believe that the Bush Doctrine would have been sustained through another presidency had things not turned sour. In fact, it is not unreasonable to conclude that the economic crisis alone was the cause of the Republican Party's reversal in 2008.

Moreover, there is a new crisis that seems unlikely to be resolved any time soon. Major national and international banks have closed, insurance companies are seeking government bailouts, and leading American automakers have gone bankrupt. At this writing, no responsible economist has suggested that the bottom of the economic spiral is even within sight as production is down in nearly every industry, sales are shockingly low, unemployment is rising, and even the health care industry is seeing layoffs. Even before taking office, President Obama cautioned that federal deficits of more than a trillion dollars would be the rule for "the forseeable future."

What will be the fate of the new American majority be in the next election if the economic troubles deepen and stagnate without signs of improvement? How will Americans view the Obama approach if foreign governments stop buying American bonds, and the Treasury Department has to print more money instead? How will we respond to the hyperinflation that results? How will we value coolheaded and patient leadership then?

We cannot know for sure whether America will reach the tipping point at which the political system can no longer be righted and the rule of law restored. As it has not happened yet, we cannot know what conditions are required for America to slip into fascism. But our history demonstrates that Americans have the capacity to react to adversity in a general direction toward fascism. It is possible that the constitutional basis of the political system will protect us if things go too far and that the courts or the electoral process will compensate for excesses. But this prospect is a slim thread on which to hang our hopes for democracy and freedom, as Judge Learned Hand wrote:

> I often wonder whether we do not rest our hopes too much upon constitutions, upon laws and upon courts. These are false hopes; believe me, these are false hopes. Liberty lies in the hearts of men and women; when it dies there, no constitution, no law, no court can save it.[24]

What we learn from the excesses of 1798, the Red Scare, the McCarthy era, and the war on terrorism is that the rule of law is always subordinate to political power. If the public wills it, the law can be ignored. This observation has held true in the United States, in Germany, and for that matter, everywhere. Americans must nourish and preserve the habit of resistance and exercise it before the opportunists have gone too far, for by then the ability to resist may be eroded to impotence. Americans must publicly question each incremental step toward fascism and, most of all, learn to venerate their country in a meaningful and substantial way rather than in vapid reverence for the flag, the military, or the president. We need to be more thoughtful and less romantic, more respectful of wisdom and experience and less populist, more global and less nationalistic, more inclusive and less racist, more questioning and less obedient.

Americans can do some practical things to reduce their chances of sliding too far toward fascism. In studying fascist movements around the world, Nancy Bermeo noted that the single best predictor of success for fascist movements is political polarization.[25] The mutual demonization of opposing parties locks up the machinery of government and makes it possible for a third group to emerge; it promises to sweep away the bickering cowards and to boldly enact the will of the people. Such movements tend to be antidemocratic because they blame the democratic process itself as the cause of the gridlock. When parties have become so polarized that all anyone—voters included—can think of is vanquishing opponents, then a sort of political disillusionment sets in, and political principles give way to an empty contentiousness.

A second useful generalization about the rise of such movements is that they tend to occur when existing democratic regimes are incompetent.[26] Government is not just a theater for ideological or political drama; it is also an essential institution to human life. People get hurt when it doesn't work. Incompetent government raises fears of economic collapse, violence in the streets, and a failure to respond to external enemies or natural disasters. This view is far more true in the current century than it was in, say, the nineteenth century, because the greater density of the world's present population requires more elaborate mechanisms of coordination and regulation to keep everyone fed and secure. So when government fails, citizens will almost always place security above freedom. This inclination is as true of the Afghans and Somalis, among whom the Taliban is again making gains, as it is of the Russians, who have sidled toward the old Soviet-style leadership and away from increasing democratic reforms.

These two generalizations offer a warning to Americans: beware those who seek always to discredit government, to blame it for the nation's ills, and to alienate citizens from its workings. Such people and groups have a strong voice in American politics today. They blame the government for imposing high taxes and wasting taxpayer money, they see it as a barrier to business competitiveness, and they rail against its intrusion in everyday life. They warn of dire consequences if the government gets into the health care business, for example, even though the rest of the modern world has surpassed the United States in health care access as well as in health outcomes. They take pains to point out how bad a job the government does at everything it undertakes and how good a job it does at stifling individual initiative and creativity. But they don't mean it. Even as they extol the virtues of small government, they bloat it with staggering defense appropriations. Even as they warn of its intrusions into the private realm, they give it the power to spy on people or to arrest them without access to the law. Their game is to alienate citizens from their government, to trivialize the vote, and to make the democratic process look ineffective and foolish. The best way to prevent fascism is to avoid alienation, to resist extreme polarization, and to remain connected to the political process.

———————

Germany was ripe for trouble when the nation faced multiple crises in the 1920s. When the Weimar government was unable to quell the distress, Germany plunged into the abyss of fascism, recovering from the nightmare only after the conflagration of total war and ruin. Only through this purifying destruction was German culture finally rid of the elements that had made Germans prone to fascist thought. Germans today, since what they call "Day One"—the day after the war ended—avoid romantic thinking and excessive veneration of the volk. They no longer place Germany *über alles*. They teach their schoolkids to avoid regimentation. They recoil from racism. Their collective memories are too abhorrent to contemplate a return to the way things were.

The German nightmare is in the past. That society fell into the abyss and by all appearances was cleansed by fire of any further appetite for fascism. Americans do not have such memories, however; we have not experienced the utter defeat and destruction of a failed political adventure gone completely mad. We still have the self-assurance to believe that it can't happen here, and that self-assurance may be our greatest weakness.

NOTES

1. Introduction

1. Rajiv Chandrasekaran, *Imperial Life in the Emerald City: Inside Iraq's Green Zone* (New York: Vintage, 2007).
2. See, for example, the CNN election polls. They included questions on twenty-one issues, including stem cell research; lesbian, gay, bisexual, and transgender (LGBT) issues; free trade; and Cuba; but none on political rights, domestic spying, or the Patriot Act. CNN, "Campaign Issues," 2008, (cited March 4, 2009) http://www.cnn.com/ELECTION/2008/issues/.

2. Cause and Culture

1. Hans Ostwald, "A Moral History of the Inflation," in *The Weimar Republic Sourcebook*, ed. Anton Kaes, Martin Jay, and Edward Dimendberg (Berkeley: University of California Press, 1994), 77.
2. George L. Mosse, ed., *Nazi Culture: Intellectual, Cultural, and Social Life in the Third Reich* (New York: Grosset & Dunlap, 1966).
3. Umberto Eco, "Ur-Fascism," *New York Review of Books,* June 22, 1995.

3. Romanticism

1. Ron Suskind, "Without a Doubt," *New York Times,* October 17, 2004.
2. From the *Niederelbisches Tageblatt,* September 12, 1936, quoted in Joachim Remak, ed., *The Nazi Years: A Documentary History* (Englewood Cliffs, NJ: Prentice-Hall, 1969), 79.
3. Peter Viereck, *Metapolitics: From the Romantics to Hitler* (New York: Alfred A. Knopf, 1941), 124.
4. Wolf Lepenies, *The Seduction of Culture in German History* (Princeton, NJ: Princeton University Press, 2006), 42.
5. Randall Collins and Michael Makowsky, *The Discovery of Society,* 6th ed. (Boston: McGraw-Hill, 1998).
6. Much of the ensuing discussion of the English, French, and American Enlightenment is informed by Jacques Barzun, *From Dawn to Decadence: 500 Years*

205

of Western Cultural Life: 1500 to the Present (New York: Perennial, 2000); James Buchan, *Crowded with Genius: The Scottish Enlightenment: Edinburgh's Moment of the Mind* (New York: HarperCollins, 2003); Gertrude Himmelfarb, *The Roads to Modernity: The British, French, and American Enlightenments* (New York: Alfred A. Knopf, 2004). Himmelfarb argues that there were three Enlightenments; the primacy of reason was stressed in the French version. However, belief in an orderly world also underlay the scientific revolution in Scotland and America, according to Buchan. In the social sciences, see also Randall Collins, *Four Sociological Traditions* (New York: Oxford University Press, 1994), 16–20.

7. Buchan, *Crowded with Genius*, 131. In Germany, universalism was largely translated into religious tolerance; see Henri Brunschwig, *Enlightenment and Romanticism in Eighteenth-Century Prussia*, trans. Frank Jellinek (Chicago: University of Chicago Press, 1974), 66.

8. Himmelfarb, *The Roads to Modernity*, 161.

9. Collins and Makowsky, *The Discovery of Society*, 22–4.

10. Brunschwig, *Enlightenment and Romanticism in Eighteenth-Century Prussia*, 65.

11. Steven Ozment, *A Mighty Fortress: A New History of the German People* (New York: Perennial, 2004), 152.

12. Brunschwig, *Enlightenment and Romanticism in Eighteenth-Century Prussia*, 246.

13. Ozment, *A Mighty Fortress*, 153–62.

14. Allen Wilson Porterfield, *An Outline of German Romanticism, 1766–1866* (Boston: Ginn & Co., 1914), 177–80.

15. Carl Schmitt, *Political Romanticism*, trans. Guy Oakes (Berlin: Duncker and Humboldt, 1919; Cambridge, MA: MIT Press, 1986). Citations are to MIT Press edition.

16. Bryan Magee, *The Tristan Chord: Wagner and Philosophy* (New York: Henry Holt, 2000), 209.

17. George Boas, ed., *Romanticism in America: Papers Contributed to a Symposium Held at the Baltimore Museum of Art, May 13, 14, 15, 1940* (New York: Russel & Russel, 1961), viii.

18. Ibid.

19. Barzun, *From Dawn to Decadence*, 470.

20. Boas, *Romanticism in America*, vi.

21. Himmelfarb, *The Roads to Modernity*, 115.

22. Ozment, *A Mighty Fortress*, 228.

23. Robert K. Massie, *Dreadnought: Britain, Germany, and the Coming of the Great War* (New York: Ballantine Books, 1991).

24. Richard J. Evans, *The Coming of the Third Reich* (New York: Penguin, 2004), 83.

25. Ibid., 83–84.

26. Alan Balfour, *Berlin: The Politics of Order, 1737–1989* (New York: Rizzoli International, 1990), 108–51.

27. Wolfgang Grothe, quoted in Peter Gay, *Weimar Culture: The Outsider as Insider* (London: W. W. Norton, 2001), 121.

28. Fritz Stern, *Einstein's German World* (Princeton, NJ: Princeton University Press, 1999).

29. Eric D. Weitz, *Weimar Germany: Promise and Tragedy* (Princeton, NJ: Princeton University Press, 2007), 361.

30. Stefan Zweig, *Die Welt von Gestern: Erinnerungen eines Europäers* (Stuttgart: Deutscher Bücherbund, 1981), quoted in Gay, *Weimar Culture*, 129–30.

31. Rudolf Kayser, "Americanism," in *The Weimar Republic Sourcebook,* 395–397. See also other selections from chapter 15, "Imagining America: Fordism and Technology."

32. Evans, *The Coming of the Third Reich,* 183.

33. Quoted in Viereck, *Metapolitics,* 17.

34. Gerald N. Grob and Robert N. Beck, *Ideas in America: Source Readings in the Intellectual History of the United States* (New York: Free Press, 1970), 128.

35. Daniel J. Boorstin, *The Americans: The National Experience* (New York: Vintage Books, 1965), 222; and Ralph H. Gabriel, *American Values: Continuity and Change* (Westport, CT: Greenwood Press, 1974), 51.

36. Gabriel, *American Values,* 54.

37. Ibid., 55.

38. Quoted in Stewart Winger, *Lincoln, Religion, and Romantic Cultural Politics* (Dekalb, IL: Northern Illinois University Press, 2003), 62.

39. Ibid., 64.

40. Peter Watson, *The Modern Mind: An Intellectual History of the 20th Century* (New York: HarperCollins, 2000), 207.

41. CBS News, "Poll: Creationism Trumps Evolution," November 22, 2004 (cited June 21, 2007) http://www.cbsnews.com/stories/2004/11/22/opinion/polls/main657083.shtml.

42. Howard Mumford Jones, *O Strange New World: American Culture: The Formative Years* (New York: Viking, 1964), 379.

43. Philip French, *Westerns: Aspects of a Movie Genre* (New York: Oxford University Press, 1977), 107.

44. Robert Pattison, *The Triumph of Vulgarity: Rock Music in the Mirror of Romanticism* (New York: Oxford University Press, 1987), 188.

45. John C. Scott, "The Mission of the University: Medieval to Postmodern Transformations," *Journal of Higher Education* 77, no. 1 (2006).

46. Mary Belenky and others, *Women's Ways of Knowing: The Development of Self, Voice, and Mind* (New York: Basic Books, 1997).

47. Bronwyn Davies, "Women and Transgression in the Halls of Academe," *Studies in Higher Education* 31, no. 4 (2006).

48. See Emily Martin, *The Woman in the Body: A Cultural Analysis of Reproduction* (Boston: Beacon Press, 1987). Also see David H. Freeman, "The Aggressive Egg," *Discovery,* June 1, 1992.

49. Kathleen Wheeler, *Romanticism, Pragmatism, and Deconstruction* (Oxford, UK: Blackwell, 1993), x.

50. See, for example, Patricia Hill Collins, *Black Feminist Thought: Knowledge, Consciousness, and the Politics of Empowerment* (New York: Routledge, Chapman and Hall, 1990).

51. Laurie Goodstein, "Teaching of Creationism Is Endorsed in New Survey," *New York Times,* August 31 2005.

52. Gary Gerstle, *The American Crucible: Race and Nation in the Twentieth Century* (Princeton, NJ: Princeton University Press, 2001), 135.

53. Steven E. Schier, *You Call This an Election? America's Peculiar Democracy* (Washington, DC: Georgetown University Press, 2003). See also E. J. Dionne, Jr., *Why Americans Hate Politics* (New York: Simon & Schuster, 1991).
54. Martha Sawyer Allen, "Politics Is a Dirty Word; Does It Have to Be That Way?" *Minneapolis Star-Tribune*, November 8, 2003.
55. Thomas E. Patterson, *The Vanishing Voter: Public Involvement in an Age of Uncertainty* (New York: Alfred A. Knopf, 2002), 63–64.
56. Ibid., 82.
57. Darrell M. West and L. Sandy Maisel, "Conclusion: Discourse and Beyond," in *Running on Empty? Political Discourse in Congressional Elections*, ed. L. Sandy Maisel and Darrell M. West (New York: Rowman & Littlefield, 2004), 229.
58. Samuel Walker, *In Defense of American Liberties: A History of the ACLU*, 2nd ed. (Carbondale: Southern Illinois University Press, 1999). See also Gerstle, *The American Crucible*, 89–91.

4. Populism

1. Evans, *The Coming of the Third Reich*, 170.
2. Ibid., 175.
3. Max H. Kele, *Nazis and Workers: National Socialist Appeals to German Labor, 1919–1933* (Chapel Hill: University of North Carolina Press, 1972).
4. George L. Mosse, *The Fascist Revolution: Toward a General Theory of Fascism* (New York: Howard Fertig, 1999), 9. This phrase, by the way, has been resurrected by contemporary politicians to claim a similarly transcendent position independent of partisan party lines. Bill Clinton used it in the 1992 campaign for the Democratic nomination, and Tony Blair has used it to similar purpose.
5. Evans, *The Coming of the Third Reich*, 180.
6. William L. Shirer, *The Rise and Fall of the Third Reich: A History of Nazi Germany* (New York: Simon and Schuster, 1960), 69–70.
7. Worth Robert Miller, "Farmers and Third-Party Politics in Late Nineteenth-Century America," in *The Gilded Age: Essays on the Origins of Modern America*, edited by Charles W. Calhoun (Wilmington, DE: Scholarly Resources Inc., 1996), 235–60.
8. Robert C. McMath, Jr., *American Populism: A Social History, 1877–1898* (New York: Hill and Wang, 1993), 135–36.
9. Sheldon Hackney, ed., "Introduction," in *Populism: The Critical Issues* (Boston: Little, Brown, 1971).
10. McMath, *American Populism*, 144.
11. Hackney, *Populism*, xi.
12. John D. Hicks, *The Populist Revolt: A History of the Farmers' Alliance and the People's Party* (Minneapolis: University of Minnesota Press, 1931), 405.
13. Miller, "Farmers and Third-Party Politics."
14. Ibid.
15. Richard Hofstadter, *Anti-Intellectualism in American Life* (New York: Alfred A. Knopf, 1963), 68.
16. George McKenna, "Populism: The American Ideology," in *American Populism*, ed. George McKenna (New York: G. P. Putnam's Sons, 1974), xii.

17. C. Vann Woodward, "The Populist Heritage and the Intellectual," *American Scholar* 29 (1960); and Richard Hofstadter, *The Age of Reform: From Bryan to F.D.R.* (New York: Alfred A. Knopf, 1955), 94–95.

18. *George Wallace: Settin' the Woods on Fire*, The American Experience, DVD, directed by Daniel Mccabe and Paul Stekler (PBS Home Video, 2000). From a conversation with Seymore Trammel, then Barbour County's district attorney, recalled by Trammel himself. The *New York Times*'s obituary of Wallace had a different version, by which Wallace swore never to be "out-segged" again.

19. McMath, *American Populism*, 11.

20. McKenna, *American Populism*, xxii.

21. Hofstadter, *Anti-Intellectualism in American Life.*

22. McKenna, *American Populism*, 213.

23. Both quotations are from Hofstadter, *Anti-Intellectualism in American Life*, 10.

24. Irwin Unger, "Critique of Norman Pollack's 'Fear of Man'," in Hackney, *Populism*, 118.

25. Hofstadter, *Anti-Intellectualism in American Life*, 12.

26. Carl Abbott, "Urban America," in *Making America: The Society & Culture of the United States*, ed. Luther S. Luedtke (Chapel Hill: University of North Carolina Press, 1992), 115.

27. Hackney, *Populism*, xii.

28. Richard Hofstadter, "The Folklore of Populism," in Hackney, *Populism*, 77–78.

29. Hofstadter, *The Age of Reform;* and Hackney, *Populism.*

30. Ralf Dahrendorf, *Society and Democracy in Germany* (Garden City, NY: Doubleday, 1967), 38.

31. Detlev J. K. Peukert, *The Weimar Republic: The Crisis of Classical Modernity*, trans. Richard Deveson (New York: Hill and Wang, 1989), 6.

32. Ibid., 66, 101.

33. Ibid., 179.

34. Ibid., 11–14.

35. Dahrendorf, *Society and Democracy in Germany*, 105.

36. Evans, *The Coming of the Third Reich*, 208.

37. Ibid.; and Claudia Koonz, *The Nazi Conscience* (Cambridge, MA: Belknap Press, 2003), 21.

38. Dietrich Orlow, *The History of the Nazi Party* (Pittsburgh: University of Pittsburgh Press, 1969), 132.

39. Evans, *The Coming of the Third Reich*, 209.

40. George L. Mosse, *The Crisis of German Ideology: Intellectual Origins of the Third Reich* (New York: Grosset & Dunlap, 1964), 98.

41. Evans, *The Coming of the Third Reich*, 211.

42. Koonz, *The Nazi Conscience*, 31.

43. Evans, *The Coming of the Third Reich*, 264.

44. Kele, *Nazis and Workers*, 29.

45. Viereck, *Metapolitics*, 39.

46. Mosse, *Nazi Culture.*

47. Eric H. Vieler, *The Ideological Roots of German National Socialism* (New York: Peter Lang, 1999), 9.

48. Pierre Ayçoberry, *The Social History of the Third Reich, 1933–1945,* trans. Janet Lloyd (New York: New Press, 1999), 68.
49. Kele, *Nazis and Workers,* 25.
50. David Schoenbaum, *Hitler's Social Revolution: Class and Status in Nazi Germany, 1933–1939* (Garden City, NY: Doubleday, 1966), 47.
51. Victor C. Ferkiss, "Populist Influences on American Fascism 1957," *Western Political Quarterly* 10, no. 2 (1957):350, 69.
52. Dane Smith, "Cheney Applauds Rural Voters, Values," *Minneapolis Star-Tribune,* August 7, 2004.
53. Joshua Kurlantzick, "The Campaign Trail: Pardon?" *New Yorker,* April 19–26, 2004.
54. Thomas Frank, *What's the Matter with Kansas? How Conservatives Won the Heart of America* (New York: Metropolitan Books, 2004), 104.
55. McKenna, *American Populism,* 245.
56. Frank, *What's the Matter with Kansas?*

5. Nationalism

1. Paul Farhi, "For Broadcast Media, Patriotism Pays," *Washington Post,* April 7, 2003.
2. George Lipsitz, "Dilemmas of Beset Nationhood: Patriotism, the Family, and Economic Change in the 1970s and 1980s," in *Bonds of Affection: Americans Define Their Patriotism,* ed. John Bodnar (Princeton, NJ: Princeton University Press, 1996).
3. Louis L. Snyder, *Roots of German Nationalism* (Bloomington: Indiana University Press, 1978), vii.
4. For definitions of this and the following types of nationalism, see Hans Kohn, *Nationalism, Its Meaning and History* (Princeton, NJ: Van Nostrand, 1955).
5. Snyder, *Roots of German Nationalism,* vii.
6. Ibid., 2.
7. Albert Goldman and Evert Sprinchorn, eds., *Wagner on Music and Drama: A Compendium of Richard Wagner's Prose Works,* trans. H. Ashton Ellis (New York: E. P. Dutton & Co., 1964).
8. Pamela M. Potter, *Most German of the Arts: Musicology and Society from the Weimar Republic to the End of Hitler's Reich* (New Haven: Yale University Press, 1998).
9. Cecilia Hopkins Porter, *The Rhine as Musical Metaphor: Cultural Identity in German Romantic Music* (Boston: Northeastern University Press, 1996), 5.
10. Snyder, *Roots of German Nationalism,* 43–49. The Grimms' compilation was added to the United Nations Educational, Scientific, and Cultural Organization's "Memory of the World" register as part of the world cultural heritage in 2005.
11. Ibid., 48.
12. Mosse, *The Crisis of German Ideology,* 26.
13. Ibid., 76.
14. Ibid., 77.
15. Snyder, *Roots of German Nationalism,* 62.
16. Vieler, *The Ideological Roots of German National Socialism,* 25.
17. Snyder, *Roots of German Nationalism,* 24.
18. Gordon A. Craig, *The Germans* (New York: Penguin, 1991), 86.

19. Liah Greenfeld, *Nationalism: Five Roads to Modernity* (Cambridge, MA: Harvard University Press, 1992), 366.
20. Mosse, *Nazi Culture*, 134.
21. David Culbert, "The Impact of Anti-Semitic Film Propaganda on German Audiences: *Jew Süss* and *the Wandering Jew*," in *Art, Culture, and Media under the Third Reich*, ed. Richard A. Etlin (Chicago: University of Chicago Press, 2002). Also Mary-Elizabeth O'Brien, "The Celluloid War: Packaging War for Sale in Nazi Home-Front Films," in Etlin, *Art, Culture, and Media under the Third Reich.*
22. Joachim Wolschke-Bulmahn and Gert Gröning, "The National Socialist Garden and Landscape Ideal: Bodenständigkeit (Rootedness in the Soil)," in Etlin, *Art, Culture, and Media under the Third Reich*, 76.
23. Both quotations are from Barbara W. Tuchman, *The March of Folly: From Troy to Vietnam* (New York: Ballantine Books, 1984), 127, 84.
24. Winthrop S. Hudson, ed., *Nationalism and Religion in America: Concepts of American Identity and Mission* (New York: Harper & Row, 1970).
25. Lawrence J. Friedman, *Inventors of the Promised Land* (New York: Alfred A. Knopf, 1975), xiii. See also Cynthia M. Koch, "Teaching Patriotism: Private Virtue for the Public Good in the Early Republic," in Bodnar, *Bonds of Affection;* and Hans Kohn, *American Nationalism: An Interpretive Essay* (New York: Macmillan, 1957).
26. Boorstin, *The Americans*, 391.
27. Paul Johnson, *A History of the American People* (New York: HarperPerennial, 1997), 423.
28. Luther S. Luedtke, "The Search for American Character," in *Making America: The Society & Culture of the United States*, ed. Luther S. Luedtke (Chapel Hill: University of North Carolina Press, 1992). See also Arthur Mann, "From Immigration to Acculturation," in *Making America*, which provides statistics showing that by 1880 all major American cities were populated predominantly by foreign-born people.
29. Boorstin, *The Americans*, 363.
30. Steven Watts, *The Republic Reborn: War and the Making of Liberal America, 1790–1820* (Baltimore, MD: Johns Hopkins University Press, 1987), 283.
31. For a good analysis of the importance of this "market revolution," see the readings in Melvyn Stokes and Stephen Conway, eds., *The Market Revolution in America: Social, Political, and Religious Expressions, 1800–1880* (Charlottesville: University Press of Virginia, 1996); and Watts, *The Republic Reborn.*
32. Arthur M. Schlesinger, Jr., *The Disuniting of America: Reflections on a Multicultural Society* (New York: W. W. Norton, 1998), 16.
33. Charles McKay, *Life and Liberty in America*, quoted in Greenfeld, *Nationalism.*
34. Boorstin, *The Americans*, 365–67. Also Wilbur Zelinsky, *Nation into State: The Shifting Symbolic Foundations of American Nationalism* (Chapel Hill: University of North Carolina Press, 1988).
35. Schlesinger, *The Disuniting of America*, 123.
36. David Waldstreicher, *In the Midst of Perpetual Fetes: The Making of American Nationalism, 1776–1820* (Chapel Hill: University of North Carolina Press, 1997).
37. Boorstin, *The Americans*, 379–82.
38. Ibid., 374–75.
39. Gerstle, *The American Crucible*, 57.

40. Ibid., 91.

41. Samuel P. Huntington, *Who Are We? The Challenges to America's National Identity* (New York: Simon & Schuster, 2004). See also John Higham, "Hanging Together: Divergent Unities in American History, June 1974," *Journal of American History* 61 (1974); Henry Steele Commager, *Jefferson, Nationalism, and the Enlightenment* (New York: George Braziller, 1975); and Jones, *O Strange New World*.

42. For example, repeated attempts were made in the late nineteenth century to amend the Constitution to include the phrase "almighty God" in its Preamble. See Gaines M. Foster, "A Christian Nation: Signs of a Covenant," in Bodnar, *Bonds of Affection*, 126.

43. Huntington, *Who Are We?* 141–43. See also Higham, "Hanging Together."

44. Dickran Tashjian, "The Artlessness of American Culture," in Luedtke, *Making America*.

45. There are those who claim that no truly American styles have been developed in various art forms. See ibid., regarding visual arts, and Leland M. Roth, "A New Architecture, yet Old," in Luedtke, *Making America*, regarding architecture.

46. Luedtke, "The Search for American Character."

47. Bennett has spawned a minor industry in publishing, with such titles as *The Book of Virtues: A Treasury of Great Moral Stories, The Book of Virtues for Young People: A Treasury of Great Moral Stories, The Children's Treasury of Virtues, The Children's Book of Heroes, The Children's Book of Faith, The Children's Book of America, Why We Fight: Moral Clarity and the War on Terrorism,* and *Our Country's Founders: A Book of Advice for Young People.* He has also entered the exceptionalism business with *America: The Last Best Hope,* in two volumes.

48. Sheldon Hackney, "A National Conversation on American Populism and Identity," *Humanities* 15, no. 6 (1994).

49. Ana M. Aizcorbe, Arthur B. Kennickell, and Kevin B. Moore, "Recent Changes in U.S. Family Finances: Evidence from the 1998 and 2001 Survey of Consumer Finances," *Federal Reserve Bulletin* 89 (2003).

50. This figure is higher than what is commonly reported, but it is more accurate because it includes indirect costs of the military such as veterans' benefits, foreign military aid, and the military's share of interest on the national debt. And the total base on which the percentage is calculated does not include Social Security funds, since they are not generated from the federal income tax. For documentation on the supplemental appropriation to fund the war on terrorism, see Congressional Budget Office, *Letter to Senate Budget Committee,* February 11, 2008 (cited June 25 2008), http://www.cbo.gov/ftpdocs/89xx/doc8971/Letter.2.1.shtml.

51. Brian E. Fogarty, *War, Peace, and the Social Order* (Boulder, CO: Westview Press, 2000), 104.

52. Commager, *Jefferson, Nationalism, and the Enlightenment,* xiii.

53. Huntington, *Who Are We?* 47.

54. Friedman, *Inventors of the Promised Land,* 57.

55. Watts, *The Republic Reborn,* 283–93. See also Higham, "Hanging Together," 13; and Robert B. Westbrook, "In the Mirror of the Enemy: Japanese Political

Culture and the Peculiarities of American Patriotism in World War II," in Bodnar, *Bonds of Affection*..

56. John Bodnar, "The Attractions of Patriotism," in Bodnar, *Bonds of Affection*.
57. Cecilia Elizabeth O'Leary, "'Blood Brotherhood': The Racialization of Patriotism, 1865–1918," in Bodnar, *Bonds of Affection*, 64. See also Waldstreicher, *In the Midst of Perpetual Fetes*, for a description of the use of national holidays and celebrations as platforms for demonstrating various interpretations of American identity.
58. Stuart McConnell, "Reading the Flag: A Reconsideration of the Patriotic Cults of the 1890s," in Bodnar, *Bonds of Affection*.
59. Lipsitz, "Dilemmas of Beset Nationhood," 255; and Higham, "Hanging Together," 17–18.
60. Schlesinger, *The Disuniting of America*, 142.
61. Frank, *What's the Matter with Kansas?*

6. Racism

1. George M. Fredrickson, *Racism: A Short History* (Princeton, NJ: Princeton University Press, 2002). While many—probably most—nations have treated various ethnic groups unequally, only in these three did the legitimate government pass entire systems of laws to officially discriminate against subordinate groups on the basis of race.
2. Stern, *Einstein's German World*, 277.
3. *Savage Acts*, videorecording, directed by Pennee Bender, Joshua Brown, and Andrea Ades Vasquez (New York: American Social History Productions, 1995). The passage is also quoted in Howard Zinn, *A People's History of the United States: 1492–Present* (New York: Perennial Classics, 2003), 315.
4. Daniel Jonah Goldhagen, *Hitler's Willing Executioners: Ordinary Germans and the Holocaust* (New York: Vintage Books, 1997), 45.
5. Lucy S. Dawidowicz, *The War against the Jews, 1933–1945* (New York: Holt, Rhinehart, and Winston, 1975), 23.
6. Ozment, *A Mighty Fortress*, 95–98.
7. Ibid., 99.
8. Dawidowicz, *The War against the Jews*, 30.
9. Peter Pulzer, *Jews and the German State: The Political History of a Minority, 1848–1933* (Detroit: Wayne State University Press, 2003), 28.
10. Ibid., 2.
11. Dawidowicz, *The War against the Jews*, 31–32.
12. Pulzer, *Jews and the German State*, 32.
13. Goldhagen, *Hitler's Willing Executioners*, 57.
14. Pulzer, *Jews and the German State*, 109-17.
15. Ibid., 129.
16. Goldhagen, *Hitler's Willing Executioners*, 77.
17. Pulzer, *Jews and the German State*, xix.
18. Michael Burleigh, *The Third Reich: A New History* (New York: Hill and Wang, 2000), 29–32; and Pulzer, *Jews and the German State*, 205.
19. Dawidowicz, *The War against the Jews*, 46.
20. Ibid., 47.
21. Burleigh, *The Third Reich*, 292.

22. Ibid., 293.

23. Ibid., 320.

24. Zinn, *A People's History of the United States*, 23–27.

25. Ibid., 12.

26. Mark S. Weiner, *Black Trials: Citizenship from the Beginnings of Slavery to the End of Caste* (New York: Vintage Books, 2004), 28–31. Whether Africans and Indians were regarded as innately different or simply culturally backward is a matter of some dispute. Zinn, for example, argues that from the very beginning of the colonies, whites viewed blacks as inherently inferior. But Ruchames, Horsman, and many others offer evidence that differences in capability were generally taken to be typical of differences among cultures and nations. See Zinn, *A People's History of the United States*, 23–33; also Reginald Horsman, *Race and Manifest Destiny: The Origins of American Racial Anglo-Saxonism* (Cambridge, MA: Harvard University Press, 1981), 98–99; and Louis Ruchames, ed., *Racial Thought in America: A Documentary History*, vol. 1 (Amherst: University of Massachusetts Press, 1969), 1–23.

27. Ibid., 31.

28. Ibid., 59.

29. Ibid., 31.

30. Ruchames, *Racial Thought in America*, 238.

31. Horsman, *Race and Manifest Destiny*, 121.

32. James Hunt, "The Negro's Place in Nature," *Anti-Abolition Tracts No. 4* (New York: Van Evrie, Horton & Company, 1868), in *Anti-Abolition Tracts and Anti-Black Stereotypes: General Statements of "the Negro Problem,"* ed. John David Smith (New York: Garland, 1993), 97–123; "The Six Species of Men," *Anti-Abolition Tracts No. 5* (New York: Van Evrie, Horton & Company, 1866), in *Anti-Abolition Tracts and Anti-Black Stereotypes*, 125–155; and Horsman, *Race and Manifest Destiny*, 140.

33. Stephan Thernstrom and Abigail Thernstrom, *America in Black and White: One Nation, Indivisible* (New York: Simon & Schuster, 1997), 31.

34. Joe R. Feagin, Hernán Vera, and Pinar Batur, *White Racism: The Basics* (New York: Routledge, 2001), 22.

35. Thernstrom and Thernstrom, *America in Black and White*, 45.

36. Alden T. Vaughan, *Roots of American Racism: Essays on the Colonial Experience* (New York: Oxford, 1995), 3.

37. Ibid., 11.

38. Ibid., 20–26.

39. Joe R Feagin, *Racial and Ethnic Relations*, 3rd ed. (Upper Saddle River, NJ: Prentice-Hall, 1989), 104.

40. Theodore W. Allen, *The Invention of the White Race*, vol. 1, *Racial Oppression and Social Control* (London: Verso, 1994), 31.

41. Ronald Takaki, *A Different Mirror: A History of Multicultural America* (Boston: Little, Brown, 1993), 194.

42. Ibid., 206.

43. Benjamin B. Ringer, *"We the People" and Others: Duality and America's Treatment of Its Racial Minorities* (New York: Tavistock, 1983), 591.

44. United States Census Bureau, *Housing Patterns*, June 27 2005 (cited March

27, 2008), http://www.census.gov/hhes/www/housing/housing_patterns/overview.html.

45. Thernstrom and Thernstrom, *America in Black and White*, 286–95, 520–25.

46. Richard Breitman, "New Sources on the Holocaust in Italy," *Holocaust and Genocide Studies* 16, no. 3 (2002): 402–14. See also Maura E. Hametz, "The Ambivalence of Italian Antisemitism: Fascism, Nationalism, and Racism in Trieste," *Holocaust and Genocide Studies* 16, no. 3 (2002):376–401.

47. Leon D. Wynter, *American Skin: Pop Culture, Big Business, and the End of White America* (New York: Crown, 2002), 5–18.

48. Ibid.

7. Authoritarianism

1. Erich Fromm, *Escape from Freedom* (New York: Farrar & Rhinehart, 1941).

2. T. W. Adorno and others, *The Authoritarian Personality*, abridged ed. (New York: Harper, 1950; New York: Norton, 1982).

3. This idea was first proposed by Adorno and others. Altemeyer reviewed the research and provided his own test of the hypothesis, concluding there was no evidence to support it. See ibid.; and Bob Altemeyer, *Enemies of Freedom: Understanding Right-Wing Authoritarianism* (San Francisco: Jossey-Bass, 1988).

4. William Stone and Laurence Smith, for example, found little difference between the authoritarianism scores of adolescents in Austria, Germany, France, and the United States. William F. Stone and Laurence D. Smith, "Authoritarianism: Left and Right," in *Strength and Weakness: The Authoritarian Personality Today*, ed. William F. Stone, Gerda Lederer, and Richard Christie (New York: Springer-Verlag, 1993), 191.

5. Goldhagen, *Hitler's Willing Executioners*, 383.

6. Stanley Milgram, *Obedience to Authority: An Experimental View* (New York: Harper & Row, 1974). Milgram actually performed a wide range of variations on the experiment—different physical environments, different actors, moving learners closer to teachers, and so on—as a way of addressing diverse interpretations of the results. His film of the original experiment is essential to understanding the subjects' motivations. See Stanley Milgram, *Obedience*, DVD, edited by Stanley Milgram (University Park: Pennsylvania State University, 1969).

7. Altemeyer, *Enemies of Freedom*, 2.

8. Goldhagen notes that in variations on the basic experiment where the teacher faces the learner directly, the rate of total obedience declines to "only" 30 percent.

9. These observations are culled from various sources: John Ardagh, *Germany and the Germans: An Anatomy of a Society Today* (New York: Harper & Row, 1987); Hyde Flippo, *The German Way: Aspects of Behavior, Attitudes, and Customs in the German-Speaking World* (Lincolnwood, IL: Passport Books, 1998); Adolph Schalk, *The Germans* (Engelwood Cliffs, NJ: Prentice-Hall, 1971); Craig, *The Germans*; and Catherine C. Fraser and Dierk O. Hoffmann, *Pop Culture Germany! Media, Arts, and Lifestyle* (Santa Barbara, CA: ABC-CLIO, 2006).

10. Greg Nees, *Germany: Unraveling an Enigma* (Yarmouth, ME: Intercultural Press, 2000), 20.

11. Ardagh, *Germany and the Germans*, 14.

12. Robert Gellately, *Backing Hitler: Consent and Coercion in Nazi Germany* (Oxford, UK: Oxford University Press, 2001), 6.

13. Nicholas N. Kittrie, *The War against Authority: From the Crisis of Legitimacy to a New Social Contract* (Baltimore: Johns Hopkins University Press, 1995), xiii; and Barrington Moore, Jr., *Authority and Inequality under Capitalism and Socialism* (Oxford, UK: Clarendon Press, 1987), 18.

14. Stephen S. Owen and Kenneth Wagner, "The Specter of Authoritarianism among Criminal Justice Majors," *Journal of Criminal Justice Education* 19, no. 1 (2008); H. Michael Crowson, "Authoritarianism, Perceived Threat, and Human Rights Attitudes in U.S. Law Students: A Brief Look," *Individual Differences Research* 5, no. 4 (2007); and Allan L. McCutcheon, "A Latent Class Analysis of Tolerance and Nonconformity in the American Public," *Public Opinion Quarterly* 49 (1985).

15. For a review of this literature, see Richard M. Doty, Bill E. Peterson, and David G. Winter, "Threat and Authoritarianism in the United States, 1978–1987," *Journal of Personality and Social Psychology* 61, no. 4 (1991). See also Stone, Lederer, and Christie, *Strength and Weakness*.

16. Elizabeth Suhay and Martha Hill, "The Structure of Public Opinion in the Wake of 9/11: Ethnocentrism, Authoritarianism, and Support of War" (paper presented at the Midwestern Political Science Association Annual Meeting, Chicago, 2004); and Andrew J. Perrin, "National Threat and Political Culture: Authoritarianism, Antiauthoritarianism, and the September 11 Attacks," *Political Psychology* 26, no. 2 (2005). Suhay and Hill used survey data as the basis for research while Perrin used letters to the editor. The ambivalent outcome of the latter study is likely the result of the way editors select readers' letters by "balancing" each letter with one of an opposite opinion.

17. Stewart J. H. McCann, "Threatening Times, 'Strong' Presidential Popular Vote Winners, and the Victory Margin, 1824–1964," *Journal of Personality and Social Psychology* 73, no. 1 (1997). See also Markus Kemmelmeier, "Authoritarianism and Candidate Support in the U. S. Presidential Elections of 1996 and 2000," *Journal of Social Psychology* 144, no. 2 (2004).

18. Irene Taviss Thomson, "From Conflict to Embedment: The Individual-Society Relationship, 1920–1991," *Sociological Forum* 12, no. 4 (1997). See also Philip Elliot Slater, *The Pursuit of Loneliness: American Culture at the Breaking Point* (Boston: Beacon Press, 1970); and Robert N. Bellah and others, *Habits of the Heart: Individualism and Commitment in American Life* (Berkeley: University of California Press, 1985).

19. The party's early history is well documented and provides fascinating insight into the mundane politics of the future Third Reich. See Shirer, *The Rise and Fall of the Third Reich*; Orlow, *The History of the Nazi Party;* and Evans, *The Coming of the Third Reich.*

20. Gellately, *Backing Hitler*, 22.

21. Karl Dietrich Bracher, "The Technique of the National Socialist Siezure of Power," in *The Path to Dictatorship 1918–1933*, ed. Fritz Stern (New York: Frederick A. Praeger, 1966).

22. Richard J. Evans, *The Third Reich in Power* (New York: Penguin, 2005).

23. Gellately, *Backing Hitler.*

8. Can It Happen Here?

1. This discussion and much of what follows regarding attacks on the Constitution come from Geoffrey R. Stone, *Perilous Times: Free Speech in Wartime from the Sedition Act of 1798 to the War on Terrorism* (New York: W. W. Norton, 2004).

2. Ibid., 96–98.

3. Ibid. See also Gerstle, *The American Crucible*, 85–94.

4. George Creel, *How We Advertised America: The First Telling of the Amazing Story of the Committee on Public Information that Carried the Gospel of Americanism to Every Corner of the Globe* (New York: Harper & Brothers, 1920), 5. Quoted in Murray B. Levin, *Political Hysteria in America: The Democratic Capacity for Repression* (New York: Basic Books, 1971).

5. Stone, *Perilous Times*, 156.

6. Ibid., 186.

7. Matt Gouras, "Montana Pardons Issued 'about 80 Years Too Late,'" *Minneapolis Star-Tribune*, 2003 (cited May 4, 2006), http://www.startribune.com/484/v-print/story/410443.html.

8. "The Enemy Within: Terror in America—1776 to Today" (Washington, DC: International Spy Museum, 2004).

9. Levin, *Political Hysteria in America*, 106–12. The present discussion of the Red Scare of 1919–20 is based largely on Levin's analysis.

10. Ibid., 93–94.

11. This and the previous Hansen quote are from ibid., 30.

12. Ibid., 28–29.

13. Ibid., 128.

14. Warren G. Harding, Boston, May 14, 1920.

15. Stone, *Perilous Times*, 212.

16. Ibid., 213.

17. Ibid., 339.

18. Ibid., 378.

19. The run-up to war is well documented, most notably by Bob Woodward and Richard Clarke. See Bob Woodward, *Plan of Attack* (New York: Simon & Schuster, 2004); Richard Clarke, *Against All Enemies: Inside America's War on Terror* (New York: Free Press, 2004); and Richard Clarke, *Your Government Failed You: Breaking the Cycle of National Security Disasters* (New York: HarperCollins, 2008).

20. Anita Miller, ed., *George W. Bush Versus the Constitution: The Downing Street Memos and Deception, Manipulation, Torture, Retribution, and Coverups in the Iraq War and Illegal Domestic Spying* (Chicago: Academy Chicago Publishers, 2006), xvi–xxiii.

21. Stone, *Perilous Times*, 553.

22. Ibid., 551.

23. Levin, *Political Hysteria in America*, 91.

24. Quoted in Stone, *Perilous Times*, 536.

25. Nancy Bermeo, *Ordinary People in Extraordinary Times: The Citizenry and the Breakdown of Democracy* (Princeton, NJ: Princeton University Press, 2003), 19.

26. David Spitz, *Patterns of Anti-Democratic Thought: An Analysis and a Criticism, with Special Reference to the American Political Mind in Recent Times* (New York: Free Press, 1965), 151.

SELECTED BIBLIOGRAPHY

Altemeyer, Bob. *The Authoritarian Specter*. Cambridge, MA: Harvard University Press, 1996.

———. *Enemies of Freedom: Understanding Right-Wing Authoritarianism*. San Francisco: Jossey-Bass, 1988.

Ayçoberry, Pierre. *The Social History of the Third Reich, 1933–1945*. Translated by Janet Lloyd. New York: New Press, 1999.

Barzun, Jacques. *From Dawn to Decadence: 500 Years of Western Cultural Life: 1500 to the Present*. New York: Perennial, 2000.

Boorstin, Daniel J. *The Americans: The National Experience*. New York: Vintage Books, 1965.

Browning, Christopher R. *Ordinary Men: Reserve Police Battalion 101 and the Final Solution in Poland*. New York: HarperPerennial, 1993.

Burleigh, Michael. *The Third Reich: A New History*. New York: Hill and Wang, 2000.

Craig, Gordon A. *The Germans*. New York: Penguin Books, 1991.

Dahrendorf, Ralf. *Society and Democracy in Germany*. Garden City, NY: Doubleday, 1967.

Dawidowicz, Lucy S. *The War against the Jews, 1933–1945*. New York: Holt, Rhinehart, and Winston, 1975.

Dionne, E. J., Jr. *Why Americans Hate Politics*. New York: Simon & Schuster, 1991.

Evans, Richard J. *The Coming of the Third Reich*. New York: Penguin, 2004.

———. *The Third Reich in Power*. New York: Penguin, 2005.

Frank, Thomas. *What's the Matter with Kansas? How Conservatives Won the Heart of America*. New York: Metropolitan Books, 2004.

Fromm, Erich. *Escape from Freedom*. New York: Farrar & Rhinehart, 1941.

Gay, Peter. *Weimar Culture: The Outsider as Insider*. London: W. W. Norton, 2001.

Gellately, Robert. *Backing Hitler: Consent and Coercion in Nazi Germany*. Oxford, UK: Oxford University Press, 2001.

Gerstle, Gary. *The American Crucible: Race and Nation in the Twentieth Century*. Princeton, NJ: Princeton University Press, 2001.

Goldhagen, Daniel Jonah. *Hitler's Willing Executioners: Ordinary Germans and the Holocaust.* New York: Vintage Books, 1997.

Gore, Al. *The Assault on Reason.* New York: Penguin, 2007.

Hackney, Sheldon, ed. *Populism: The Critical Issues.* Boston: Little, Brown, 1971.

Himmelfarb, Gertrude. *The Roads to Modernity: The British, French, and American Enlightenments.* New York: Alfred A. Knopf, 2004.

Hobsbawm, Eric. *The Age of Extremes: A History of the World, 1914–1991.* New York: Vintage Books, 1996.

Hofstadter, Richard. *Anti-Intellectualism in American Life.* New York: Alfred A. Knopf, 1963.

———. *The Paranoid Style in American Politics and Other Essays.* New York: Alfred A. Knopf, 1965.

Johnson, Paul. *A History of the American People.* New York: HarperPerennial, 1997.

Kaes, Anton, Martin Jay, and Edward Dimendberg, eds. *The Weimar Republic Sourcebook.* Berkeley: University of California Press, 1994.

Kershaw, Ian. *The Nazi Dictatorship: Problems and Perspectives of Interpretation.* London: Edward Arnold, 1985.

Koonz, Claudia. *The Nazi Conscience.* Cambridge, MA: Belknap Press, 2003.

Levin, Murray B. *Political Hysteria in America: The Democratic Capacity for Repression.* New York: Basic Books, 1971.

Lewis, Sinclair. *It Can't Happen Here.* London: Cape, 1935; New York: Signet Books, 1970.

Magee, Bryan. *The Tristan Chord: Wagner and Philosophy.* New York: Henry Holt, 2000.

McKenna, George, ed. *American Populism.* New York: G. P. Putnam's Sons, 1974.

Milgram, Stanley. *Obedience to Authority: An Experimental View.* New York: Harper & Row, 1974.

Mosse, George L. *The Fascist Revolution: Toward a General Theory of Fascism.* New York: Howard Fertig, 1999.

Orlow, Dietrich. *The History of the Nazi Party.* Pittsburgh: University of Pittsburgh Press, 1969.

Ozment, Steven. *A Mighty Fortress: A New History of the German People.* New York: Perennial, 2004.

Peukert, Detlev J. K. *The Weimar Republic: The Crisis of Classical Modernity.* Translated by Richard Deveson. New York: Hill and Wang, 1992.

Pulzer, Peter. *Jews and the German State: The Political History of a Minority, 1848–1933.* Detroit: Wayne State University Press, 2003.

Rorty, Richard. *Objectivity, Relativism, and Truth.* Vol. 1. Cambridge, UK: Cambridge University Press, 1991.

Snyder, Louis L. *Roots of German Nationalism.* Bloomington: Indiana University Press, 1978.

Stern, Fritz. *Einstein's German World.* Princeton, NJ: Princeton University Press, 1999.

———. *The Politics of Cultural Despair: A Study in the Rise of the Germanic Ideology.* Berkeley: University of California Press, 1961.

Stone, Geoffrey R. *Perilous Times: Free Speech in Wartime from the Sedition Act of 1798 to the War on Terrorism.* New York: W. W. Norton, 2004.

Vieler, Eric H. *The Ideological Roots of German National Socialism.* Edited by Peter
    M. Daly, McGill European Studies. New York: Peter Lang, 1999.
Viereck, Peter. *Metapolitics: From the Romantics to Hitler.* New York: Alfred A. Knopf,
    1941.
Weitz, Eric D. *Weimar Germany: Promise and Tragedy.* Princeton, NJ: Princeton
    University Press, 2007.
Zinn, Howard. *A People's History of the United States: 1492–Present.* New York:
    Perennial, 2003.

INDEX

abolition movement, 46, 51, 55, 107, 117, 140, 164
Adams, John, 45, 46, 51, 178
Addams, Jane, 180–81
Afghanistan, 13, 21; war in, 2, 13, 26, 115, 119
Ahnenerbe, 99
al Qaeda, 192
Alien and Sedition Acts, 178–79
Altemeyer, Bob, 156–57
American Legion, 183, 185
American Protective League, 181–83
Americanism, in Germany, 42, 162
Anschluss. See Austria, annexation of
anti-communism: in Germany, 6, 43, 58, 78–79, 134, 162, 170–71; in U.S., 51–52, 68, 184–90
anti-Semitism, German, 17, 19; in Europe, 126–27; and Martin Luther, 128; under National Socialism, 79, 99–101, 123–24, 135, 148–49; and nationalism, 59, 93–94, 99–100, 119, 132; origins of, 125–30; propaganda, 100, 135; and racial theory, 119, 124–25. *See also* Holocaust; Jews
art, 83, 92, 97, 112; Enlightenment, 30, 32, 37; modern, 17, 40–41, 54, 61, 70; and National Socialism, 61–62, 70, 72; romantic, 35–38, 44, 47
Aufklärung. See Enlightenment, German
Auschwitz. *See* extermination camps

Austria, annexation of (*Anschluss*), 91, 135
authoritarian personality, 154–57
authoritarianism, 18; American, 163–67; experimental findings, 153–57; German conformity and obedience, 97–98, 158–163; "right-wing authoritarianism," 156–57
"axis of evil," 193

Beer Hall Putsch. *See* Munich putsch
Beethoven, Ludwig von, 40
Bennett, William, 3, 113
Bill of Rights, 106, 168; violation of, 1, 5, 174, 177–79, 192–97. *See also* Constitution of the United States
Bismarck, Otto von, 91, 96–97, 131–32, 160
Bonaparte, Napoleon, 34, 91, 97, 103
book burning, 96, 171
Bryan, William Jennings, 23, 46, 65, 68, 80
bureaucracy, 55, 62, 74–75, 84, 130
Bush, George H. W., 82, 84, 191
Bush, George W., 1, 4, 82, 115, 166; administration, 1–8, 27, 192–93, 195; doctrine, 8, 119, 121, 200

Carter, Jimmy, 8, 52, 81
Census, U.S., 138, 148 151
Chamberlain, Neville, 6
Cheney, Richard, 3, 82, 83, 193, 199

ABOUT THE AUTHOR

BRIAN E. FOGARTY is a professor of sociology at St. Catherine University in St. Paul, Minnesota. He has written for a variety of publications, including the *Aspen Institute Quarterly, Peace and Change,* and the *Minneapolis Star-Tribune.* Fogarty received the university's Carol Easley Denny Award and previously published *War, Peace, and the Social Order* (Westview, 2000). He lives in St. Paul, Minnesota.